Tumult of Images

COSTERUS NEW SERIES 100

Series Editors:
C.C. Barfoot, Hans Bertens, Theo D'haen
and Erik Kooper

Tumult of Images

Essays on
W.B. Yeats and Politics

Edited by Peter Liebregts
and Peter van de Kamp

The Literature of Politics,
The Politics of Literature
Proceedings of the Leiden
IASAIL Conference: Volume 3

General editors: C.C. Barfoot,
Theo D'haen and Tjebbe A. Westendorp

Rodopi *Amsterdam-Atlanta, GA 1995*

CIP-gegevens Koninklijke Bibliotheek, Den Haag

Tumult

Tumult of images : essays on Yeats and politics / eds.
Peter van de Kamp and Peter Liebregts. - Amsterdam -
Atlanta, GA 1995 : Rodopi. - (The literature of politics,
the politics of literature ; 3) (Costerus, ISSN 0165-9618 ; 100)
ISBN 90-5183-779-8 geb.
Trefw.: Yeats, William Butler ; essays / poëzie en
politiek ; Ierland ; geschiedenis.

Cover design: Hendrik van Delft

© Editions Rodopi B.V.
    Amsterdam - Atlanta, GA 1995

Printed in The Netherlands

CONTENTS

BIBLIOGRAPHICAL NOTE

The works by W.B. Yeats listed below will be referred to by abbreviation and page number throughout the text and notes. In the case of Finneran's edition of the poetry (*PNE*) the reference is to the number of the poem.

Au	*Autobiographies*, London, 1980.
AV B	*A Vision* (1937), London, 1962.
CP	*Collected Poems*, London, 1982.
CPl	*Collected Plays*, London, 1982.
E&I	*Essays and Introductions*, London, 1961.
Ex	*Explorations*, London, 1962.
L	*The Letters of W.B. Yeats*, ed. Allan Wade, New York, 1955.
LNI	*Letters to the New Island (A New Edition)*, eds George Bornstein and Hugh Witemeyer, London, 1989.
Mem	*Memoirs: Autobiography-First Draft, Journal*, ed. Denis Donoghue, London, 1972.
Myth	*Mythologies*, London, 1959.
PNE	*The Poems: A New Edition*, ed. Richard J. Finneran, London, 1984.
UP1	*Uncollected Prose by W.B. Yeats, Vol. I: First Reviews and Articles 1886-1896*, ed. John P. Frayne, London, 1970.
UP2	*Uncollected Prose by W.B. Yeats, Vol. II: Reviews, Articles and Other Miscellaneous Prose 1897-1939*, eds John P. Frayne and Colton Johnson, London, 1975.
VP	*The Variorum Edition of the Poems of W.B. Yeats*, eds Peter Allt and Russell K. Alspach, New York, 1973.
VPl	*The Variorum Edition of the Plays of W.B. Yeats*, ed. Russell K. Alspach, New York, 1966.
VSR	*The Secret Rose: Stories by W.B. Yeats: A Variorum Edition*, eds Phillip L. Marcus, Warwick Gould and Michael J. Sidnell, Ithaca and London, 1981.

INTRODUCTION

... politics, for a vision-seeking man, can be but half achievement, a choice of an almost easy kind of skill instead of that kind which is, of all those not impossible, the most difficult.
                                                    W.B. Yeats, "Ireland After Parnell"

The 1991 IASAIL conference, held in Leiden, had as its theme politics in Anglo-Irish literature. Since the essays in this book are based on papers on W.B. Yeats presented at this conference, the reader might expect further contributions to the debate which was launched by W.H. Auden when he put Yeats, shortly after the latter's death, into the witness box on charges of social insensitivity. Auden's council for the defence won the day with the observation that however "false or undemocratic [Yeats's] ideas, his diction shows a continuous evolution towards what one might call the true democratic style".[1] Yet no verdict was reached in "The Public *v.* the Late Mr. William Butler Yeats" (1939), and the trial has continued. In 1965 Conor Cruise O'Brien took Yeats to court for his fascism, prosecuting him on the grounds that the poetry of this "public man" cannot be divorced from his politics. Twenty-one years after his prosecution, Dr O'Brien repeated his famous accusation almost verbatim at the Yeats Summer School.

The case had not been allowed to rest. In the 1980s, a host of circumstantial evidence was published, providing more nuanced deliberations for the defence. Elizabeth Butler Cullingford, in her *Yeats, Ireland and Fascism* (1981), pleaded that Yeats pursued a consistent course of ardent nationalism. One commentator has remarked that Cullingford left us with the impression that Yeats ended up as an old young-Fine Gaeler. Grattan Freyer's *W.B. Yeats and the Anti-Democratic Tradition* (1981) traced "the evolution of Yeats's political ideas and their interplay in the intellectual climate of his age", giving a special niche to the Nietzschean element in his thought, "the rating of personality and

---

1. W.H. Auden, "The Public *v.* the Late Mr. William Butler Yeats", originally published in *The Partisan Review*, VI/3 (Spring 1939), reprinted in *W.B. Yeats*, ed. William H. Pritchard, Penguin, 1972, 2.

energy over logic and humanitarianism".[2] Bernard G. Krimm, in *W.B. Yeats and the Emergence of the Irish Free State. 1918-1939: Living in Explosion* (1981) took Dr O'Brien to task by showing precisely how Yeats used the media to further his political cause, and particularly to deliberate against the reactionary forces of the new Ireland. And Paul Scott Stanfield, in *Yeats and Politics in the 1930s* (1988) showed in great detail how "politics impinged upon Yeats's awareness as they did on everyone else's".

In Ireland in the 1980s, the debate about Yeats's politics was placed in the larger framework of the "Irish Identity", the ramifications of which informed the leading Irish cultural journal *The Crane Bag*. It provided a lively forum for conflicting views on Ireland's post-colonial heritage, and has — unjustly — been held responsible for a polarization of two of modern literature's all-time greats: Yeats, the old-style nationalist fuddy-duddy "gummy Granny" vs. Joyce, the innovative socialist internationalist. One of the most controversial — and oft-quoted — contributions to the assessment of Yeats's contributions to the shaping of the Irish Republic was made by Declan Kiberd, when tongue-in-cheek he implied in "Inventing Irelands" that Yeats had a hand in the ideology of De Valera's Jansenistic Republic.

At the end of these roaring Eighties Donna Gerstenberger summed up the hive of politicizing Yeats with commendable back-spin; she wrote in "W.B. Yeats: Politics and History": "It has become fashionable in recent years to seek the right label for W.B. Yeats's political views as if to succeed were to settle things once and for all and to free contemporary poets and readers from a masterful influence that has been at times embarrassing and at others stultifying."

Leiden in 1991 seemed to offer an arena for various assessments of Yeats's politics — to have it all out. Several of the speakers had played a leading part in the political debate of the 1980s. It was pursued by none.

Yet the political issue was not skirted. A glance at our selection will suffice to show the prominence of the word "politics", from Cullingford's ero-political reading of Yeats's later ballads to Meihuis' discussion of Yeats's engagement in the light of apartheid. Leiden marked a shift in the interpretation of the word "politics", and a concomitant shift in the interest in Yeats's politics.

It is almost two decades since John Fekete published his *Critical Twilight*, in which he took New Criticism to task for its autonomous

---

2. Grattan Freyer, *W.B. Yeats and the Anti-Democratic Tradition*, Dublin, 1981, 2 and 23.

fallacy, arguing that any critical act is ideological. The argument had been put forward by critics like Lionel Trilling, Georg Lukacs and Jonathan Culler; but their credibility had remained tainted by their ideology. Only with the demise of the Eastern Bloc and the rise of revisionism, feminism, post-colonialism and deconstructionism has the fallacy of value-free, autonomous criticism been unmasked, even though as late as 1990 Catherine Belsey and Jane Moore felt the need to point out, in *The Feminist Reader*, that "there is no innocent or neutral approach to literature: all interpretation is political".[3]

This observation is manifest in our selection. It shines through the deliberative conclusions of Meihuis ("... in South Africa today poetry and politics are still both undermined by a pervasive dualism, which, incorporating and mirroring the polarizing simplifications of apartheid, has held us so long in its thrall") and Furomoto ("true nationality must be based upon the individual freed from national idiosyncrasy and an ability to look at oneself through an ever-widening perspective of history"). It informs Parkin's and Martin's observation that Yeats's politics of myth subsume the myth of politics, and Schwall's feminist reading of Yeats's "hysterica passio". In fact, it lies at the basis of the re-assessments that form the thrust of this book, be they a revaluation of Yeats's role in Ireland's Literary Renaissance or of his recruitment of Homer — and "solider" Aristotle.

All contributions bear out that the question of Yeats's politics extends far beyond party politics, and is filtered through our reading of a vacillating poet, whose ability to renew himself T.S. Eliot singled out as his greatest achievement. This is the very human Yeats who — in terms of a well-worn platitude — as a young Morrisite socialist had a heart, and as a conservative senator had a head.

However, the fact that this collection of essays does form part of a series of publications on Politics in Anglo-Irish Literature would make it unforgivable if we skirted that most contentious of issues, whose insistence is exemplified by its well-nigh everpresence on the programme of the annual Sligo Yeats Summer School, *viz.* the politics of Yeats in what Ellmann has termed his second puberty. The fact that writers of the calibre of Frank O'Connor, Richard Ellmann and Elizabeth Cullingford have all commented on the colour of Yeats's shirt in the Kildare Street Club in 1933 is proof of the detail with which this issue has been researched. Needless to say, the scope of an introduction precludes such detail. Instead of taking arms against a sea of authoritative studies, we

---

3. *The Feminist Reader: Essays in Gender and the Politics of Literary Criticism*, eds Catherine Belsey and Jane Moore, London, 1989, 1.

will limit our contribution to a critical analysis of Yeats's most politically contentious publication, "Three Songs to the Same Tune", and that in a version that has escaped critical attention.[4]

Let him finish his song: "Down to the tune of O'Donnell Abu"
Most of the debate of Yeats's politics has focused on the last ten years of his life, undoubtedly because Yeats was politically most controversial then, flirting with fascism, involved with the Army Comrades Association and propagating eugenics. The political frame of reference of this later Yeats is still far from fixed. There is no consensus about his involvement in politics. Opinions vary as to whether he intended to make political statements at all, which of his works should be considered politically, how these statements should be interpreted in the light of the Irish and European politics of his day, and what Yeats's own attitude was towards these statements. In the few cases where Yeats provides unambivalent commentary on his political work there is still considerable doubt about the import of this commentary.

On the Boiler is a case in point. Yeats writes about this manifesto to Maud Gonne, on 16 June 1938: "For the first time I am saying what I believe about Irish and European politics." (L:910) He had commended this *Fors Clavigera* in almost the same words to Dorothy Wellesley in December of the previous year. Yet despite Yeats's assertion, many critics have cast doubts on the political contentiousness of his pamphlet. Ellmann in *Yeats: The Man and the Masks* maintains that *On the Boiler* "is chiefly a declaration that politics are irrelevant".[5] T. Augustine Martin in "Who Stalked Through the Post Office?" (1978) claims that it "has very little to do with party politics on the one hand or with European doctrines of race and power on the other".[6] Shirley Neuman, in *Some Myth: Yeats's Autobiographical Prose* (1982), calls it "a last autobiographical gesture". And Sandra F. Siegel, in "Yeats's Quarrel with Himself: The Design and Argument of *On the Boiler*", the most comprehensive study of the pamphlet to date, disputes Yeats's claim by pointing out that the work does not present a clear expression of his

---

4. UCD Archives P24/1554 consists of two letters to Ernest Blythe, one in envelope, and three typescripts of the songs. According to Seamus Helferty, UCD Archivist, the papers were consulted by Moira MacEntee. Neither Dr MacEntee nor Dr Conor Cruise O'Brien have, to our knowledge, published these documents, or referred to these documents in print.

5. Richard Ellmann, *Yeats: The Man and the Masks*, Oxford, 1979, 279.

6. *The Crane Bag*, II (1978), 173.

beliefs.[7] "In each section of the essay", she points out, "Yeats advances an argument and then proceeds to devalue or repudiate the view he has seemed to uphold".

Of course, the dialectic that Siegel discerns in *On the Boiler* applies to much of Yeats. It could even be argued that it furnishes his Unity of Being with the passion which informs his conclusion that "Man can embody truth but he cannot know it". And it has been proffered as a counter-argument to those who discern embarrassing political tendencies in this later Yeats. But, like anything in Yeats that appears to allow for abstraction, it can give rise to superimpositions that take away from the integrity of his individual statements: Unity of Being does not preclude the integrity of the parts that make up the whole.

Siegel warns against "isolating passages from their contexts" because for Yeats "argument, whether political or poetic, was a mode of discovery." As a counter-argument to his political contentiousness, this view may prove limiting; it removes the responsibility and vitality from any of Yeats's statements, robs them of their direct synchronic context and relevance, and may even lead to critical wish-fulfilment, suggesting that the great poet does not really mean what his political self says.

In her perceptive analysis of *On the Boiler*, Siegel convincingly exposes the shortcomings in Yeats's argument, the inconsistencies and incoherences, but her conclusion, that these are deliberate deflations of that argument, could be interpreted as approaching the intentional fallacy.

Siegel rightly stresses the importance of co-text and context in Yeats. And her conclusions are justifiable, not only in the light of the extrapolation of the dialectic method, but also — or even more so — because, as she points out at the start of her essay, Yeats explains more than once that he speaks in the guise of Mad McCoy, the old "mad ship's carpenter" who in his childhood "used to preach from the top of an old steamboat boiler on the Sligo keys [*sic*]".

In 1922, AE wrote to Katharine Tynan:

> Yeats has come to live in Dublin. His address is 82 Merrion Sq. just two doors from this but I don't see him often. He has wrapped himself around with a mask of some kind and I never can find the natural human being. I am a disciple of Lao Tze the Chinese sage whose scripture the Tao Te King was the gospel of being natural. I prefer the country to the city, the work of Heaven to the work

---

7. Sandra F. Siegel, "Yeats's Quarrel with Himself: The Design and Argument of *On the Boiler*", *Bulletin of Research in the Humanities*, LXXXI/3 (Autumn 1978), 349-68.

of man and I think Willie was not contented with the poet Heaven made but tries to remake himself over again.[8]

Sixteen years later, in "An Acre of Grass" Yeats confirms AE's suspicions, stating explicitly that he exploits the dramatic monologue:

> Grant me an old man's frenzy,
> Myself must I remake
> Till I am Timon and Lear
> Or that William Blake
> Who beat upon the wall
> Till truth obeyed his call

(*CP*:347; *PNE*:332)

It is surprising that no critic has yet fully pursued the analogies between Yeats's frenzy and that of Shakespeare's outcast from Athens, the more so because critic after critic has pointed out Yeats's isolation after the death of Lady Gregory on 22 May 1932. We learn that Yeats's late poems "spill out with ... bitterness and loneliness", that the whole of *Wheels and Butterflies* shows "how extraordinarily alone Yeats was", that, by 1932, he stood "above the shifting tides of popular opinion", as Parnell had done, and that by 1934 Yeats was the "only Parnellite left". Of course, in reality it remains to be seen how "alone" Yeats was. In principles and aesthetics the Nestor of English verse, he could boast many like-minded souls — more than most poets can. Nor was he alone in his political convictions; as a matter of fact, as he himself admits in "The Stirring of the Bones" (*Au*:362-63), Yeats's Parnellite convictions grew when they were no longer relevant, in the 1930s. As a youngster, as Katharine Tynan recorded in an as yet unpublished document, Yeats had been too timid to engage with the fervour of his youthful eyes in the furious debate on the Parnell affair.

Yeats's alienation forms part of his Timon-like mask, which is more convincing than his masks of Blake or Lear — or Swift for that matter. In his later poems, Yeats alludes to a small band of Shakespeare's characters, Cordelia, Ophelia, Hamlet, Lear and Timon of Athens, with whose tragic gestures he felt affinity. Of these dying Shakespeareans, Timon with his misanthropy seems to have fitted his "fanatic heart" best. Indeed, the fascination with a hatred that "can have no expression in

---

8. Unpublished letter in the Katharine Tynan estate.

action"[9] engaged the later Yeats. In 1936, in a letter to Olivia Shakespear, he for instance, expresses his sympathy for Aldous Huxley's "sadistic hatred of life" (*L*:852), although he disliked the man. In the same year, he analyses his "periodical outbursts of political hatred". Two years before, he had tried to justify this rage in "Ribh considers Christian Love insufficient":

> I study hatred with great diligence,
> For that's a passion in my own control,
> A sort of besom that can clear the soul
> Of everything that is not mind or sense.
>
> Why do I hate man, woman or event?
> That is a light my jealous soul has sent.
>
> (CP:330; PNE:313)

What attracted the alienated Timon's rage to Yeats was its expression of tragic joy. Yeats had long been fascinated by Timon's tragic end. In "The Symbolism of Poetry" (1900; *E&I*:156), he had quoted the following for their enchanting rhythm:

> Timon hath made his everlasting mansion
> Upon the beached verge of the salt flood;
> Who once a day with his embossed froth
> The turbulent surge shall cover,

He had singled out Timon's ordering his tomb as a moment of pure tragedy in "Poetry and Tradition" (1907), and he again refers to Timon's "unmixed passion, 'the integrity of fire'" in "The Tragic Theatre" (1910; *E&I*:240). There are reverberations of Timon's epitaph in Yeats's *siste viator*:

> *Here lies a wretched corse, of wretched soul bereft:*
> *Seek not my name: A plague consume you wicked caitiffs left!*
> *Here lie I Timon; who, alive, all living men did hate:*
> *Pass by, and curse thy fill; but pass, and stay not here thy gait.*
>
> (V.4.70-73)

---

9. Letters to Ethel Mannin, 26 Oct. and 11 Dec. 1936; see *L*:863-64 and 872-73.

Dowden had written of the Athenian that "his rage implies the elements of a possible nobleness in him; he cannot acclimatize himself, as Alcibiades can, to the harsh and polluted air of the world".[10] Yeats's hatred is similarly directed against the State; there are echoes in Yeats of Timon's observations that "The senators shall bear contempt hereditary,/ The beggar native honour" (IV.3.10-11), and that

> ... All's obliquy;
> There's nothing level in our cursed natures
> But direct villainy. Therefore be abhorr'd
> All feasts, societies, and throngs of men!
>
> (IV.3.18-21)

Moreover, Yeats's fascination with violence, his "magic drum", is reflected in Timon's advice to Alcibiades:

> ... Follow thy drum;
> With man's blood paint the ground, gules, gules.
> Religious canons, civil laws are cruel;
> Then what should war be?
>
> (IV.3.59-62)[11]

Despite these parallels, the one insurmountable problem with Yeats's dramatic monologues is that they are not readily identifiable as such. This is borne out by the fact that even an in-depth anatomy of Yeats's rancour like Joseph M. Hassett's *Yeats and the Poetics of Hate* (1986) does not mention the figure of Timon. We would love to ascribe Yeats's politically tainted songs of the 1930s to a *dramatis persona*, and claim *he*

---

10. Quoted by Evangeline O'Connor in *Who's Who and What's What in Shakespeare* (1887), New York, 1978, 370.

11. There are further parallels between the later Yeats and the *dramatis personae* in Shakespeare's plays of the Greek and Roman state. Yeats's insistence on "measure" reflects Ulysses' soliloquy on "degree" in *Troilus and Cressida*, and his desire for War and contempt for the mob is reminiscent of that of the servants in *Coriolanus*: "Let me have war, say I. It exceeds peace, as far as day does night .... Peace is a very apoplexy, lethargy; mulled, deaf, sleepy, insensible; a getter of more bastard children than war's a destroyer of men" (IV.5.228-32). In *My Father's Son*, London, 1971, 152, Frank O'Connor recalled that Yeats demanded that the Abbey should produce *Coriolanus* "in coloured shirts, in the hope that, as in France, a Dublin audience might riot and he could defend the message of the play". O'Connor refused, "not wanting to have any part in Fascist propaganda". The play was finally produced in Renaissance costume, nearly bankrupting the theatre.

does not "sing a the before [O'Rahilly's] name"; we would feel more comfortable if his facetious joke on mariolatry — "St. Joseph thought the world would melt/But liked the way his finger smelt" — could be attributed to a fictitious character. But, knowing that Yeats sympathized with the O'Rahilly's cause and that he was at loggerheads with the Catholic hierarchy and the Censorship in Ireland, we cannot do so with certainty. Yeats's use of the dramatic monologue is comparable to his symbolic strategy of making that which is determined indeterminate and that which is undetermined determined. We may suspect irony, but it is not sustained, as it is in, say, Pope, Swift or Browning. Yeats does not provide that double perspective which allows us to postulate that, in ridicule, he means the opposite of — or at least something else than — what he is saying.

The only mask that Yeats sustained with some consistency was that description of his personality in *A Vision* (1937); men in Phase 17 are

> almost always partisans, propagandists and gregarious; yet because of the *Mask* of simplification which holds up before them the solitary life of hunters and of fishers and "the groves pale passion loves", they hate parties, crowds, propaganda (*AV B*:143).

This personality shines through "Politics" for instance. The poem cannot be read as merely a final expression of Yeats's longing for physical passion, but rather as the final postulation of a Yeatsian dilemma. The poet who in "The Lake Isle of Innisfree" resolved to go West but did not budge from London's pavements grey does — or rather, fails to do — the same in "Politics". In the latter he remains in the company of politicians; and, as a political interlocutor, he *is* trying to fix his attention "on Roman or on Russian/Or on Spanish politics".

That for Yeats as politician or as poet the grass was always greener on the other side of the hill does not take away from the fact that he is standing on that other side. It may account for his conflicting attitude towards politics in the 1930s. In 1937, for instance, he can acquaint his correspondents of the fact that he has "a horror of politics" (Feb. 11; *L*:881), that he is "finished" with politics "for ever", and then do a *volte face* and write "... for the first time in my life I am saying what are my political beliefs" (Dec. 17; *L*:902). This duality between hating propaganda and being drawn to it may also help to explain why different commentators hold different opinions on Yeats's success as a politician. Grattan Freyer, for instance, shows Yeats's political shrewdness, particularly in his P.R. — for instance his timing the publication of "Roger Casement" on the air waves and in De Valera's *Irish Press* —

whereas W.B. Stanford holds that as a politician Yeats fell short of the mark because of his lack of P.R. — specifically his "impishness, or recklessness, or callousness of speech" (reflecting the amusement with which Yeats had considered politics in 1924).[12]

But Yeats's duality does not take away from the fact that he had his say on hot political issues. He did not only make poetry out of quarrels with himself, but also out of his quarrels with others. He was partisan in print to, for instance, the IRB, the Irish Literary Society, the Lutyens plans for a Dublin Ponte Vecchio, the Abbey and the Lane paintings. In fact, he exploited a variety of propagandistic strategies, including the personal attack — of William Martin Murphy in "To a Wealthy Man who promised a Second Subscription to the Dublin Municipal Gallery if it were proved the people Wanted Pictures" — and personal praise — of Dr MacCartan in "Dedication" — to the deliberative call to arms — to the Parnellites in "Mourn — and then Onward!". There is no reason why Yeats should not be held accountable for his actions, even though they were presented in — sometimes great — poetry.

The writer of "Three Songs to the Same Tune" was a dab hand at trying to stir up support; he may have needed little incitement to do so once again, being true to the side of his personality which quarrelled with others in verse. It is not the fact that Yeats deigned to write propaganda that startles us in these songs, but the nature of this propaganda. We associate Yeats the propagandist with harmless aesthetic, and unpopular, causes. Hence our amusement at his purported rebuke of the Easter rebels. However, in these "Three Songs" Yeats was dealing with a political ideology which seemed menacingly popular in large parts of Europe, and which also had its followers in Ireland (John A. Costello, for instance, boasted in the Dáil on 2 February 1934 that the "Blueshirts will be victorious in the Irish Free State" just as "the Blackshirts were victorious in Italy" and "the Hitlershirts" in Germany).

This seems so out of character that it requires a brief historical perspective. Yeats had left the Senate in 1928 because he "was tired in himself rather than tired of the Senate".[13] In the Senate, he had made significant contributions to the Irish coinage committee, and as 'a sixty year old smiling public man' to education — a subject to which he returned time and again as an *éminence grise* and a family man — after having decided in 1900 that it was "one of our illusions .... Progress is

---

12. W.B. Stanford, "Yeats in the Irish Senate", *REL*, IV/3 (July 1963), 76.

13. Stanford, 80.

miracle, and it is sudden" (*E&I*:171-72). And he had spoken out with rhetorical eloquence in favour of divorce.

Yeats's rodomontade was in the finest of Anglo-Irish traditions,[14] but this tradition had now come under threat from the intolerance of the most powerful force in the New Ireland, the middle class Church and State. The former denounced Yeats. *The Catholic Bulletin* of July 1925, for instance, qualified his speech as "satanic arrogance"; and this Catholic hostility lasted. The Bishop who talks to Crazy Jane had tried to ostracize Yeats; and his Catholic cause was in great appeal: at the International Eucharistic Congress in the Summer of 1932 about a million people attended Mass in the Phoenix Park, to the disgust of most prominent poets.[15]

In 1932, this Catholic middle class was responsible for a dramatic shift in government. On 22 February 1932, Sean MacEntee claimed that Fianna Fail had won the Catholic vote.[16] Some two weeks later, De Valera's first Fianna Fail government took office. Yeats's fear of Ireland severing the Commonwealth bonds with England were realized. In July, De Valera withheld the Land Annuities from the British Treasury; Britain

---

14. W.E.H. Lecky, for instance, had written: "Ever since the dawn of public opinion, there has been a party which has maintained that the goal to which Irish patriots should tend, is the recognition of their country as a distinct and independent nationality, connected with England by the crown; that in such a condition alone it could retain a healthy political life, and could act in cordial cooperation with England; that every other system would be transient in its duration, and humiliating and disastrous while it lasted. To this party all the genius of Ireland has ever belonged ... Swift and Molyneux originated the conception; Burke aided it when he ... denounced the penal laws and the trade restrictions that shackled the energies of Ireland; Sheridan, when he exerted all the eloquence to oppose the union; Flood, when he formed the national party in parliament; Grattan, when he led that party in its triumph and its fall" *(Clerical Influences, an Essay on Irish Sectarianism and English Government*, Dublin, 1911, 45-46).

15. We may read in the *Irish Times* of 13 December 1932: "What has our self-concentrated nationality given the world? ... have we produced a single theologian of whom the world has heard? ... We have not produced such figures, because even in religion we were isolated, and confined ourselves to mere pieties rather than to the lofty athletics of philosophy. We can, of course, with our talent for organisation, get a million people on their knees before an altar in the Park; but did there come out of all that piety a single vision, a song, a music, any visible sign that the sacrifice was accepted and the fiery tongues had descended?"

16. Joseph Lee, *Ireland, 1912-1985: Politics and Society*, Cambridge, 1989, 177.

responded by imposing duties on Irish exports, and the Economic War with Britain had begun.

Yeats was "a Cosgrave man"; Cosgrave had appointed him to the Senate; as Abbey Director Yeats had a working relationship with Cosgrave's Minister of Finance, and he distrusted de Valera's *Fianna Fail* Ireland, believing that the country was now in the hands of the "Paudeens" Yeats had always despised. In fact, his distrust was mild in comparison to that of his "first friend and enemy", AE. Frank O'Connor recalls how AE

> was becoming more and more angry and afraid before the new Establishment of priests and politicians, particularly Sean MacEntee and de Valera. One night he really frightened me by cursing de Valera in the way I had seen old women in Cork curse.
> "I curse that man as generations of Irishmen to come will curse him — the man who destroyed our country."[17]

A brief résumé of Yeats's reaction should suffice. In 1932 he observed that "Ireland, like Russia, Italy and Germany has entered into a period of fanaticism".[18] In February of the following year, he agreed with Olivia Shakespear's comparison of De Valera with Hitler and Mussolini (*L*:806). In March he met De Valera, and was impressed by the man's "simplicity and honesty" (*ibid.*); still, he did not warm to his policies — including the cutback on funding for the Abbey. In April, he is engaged, with an "ex-cabinet minister, an eminent lawyer, and a philosopher" in working out "a social theory which can be used against Communism in Ireland — what looks like emerging is Fascism modified by religion" (*L*:808). The ex-cabinet minister was Ernest Blythe, a protestant who had served as Minister for Finance under Cosgrave from 1922, and had taken over the post of Vice-President after O'Higgins' death. Under the pseudonym of "Onlooker", Blythe was probably responsible for the stirring columns in the *United Irishman*, the Blueshirts' organ in 1933. On 17 June, 1933, "Onlooker" writes:

---

17. O'Connor, 107. AE had been one of the editors of Sir Horace Plunkett's *The Homestead*, the journal for the Irish Cooperative Movement—which Joyce called the "pig's paper". It amalgamated with *The Irish Statesman* in 1923, and was edited by AE until it folded in 1930. After its demise, it has been convincingly argued, Yeats founded the Academy to continue intellectual opposition to Ireland's mainstay Catholic dogma.

18. "Modern Ireland", a lecture delivered on Yeats's last American tour; quoted in Paul Scott Stanfield, *Yeats and Politics in the 1930s*, London, 1988, 17.

They think that all parliaments gabble too much and they are not at all sure that the national will can be properly ascertained by merely counting heads. They are generally without respect for an electoral system which enables men without ability, industry, patriotism, or common honesty to become members of the Nation's parliament more readily than the best men in the community.

Yeats warmed to the Fascist cause. In July he writes to Olivia Shakespear:

Politics are growing heroic. De Valera has forced political thought to face the most fundamental issues. A Fascist opposition is forming behind the scenes to be ready should some tragic situation develop. I find myself constantly urging the despotic rule of the educated classes as the only end to our trouble (*L*:811-12).

Fascism was in the air, and its odour had wafted into Ireland: in May 1933, the Blueshirts adopted the arm salute, greeting their leader with "shouts of 'Heil', pronounced sharply".[19] Indeed, it had been in the air before the ACA was formed. In 1927, the funeral of Kevin O'Higgins, "the Irish Mussolini", Yeats's "sole statesman", had been amply attended by Italian Blackshirts. Mussolini's answer to democracy had received praise from numerous writers within and outside Ireland. Even the gentle Katharine Tynan — the first woman to whom Yeats proposed — the Irish First World War poetical answer to Florence Nightingale, remembered for her meek "Sheep and Lambs", had entrusted to print her praise of Mussolini, and condemnation of the money-spinning German Jew. The Irish interest in Mussolini's "anti-party" with its ideal of a corporate state had been intensified by the papal *Quadragesimo Anno*. And Professor Michael Tierney of University College Dublin was adamant that it was "a complete mistake to suppose that Italian Fascism is merely a crude individual or party dictatorship".[20]

Yeats's closest ally was Captain Dermot MacManus, "his head full of vague Fascism, probably got from me" (*L*:815). MacManus introduced Yeats to O'Duffy, the Irish answer to Mussolini. In the Cosgrave years it had been rumoured that, together with Blythe, O'Duffy wanted an army coup. In August 1932, O'Duffy had taken over the leadership of

---

19. D. Thornly, "The Blueshirts" (1967), quoted in Theodore Hoppen, *Ireland Since 1800: Conflict and Conformity*, London, 1989, 181.

20. *Ibid*.

the newly founded Army Comrades Association from T.F. O'Higgins, Kevin O'Higgins's brother, and Yeats may have pictured O'Duffy as an O'Higgins incarnate — until their first meeting. Yeats had not done his homework. He was unaware that the former general, when Commissioner of the Garda, had criticized Irish dance gatherings as "orgies of dissipation, which in the present state of legislation the police are powerless to prevent".[21] MacManus claimed that after the interview Yeats had called O'Duffy an "uneducated lunatic" (what O'Duffy thought of the nutshell version of *A Vision* that Yeats presented at this meeting, with references to Swift's "bent and current" and allusions to Hegel and Spengler, is open to conjecture). In writing, Yeats was less outspoken; he told Olivia Shakespear, "I did not think him a great man though a pleasant one, but one never knows, his face and mind may harden or clarify" (*L*:813).

It did not, as Yeats points out in the final stanza of "Parnell's Funeral" in 1934. Yet in 1933 Yeats lived in hope. On August 17, he informs Olivia Shakespear:

> The papers will have told you of the "blue shirt" excitement here. The government is in a panic and has surrounded itself with armed men and armoured cars. The blue shirts are starting up all over the country .... The organization is for an independent Ireland within the commonwealth. Whether it succeeds or not in abolishing parliamentary government as we know it to-day, it will certainly bring into discussion all the things I care for (*L*:813-14).

On September 20, he writes with detachment about "our political comedy":

> Act I. Capt. MacManus ... decided that Gen[eral] O'Duffy should be made leader of a body of young men, formed to keep meetings from being broken up. He put into O'Duffy's head — he describes him as "a simple peasant" — Fascist ideas and started him off to organise that body of young men. Act II. Some journalist announced that 30,000 of these young men were going to march through Dublin on a certain day (the correct number was 3,000). Government panic. Would not O'Duffy, who had once been head of the army, and more recently head of the police, march on the Government with 30,000, plus army and police? Result, martial law — in its Irish form — armoured cars in the streets, and new

---

21. D.F. Keogh, *The Vatican, the Bishops and Irish Politics. 1919-1939*, Cambridge, 1986, 164.

police force drawn from the I.R.A. to guard the government, and O'Duffy's organization proclaimed. Act III. O'Duffy is made thereby so important that Cosgrave surrenders the leadership of his party to O'Duffy and all the opposition united under him. Two months ago he was unknown politically ... (*L*:815).

Critics have taken this commentary as a first signal of Yeats's disenchantment with the Blueshirts. Edward O'Shea conjectures that Yeats "saw earlier than most that O'Duffy was not the leader he sought, and that his realization came with the events of August 1933, after O'Duffy's planned march to Glasnevin Cemetery in commemoration of Griffith, Collins, and O'Higgins was aborted".[22] Stanfield agrees with O'Shea's claim that Yeats's disenchantment is due to the Blueshirts' subsequent embracing of party politics — after De Valera's prohibition, the ACA joined forces, in September, with the new Centre Party and Cumann na nGaedhael to form the United Ireland party, which soon became Fine Gael. We know that Yeats's "fascist" ideology was somewhat at variance with that of O'Duffy. Yeats, as Cullingford observes, "took the essentials of fascism to be order, hierarchy, discipline, devotion to culture, and the rule of the most educated".[23] A "simple peasant" hardly embodied Yeats's last two criteria.

O'Shea claims that equally important for arguing Yeats's disavowal is the first publication of "Three Songs" in *The Spectator* on 23 February 1934.[24] This refutes the view presented by Ellmann, in *Yeats: The Man and the Masks* that "in February 1934, still toying with the unofficial army, [Yeats] wrote some marching songs for O'Duffy's men .... But by August of the same year he had realized his error and rewrote the poems so that nobody could sing them".[25] Ellmann's view is anachronistic, for Yeats began to dissociate himself from the Blueshirts even before he started to compose the songs.

So whom did Yeats write these songs for, when, and with what purpose? And why did he get them first published in, of all places, *The Spectator*? Yeats's references to the songs and the Blueshirts have led to various conjectures. His first mention of the Songs is in a letter to Olivia Shakespear, postmarked 30 November 1933:

---

22. Edward O'Shea, "Yeats's 'Three Songs to the Same Tune'", *Yeats: An Annual of Critical and Textual Studies*, IV, Ann Arbor, 1986, 130.

23. Elizabeth Cullingford, *Yeats, Ireland and Fascism*, London, 1981, 202.

24. O'Shea, 131.

25. Ellmann, 277.

> I am slightly suffering from blood pressure and an attempt to write
> a new national song — three versions to the tune of O'Donnell
> Abu to be sung at the Abbey Theatre (*L*:818).

From this note, it cannot be concluded that Yeats intended them for a
nationalist street movement — but rather for a *national* theatre, where,
as Freyer has shown so convincingly, Yeats was not weary of reacting
artistically to political issues of the day. However, Yeats's comments in
a postscript to the publication of the songs in *Poetry*, dated "August,
1934", point in a different direction. He writes:

> Because a friend belonging to a political party wherewith I had
> once some loose associations, told me that it had, or was about to
> have, or might be persuaded to have, some such aim, I wrote
> these songs. Finding that it neither would nor could, I increased
> their fantasy, their extravagance, their obscurity, that no party
> might sing them (*VP*:837).

O'Brien was baffled by the disparity between the "evidence" of Yeats's
political engagement in his letters and the picture in this postscript of
Yeats "moved by an impulse, and misled by a friend, into a political
gesture which he later regretted". Whereas O'Brien questioned its
veracity, O'Shea warned against taking Yeats's commentary at face
value:

> In "Three Songs" we quite naturally and confidently regard the
> poems themselves as the "fictional texts" and the Commentary as
> "the historical text," and we are likely to privilege the latter
> without realizing that in fact both texts are fictional. There is only
> one persona here, the poet-as-adjustor, the poet-as-arranger, and
> we must look elsewhere for the "historical" author, W.B.
> Yeats.[26]

In fact, Yeats is not misleading us; nor was he misled. His account
merely lacks specificity of date and person. The "friend" Yeats refers to
was Ernest Blythe, who shared Yeats's interests in The Abbey (under
Cosgrave he had granted the company its 1,000 annual subsidy, and he
would become its director in 1939) and with whom Yeats had tried to
work out the Blueshirt philosophy. On the same day that he wrote to
Olivia Shakespear, he sent Blythe a promised "typed copy of that third

---

26. O'Shea, 135.

song".[27] It can be inferred that Yeats finished the songs by November 30, and that he must have worked on them in this month. It can further be inferred that Blythe must have convinced Yeats that he might be able to put the songs to use for "a political party", justifying their part "in the casual comedy". That Blythe did not find a forum for the songs can be inferred from a letter Yeats wrote to him in February 1934:

> Dear Blythe: I send you those songs. "The Spectator" printed them at once, which is the reason why they are huddled away in a corner. The third has probably not reached its final form, but as there is no question of it being sung that hardly matters. I went through the first two verses of the first song, & all the second song syllable by syllable with Larchet & got his general approval of the rest, but a singer might want some other change, which I should be always ready to make.[28]

John F. Larchet, Senior Professor at the Royal Irish Academy of Music since 1920, was Professor of Music at University College Dublin, and musical director of The Abbey. That Yeats, tone deaf, solicited his help in musicalizing his songs is proof of how serious Yeats was in his wish to get them sung; he ends his note to the songs in *The Spectator*:

> I read my songs to friends, they talked to others, those others talked, and now companies march to the words "Blueshirt Abu," and a song that is all about shamrocks and harps or seems all about them, because its words have the particular variation upon the cadence of "Yankee Doodle" Young Ireland reserved for that theme. I did not write that song; I could not if I tried. Here are my songs. Anybody may sing them, choosing "clown" and "fanatic" for himself, if they are singable — musicians say they are, but may flatter — and worth singing.

Yeats had explicitly left shamrocks out of a list of Irish emblems, presented in 1932, which he claimed had "ascended out of sentimentality, out of insincere rhetoric, out of mob emotion".[29] The Irish libretto to a popular American tune which Yeats refers to was "God Save Ireland" (1867), commemorating the Manchester Martyrs, by T.D. Sullivan.[30] To

---

27. UCD Archives P/24/1554 (a) 2.

28. UCD Archives P24/1554 (a) (1).

29. Quoted in Stanfield, 14.

30. See Peter van de Kamp, "Whose Renaissance?", in this volume, 165 below.

To Yeats's disapprobation, it had received immense popularity in the 1880s, epitomizing the sentimental propaganda that had stirred the Young Ireland movement to which Yeats had belonged. In one of those strange intertextual ironies, Yeats actually seems to allude to it in the last stanza of the second song; the hanging of Yeats's zealot brings to mind Sullivan's

> High upon the gallow-tree
> Swung the noble-hearted Three,
> By the vengeful tyrant stricken in their bloom;
> But they met him face to face,
> With the courage of their race,
> And they went their souls undaunted to their doom.
> "God save Ireland!" said the heroes;
> "God save Ireland!" said they all:
> "Whether on the scaffold high
> Or the battle-field we die,
> Oh, what matter, when for Erin dear we fall!"

Between November, and Yeats's completion of the songs' first version, and the third week of February, when Yeats had completed another version, the political climate had obviously changed. Yeats points this out in his note to the *Spectator* publication:

> In politics I have but one passion and one thought, rancour against all whom, except under the most dire necessity, disturb public order, a conviction that public order cannot persist without the rule of educated and able men .... Some months ago that passion laid hold upon me with the violence which unfits the poet for all politics but his own. While the mood lasted, it seemed that our growing disorder, the fanaticism that inflamed it like some old bullet imbedded in the flesh, was about to turn our noble history into an ignoble farce. For the first time in my life I wanted to write what some crowd in the street might understand and sing; I asked my friends for a tune; they recommended that old march, "O'Donnell Abu."

It is plain from our chronology that the "fanaticism that inflamed" Ireland does not only refer to De Valera's government, but also to the Blueshirt opposition; they had enacted the "ignoble farce" Yeats had described to Olivia Shakespear in his letter of 20 September. Yeats's initial purpose for the songs, then, was not as a support for the Blueshirts, but rather to set them on their proper course. Yeats goes on to describe in some detail the inception of the songs:

I first got my chorus, "Down the fanatic, down the clown," then
the rest of the first song. But I soon tired of its rhetorical
vehemence, thought that others would tire of it unless I found
some gay playing upon its theme, some half-serious exaggeration
and defence of its rancorous chorus, and therefore I made the
second version. Then I put into a simple song a commendation of
the rule of the able and the educated, man's old delight in
submission; I wrote round the line "The soldier takes pride in
saluting his captain," thinking the while of a Gaelic poet's lament
for his lost fathers: "my fathers served their fathers before Christ
was crucified."

O'Shea sees in Yeats's arrangement of the songs a "movement from
vehemence to moderation, a tempering of initial fanaticism with
somewhat greater reserve", reflecting the moderation of Yeats's own
fervour to the cause.[31] Actually, Yeats had initially arranged the songs
in a different, and rhetorically more deliberative, order. Yeats enclosed
a typescript, with corrections in hand, of an older version of the songs
in his letter to Blythe.[32] We print them here side by side with the
version in *The Spectator*.

In their initial arrangement, the songs open with a reiteration of the
autocratic and intellectocratic beliefs Yeats had posited in "Blood and the
Moon", "in mockery of a time/Half dead at the top". "Muck in the
yard" was general all over Europe, with the "clown" in England, the
"fanatic" in Ireland, and the "tyrant" in Germany (or any other
permutation of these three). Modern Europe had "known no men more
powerful" than Goldsmith and Swift, Berkeley and Burke. They had
made Ireland a victorious nation, in league with ancient Greece and
Babylon. Radical as a spreading laurel tree, these nations can stay the
wind of anarchy "bred on the Atlantic" by complying with the dictum
Yeats had been first acquainted with from his study of arcana: "As above
so below." Yeats had commended O'Duffy to Olivia Shakespear in 1933
as "autocratic, directing the movement from above down as if it were an
army" (*L*:813). By taking pride in the rule of the One through the Few

31. O'Shea, 132.

32. It cannot yet be ascertained whether these are typescripts sent to Blythe in
1933 — the third despatched on 30 November — or whether they were enclosed in
Yeats's letter to Blythe in February 1934. The textual differences between these
versions of the songs and the ones published in *The Spectator*, the difference in their
order, and the corrections in hand seem to point to the earlier date. However, their
rearrangement refutes this argument, unless we believe that Yeats in his *Spectator*
note was lying about the order of their inception in his *Spectator* note.

for the Many, this army would lift its song like an autocratic wind against all the dead wood.

These roots are provided in the shape of "grandfather" in the second "version". He prefigures the "indomitable Irishry" of Yeats's "Credo" in "Under Ben Bulben" scorning "the sort now growing up/All out of shape from toe to top". Like Attis' image, he hangs from the tree, a martyr to the cause. This martyrdom precedes that of the Easter Rising; it did not produce a terrible beauty, but an organic symmetry, based on ancient lineaments of gratified desire that began Ireland's might. From "cavern, crevice or hole" it defends Ireland's soul — and can be heard faintly shouting "Rejoice". This martyrdom forms the incitement of the third version, which stands as the most rhetorical poem that Yeats ever wrote. Its insistent anaphora, "Justify all", rises to a crescendo climaxing in the inevitably deliberative conclusion:

> This is the moment weighs all in a balance
> Keep order, leadership, nerves that are steel ....

That moment had passed in February 1934, as their publication in a tempered form in *The Spectator* bears out. But why did Yeats change these two lines into: "Fail, and that history turns into rubbish,/All that great past to a trouble of fools"? What happened between November 1933 and the third week of February 1934 that led him to revise the poem? One may speculate, as we have done above, that the revision was caused by Yeats's changing attitude to the movement of the Blueshirts. Or one might go a step further and attempt to see the composition of these songs in the context of European history of this period.

In February 1934 the executive power in France had been severely weakened by the rapid change of governments in the past few years. At the beginning of February, prime minister Edouard Daladier headed the eighth French cabinet since January 1932. This evident weakness of the constitution was eagerly exploited by communist and fascist agitators. On the 6th of February 1934 members of the fascist *Action française*, of the communist-orientated *Association Républicaine des Ancient Combattants*, and of the authoritarian-conservative *Croix de Feu* combined their forces and marched to the Place de la Concorde where they decried the lassitude of both government and parliament. This demonstration led to an extremely violent confrontation with the police, as a result of which 15 people were killed and more than 2,000 were injured. Especially the right-wing demonstrators were to blame for this bloody outcome of the political gathering. Daladier partly abated the agitation by his resignation, after which Gaston Doumergue formed a national government. However, this did not stop the communists from marching the streets again, now as a protest against the growth of fascism in France. They probably did this to make up for the disastrous result of their having joined forces with them a few days before, which had raised many questions in the minds of their supporters. Yet again violence reigned when the forces of the political left and right clashed in the streets of Paris, causing another high number of casualties. As a result the communists and socialists organized a general strike on 12 February to demonstrate against any possible take-over of the Republic by the fascists and/or royalists. Though eventually France would find itself in smoother waters again, these events in the first two weeks of February could give the impression to anyone with an interest in European politics that the ruling class had already made or was about to make way for mob rule — a practical demonstration of a terrible thought that was to haunt Yeats in the 1930s and which was one the reasons for him to write that pamphlet of political advice, *On the Boiler*. We do not know how well informed Yeats was about the political turmoil in France, but the fact that his revisions of his marching songs and the threat of mob rule in France took place in about the same period of time offers some food for thought.

Despite, or perhaps through the revisions, Yeats cherished these songs because they represented his firm beliefs, which he had put into poetry before and was to entrust to that medium again. By February 1934, Yeats knew that what he sung "was what lost" and that he had nothing else to spur him into song. He presents them in the order of inception in February 1934 as testimonial evidence of his own convictions, political and aesthetic. O'Shea has pointed out how Yeats tempered his songs in his reworkings from 1934 to 1938. Some critics have tried to link them to *A Vision*. In their final version, Yeats meta-poetically sums up their importance in his Unity of Being and their relevance to his lunar philosophy:

> *Robbers had taken his old tambourine,*
> *But he took down the moon*
> *And rattled out a tune;*
> *Robbers had taken his old tambourine.*

That Yeats revised the songs time and again, adding refrains which comment ironically on the main argument, is proof of the fact that Yeats — before the eyes of the world — showed himself repentant of a cause he soon abandoned. Yet this may not come as a surprise because, as we have stated earlier, "vacillation" is a recurring keyword when it comes to analysing the poet's thought. In a note to "The Bounty of Sweden", the concluding part of *Autobiographies* which he finished in January 1924, Yeats had claimed that the "danger to art and literature comes to-day from the tyrannies and persuasions of revolutionary societies and from forms of politics and religious propaganda" (*Au*:580-81). Ten years later, however, he had created with his marching songs that very type of "literature of revolutionary propaganda". Yet in his own endless remaking of the self and of the work, he soon rejected the first version of these poems, and revised them to bring them more in line with that statement made in "The Bounty of Sweden". Thus Yeats once again turned full circle in the gyre of his life.

Spectator (23 February 1934)

"Three Songs to the Same Tune"

I

Soldiers take pride in saluting their Captain,	Soldiers take pride in saluting their Captain,
The devotee proffers a knee to his Lord,	The devotee proffers a knee to his Lord,
Some take delight in adoring a woman.	Some take delight in adoring a woman.
What's equality? — Muck in the yard:	What's equality? — Muck in the yard:
Victorious ~~Renowned~~ Nations grow	Historic Nations grow
From above to below	From above to below.
Those fanatics all that work would undo	Those fanatics all that we do would undo;
Tyrant, fanatic, clown	Down the fanatic, down the clown,
Down, down, hammer them down	Down, down, hammer them down,
Down to the tune of O'Donnell Abu!	Down to the tune of O'Donnell Abu.
When Nations are empty up there at the top,	When Nations are empty up there at the top,
When order has weakened or faction is strong	When order has weakened or faction is strong,
Time for us all Boys, to hit on a tune Boys,	Time for us all boys, to hit on a tune boys,
Take to the roads and go marching along.	Take to the roads and go marching along;
Lift, lift, lift up the tune	Lift, every mother's son,
Marching, marching like one	Lift, lift, lift up the tune.
Those fanatics all that work would undo	Those fanatics all that we do would undo;
etc etc	. . . .
Soldiers take pride in saluting their captain,	Soldiers take pride in saluting their captain,
Where are the captains that govern mankind?	Where are the captains that govern mankind?
What happens a tree that has nothing within it?	What happens a tree that has nothing within it?
O O A marching wind, ~~and~~ a blast of the wind	O marching wind, O a blast of the wind,
Marching, marching along,	Marching, marching along.
Lifting, lifting its song.	Lift, lift, lift up the song.
Those fanatics all that work would undo	Those fanatics all that we do would undo;
etc. etc..........	. . . .

[UCD Archives P24/1554 (b) (ii)]

~~Second Version~~

~~Grandfather said in the great Re~~bellion;
Ma̶n̶ε̶x̶x̶i̶x̶x̶g̶u̶n̶d̶xand a ~~girl might be b~~

SECOND VERSION

Grandfather said in the great Rebellion:
'Hear gentlemen, ladies and all mankind
Money is good and a girl might be better
But good strong blows are delights to the mind
Come march, singing this song
Swinging, swinging, along

'Those fanatics all that work would undo
Tyrant, fanatic, clown,
Down, down, hammer them down
Down to the tune of O'Donnell Abu!

        followed
      but she ~~went with~~ another
'A girl I had once ~~and another man took~~ her,
Money I had and it went in the night,
Strong
A̶n̶d̶ drink they say is the ruin of a man,
But a
A̶ righteous cause and the blows are delight
Come march, singing this song

        etc., etc.,

Money is good and a girl might be better
No matter what happens or who takes the fall
But a   and
A̶ righteous cause — ~~but~~ the rope gave a jerk there
He said no more for his throat was too small
Come march, singing this song,

        etc., etc.,

Spectator (23 February 1934)

II.

Grandfather said in the great Rebellion:
Hear gentlemen, ladies and all mankind,
Money is good and a girl might be better,
But good strong blows are delights to the mind.
Come march, singing this song,
Swinging, swinging along.

Those fanatics all that we do would undo;
Down the fanatic, down the clown,
Down, down, hammer them down,
Down to the tune of O'Donnell Abu.

A girl I had, but she followed another;
Money I had and it went in the night;
Strong drink I had, and it brought me sorrow;
But a good strong cause and the blows are delight.
Come march, singing this song,
Swinging, swinging along.
. . . .

Money is good, and a girl might be better
No matter what happens or who takes the fall,
But a good strong cause — and the rope gave a jerk
there,
He said no more for his throat was too small,
Come march, singing this song,

. . . .

Spectator (23 February 1934)

THIRD VERSION

Justify all those renowned generations
That left their bodies a meal for the wolves
That left their homesteads a lair for the foxes
Lived banished men, or had hidden themselves
In cavern, crevice or hole
Defending Ireland's soul

Those fanatics all that work would undo
Tyrant, fanatic, clown,
Down, down, hammer them down
Down to the tune of O'Donnell Abu!

Justify all those renowned generations
     have sunk
Justify all that ~~sank~~ in their blood
Justify all that have died on the gallows
     hid, or have
Justify all that have ~~hidden or~~ stood,
Or have marched the night long
Singing, singing a song

Those fanatics all that work would undo
        etc. etc.

This is the moment weighs all in a balance
Keep order, leadership, nerves that are steel,
Or mock the memory of the Red O'Donnell,
Mock the memory of the great O'Neill,
Mock Emmet, mock Parnell
All the renownéd that fell.

Those fanatics all that work would undo
        etc. etc.

I.

Justify all those renowned generations;
They left their bodies to fatten the wolves,
They left their homesteads to shelter the foxes,
Fled to far countries, or sheltered themselves
In cavern, crevice, or hole,
Defending Ireland's soul.

Those fanatics all that we do would undo;
Down the fanatic, down the clown,
Down, down, hammer them down,
Down to the tune of O'Donnell Abu.

Justify all those renowned generations,
Justify all that have sunk in their blood,
Justify all that have died on the scaffold,
Justify all that have fled or have stood,
Or have marched the night long,
Singing, singing a song.

Those fanatics all that we do would undo;
. . . .

Fail, and that history turns into rubbish,
All that great past to a trouble of fools;
Those that come after shall mock O'Donnell,
Mock at the memory of both O'Neills,
Mock Emmett, mock Parnell,
All the renown that fell.

Those fanatics all that we do would undo;
. . . .

POLITICS AND THE YEATSIAN APOCALYPSE

AUGUSTINE MARTIN

Apocalypse

In the Christian Dispensation the word "apocalypse" denotes the revelation granted to John the Evangelist, on the Isle of Patmos; foretelling the end of the world and the signs and wonders accompanying it. That last book of the New Testament which Catholics call The Apocalypse of St John is usually referred to as the Book of "Revelations" in the Protestant tradition. The term apocalypse has otherwise been largely used to mean any kind of revelation involving the end of the world, or at least the end to some decisive phase in the world's history marked by signs and portents. The word "millennial" is often used to describe the apocalyptic process whether it be lineal and terminal, on the one hand, or cyclical and recurrent, on the other. In the former case eschatologists speak of a last battle between good and evil, calling it "Armageddon"; in the latter case they speak of a "New Dispensation". The "cyclical" version of historic process was also favoured in the pre-Christian world, notably in the thought of Plato.

Though Yeats is regarded as eminently a poet of apocalypse, none of these key words occurs in his poetry—with the exception of "revelation" which makes its sole and thunderous entry in "The Second Coming". Their absence is not remarkable in itself. The reason may be purely aesthetic — as words they are rather dry and abstract in texture; and none of them moves easily to the iambic beat of English verse.

The study of apocalypse developed its own intellectual discipline: Eschatology: contemplation of the last four things, Heaven, Hell, Death and Judgment. I have checked in the *Concordance* to see how they fare in Yeats's poetical economy.

JUDGMENT: makes four appearances, two of them germane to our theme: "Crazy Jane on the Day of Judgment" and "The Man and the Echo", the second profoundly significant as the poet "stands in judgment on his soul" and thereafter "sinks at last into the night".

HEAVEN and its variations occupy almost a page of the *Concordance*. About a quarter are used with relevance to our concern, others being merely decorative or conventional as with "He Wishes for the Cloths of Heaven". A pattern recurs in the early poems associated with what I provisionally term "soft-core apocalypse": thus *The Wanderings of Oisin* foretells that "earth and heaven and hell would die"; *The Shadowy Waters* foresees a time "when earth and heaven would be folded up" or alternatively "when heaven and earth are withering"; the early "Rose" poems presage that "peace of heaven with hell" of which Blake had so frequently written. I call these "soft-core" because they are not accompanied by historical violence and are thus distinguished from his later poems of apocalypse written after 1917. They are part of what Yeats himself called "the poetry of longing and complaint, the cry of the heart against necessity".

It is characteristic of this soulful early mood that in *The Island of Statues* "all night long the heavens weep and weep" while later, in sharp contrast, "heaven yawns" and its joints "crack" in "Crazy Jane Reproved". In "The Tower" the human soul leaps into a "desolate heaven", while finding positive injustice in the world epitomized by the title of "The Cold Heaven". In the apocalyptic sense, heaven, singular and plural, has a notably active force in the later poems, "blazing into the head" in "Lapis Lazuli", controlling the stars in "Veronica's Napkin"; labouring and sighing in "The Lady's Third Song", and "opening" momentously as "gyres run on" in "Under Ben Bulben". The adjectival form understandably, as with "all heavenly glory" in "Among School Children", is mostly honorific and benign.

HELL: curiously the word occurs only thirteen times and its apocalyptic reference is confined to its association with Heaven in the early poems noted above.

DEATH: like all serious poets Yeats is much possessed with it. Together with its morphemes, death takes up four pages of the *Concordance*, a vivid minority of the references being relevant to the apocalyptic theme: "God's death" is but a play in the "Two Songs" from *The Resurrection*; that inscrutable "crime of death and birth" enlivens the "Dialogue of Self and Soul"; in "Upon a Dying Lady" the heroine joins those legendary world-shakers,

> Achilles, Timon, Babar, Barhaim, all
> Who have lived in joy and laughed into the face of Death.

(*CP*:179; *PNE*:179)

In "Blood and the Moon" he asks

> Is every modern nation like the tower,
> Half dead at the top?
>
> *(CP*:269; *PNE*:243)

"Agamemnon dead" in "Leda and the Swan" marks the fall of the Trojan world; "Children dazed or dead" are victims of the crumbling gyre, with the "Crazed Moon ... staggering in the sky"; because of "those new dead" in "The Spirit Medium" the speaker clings to the solace of spade and earth.

I now want to distinguish Yeats's early intimations of apocalypse from his later — without, I hope, compromising the continuity between them. A passage from his celebrated Introduction to *The Resurrection* — a play of later, "hard-core apocalypse" — provides the necessary perspective,

> When I was a boy everyone talked about progress, and rebellion against my elders took the form of aversion to that myth. I took satisfaction in certain public disasters, felt a sort of ecstasy at the contemplation of ruin, and then came upon the story of Oisin in Tir na nOg, and reshaped it into my "Wanderings of Oisin".... Presently Oisin and his islands faded and the sort of images that came into "Rosa Alchemica" and "The Adoration of the Magi" took their place. Our civilisation was about to reverse itself, or some new civilisation was about to be born from all that our age rejected, from all that my stories symbolised as a harlot, and take after its mother; because we had worshipped a single god it would worship many or receive from Joachim of Flora's Holy Spirit a multitudinous influx (*VPl*:932).

Yeats sees in *The Wanderings of Oisin* and these two stories a unity of concern not immediately visible to the reader, chiefly because he did not carry through his plans for the poem. He had planned for it "an elaborate metaphor of a breaking wave intended to prove that all life rose and fell in the poem" and the hero, having experienced Christian revelation, was to have "passed in death over another sea to another island" (*ibid.*).

I have discussed elsewhere the apocalyptic structure of *The Secret Rose* (1897), which had been first planned so as to end with "The Adoration of the Magi".[1] The volume would then have encompassed the

---

1. Augustine Martin, "Apocalyptic Structure in Yeats's *Secret Rose*", *Studies*, LXIV/253 (Spring 1975), 24-35.

"twenty centuries of stony sleep" of the Christian era, enacted the savage Nativity and Epiphany of a New Dispensation, and thus supplied the millennial continuity abandoned in the execution of *The Wanderings of Oisin*.

The figure of Michael Robartes presides over "Rosa Alchemica" and "The Adoration of the Magi". The character is based on MacGregor Mathers whom Yeats met in London around 1888 and whose Order of the Golden Dawn Yeats joined in 1890. This occult sodality becomes the Order of the Alchemical Rose in these millennial stories. Mathers was convinced that the present world was doomed to perish in some vast holocaust:

> He began to foresee changes in the world, announcing in 1893 or 1894 the imminence of immense wars .... Was this prophecy of his, which would shortly be repeated by mediums and clairvoyants all over the world, an unconscious inference taken up into an imagination brooding upon war, or was it prevision? (*Au*:336)

Yeats's own field research threw up the ubiquitous belief among Irish country people in the Battle of the Valley of the Black Pig, a prophecy informing several poems in *The Wind Among the Reeds*. In a prose sketch entitled "War", published in the 1902 edition of *The Celtic Twilight*, he reports a conversation he had with an Irish countrywoman:

> And presently our talk of war shifted, as it had a way of doing, to the battle of the Black Pig, which seems to her a battle between Ireland and England, but to me an Armageddon which shall quench all things in Ancestral Darkness ... (*Myth*:111).

In a note to his lyric, "The Valley of the Black Pig" he writes,

> I have myself heard said that the girths shall rot from the bellies of the horses, because of the few men that shall come alive out of the valley (*VP*:161).

And in the lyric itself

>   ... unknown spears
> Suddenly hurtle before my dream-awakened eyes,
> And the clash of fallen horsemen and the cries
> Of unknown perishing armies beat about my ears.
> (*CP*:73; *PNE*:60)

while the speaker grows "weary of the world's empires".

This final phase introduces the last word I want to chase in the *Concordance*, that most crucial of all Yeats's apocalyptic words — "world". Like Martha Clifford in *Ulysses*, Yeats "does not like that world".

WORLD, with its morphemes takes up three pages of the *Concordance*: about half of these are conventional — "They have gone about the world like wind". There are then two crucial and related senses of the word, both of them related to our theme.

There is the biblical, New Testament, sense of "world", the sense in which, according to the Parable of the Unjust Steward, the "children of this world are wiser in their generation than the children of light"; the same sense in which the Christian, with baptism, renounces "the World, the Flesh and the Devil". The most schematic example of this usage is in "Beggar to Beggar cried" where the speaker finds it "time to put off the world" in order to — "make my soul" and to "rid me of the devil in my shoes ... And the worse devil that is between my thighs". But the idea is already prominent in "The Song of the Happy Shepherd" where the "sick children of the world" are warned against scientific materialism, and later, in "Adam's Curse" where the poetic spirit exclaims against the

> ... bankers, schoolmasters, and clergymen
> The martyrs call the world.
>
> (*CP*:89; *PNE*:83)

This biblical sense of "world" is, of course, closely related to its use in English Romantic poetry: in Wordsworth's "the world is too much with us" it is seen as the enemy of the health-giving and upper-case "Nature".

(With Yeats "nature" has no such status, it is largely an indifferent, often a destructive force; but most significantly it connotes material process as opposed to the eternity of the soul and of art. The poet in "Sailing to Byzantium" is "out of nature", free to contemplate its process. God will eventually "burn nature with a kiss" as in "The Man who Dreamed of Fairyland". "Earth", on the other hand, is mostly seen affectionately: "The old earth's dreamy youth" is a source of inspiration and healing to the Happy Shepherd.)

The second sense of the "world" is a place which is soon to pass away. Considering its first meaning this consummation is devoutly to be wished, and is repeatedly wished in the lyrics. The exemplary poem here is "He Mourns for the Change that has come upon him and his Beloved, and longs for the End of the World" in *The Wind among the Reeds*

(1899), which is, with *The Secret Rose*, his summary *fin-de-siècle* statement, epitome of his "soft-core apocalypse". Already in *Oisin* we have seen "God shake the world with restless hands"; in "The Rose of the World" the poet "and the labouring world are passing by"; "time and the world are ever in flight" in "Into the Twilight"; in "The Blessed" again "time and the world are ebbing away".

How this world is to end, whether with a bang or a whimper, is never quite clear. Yeats's letters of the period show, here and there, a man sniffing the wind for rumours of wars. Apocalyptic doctrine does ordain — as far back as in Plato's *Laws* — that the moments of change must involve violence. Yeats himself had exclaimed, after seeing Alfred Jarry's *Ubu Roi*:

> After Stephane Mallarmé, after Paul Verlaine, after Gustave Moreau, after Puvis de Chavannes, after our own verse, after all our subtle colour and nervous rhythm, after the faint mixed tints of Conder, what more is possible? After us the Savage God (*Au*:349).

But is that savage god, who brings down the philistine fabric of Victorianism, destined to "preside" over the new dispensation making it an age of brutal anarchy? Or is he merely the agent of change, a portent of apocalypse, like the "boar without bristles" that comes out of the West in "He mourns for the Change"? And what is his relationship to the rough beasts and rampant swans of the later "hard-core" apocalyptics? To arrive at an answer it will help to look again at "Rosa Alchemica" and "The Tables of the Law".

The narrator of "Rosa Alchemica", a lapsed Rosicrucian, is still a practitioner and scholar of alchemy on which he is writing a book when the story opens. Alchemy was the central sacrament of these Rosicrucians — fictional counterparts of the Golden Dawn — who had derived it in turn from Hermetism and Theosophy. The narrator reveals that the true alchemist "sought to fashion gold out of common metals merely as part of an universal transformation of all things into some divine and imperishable substance". The book he is writing is intended as a "fanciful reverie over the transmutation of life into art, and a cry of measureless desire for a world made wholly of essences" (*VSR*:126).

His reverie is interrupted by Michael Robartes who conveys him to the temple of the Alchemical Rose which stands on the Atlantic coast, lecturing him as they go on the imminent return of the pagan gods, Celtic and Classical. When the narrator performs the dance of initiation he notices an image of the Alchemical Rose on the ceiling and, on the floor, the face of "a pale Christ on a pale cross". (It is worth noting that the story appeared side by side with an essay by Havelock Ellis on Nietzsche in *The Savoy*, April 1896). When he asks for an explanation he is told that the dancers desire "to trouble His unity with their multitudinous feet" (*ibid.*:146).

In "The Tables of the Law" the same narrator recalls that Owen Aherne had believed "that the beautiful arts were sent into the world to overthrow nations, and finally life herself, by sowing everywhere unlimited desires, like torches thrown into a burning city", a belief given weight later "by the fermentation of belief which is coming upon our [Irish] people with the reawakening of their imaginative life" (*ibid.*:151).

In "The Adoration of the Magi" the same narrator — waiting in dread of "that inquietude of the veil of the temple, which M. Mallarmé considers a characteristic of our times" (*ibid.*:165) — is visited by three old Irish storytellers from a western island. They had been reading Virgil's "Messianic Eclogue" — Yeats mentions the Fifth while clearly meaning the Fourth Eclogue — when a voice comes to them over the waters telling them to set out for Paris where a dying woman will give them "the secret names of the gods" which when intoned bring back the Immortals (*ibid.*:166). They make the journey, finding a beautiful, dying Irishwoman in a Parisian brothel. As they kneel by the bedside they hear the voice of Hermes telling them to "bow down before her ... that the Immortals may come again" (*ibid.*:168).

The voice continues: "When the Immortals would overthrow the things of to-day and bring in the things that were yesterday, they have no-one to help them, but one whom the things that are to-day have cast out ... this woman has been driven out of time and has lain upon the bosom of Eternity." Hermes goes on to announce that "another Argo shall carry over the sea, and another Achilles beleaguer another Troy" (*ibid.*:169). In time the woman revives long enough to intone the secret names of the Irish gods and other names "till the spirit went out of her body" (*ibid.*:170). A final name they do not catch, but it is explained to them that it was that of a "symbolist painter" who attended the Black Mass and had "taught her to see visions and to hear voices" (*ibid.*:171).

(In a 1925 version Yeats altered the story to accord with the "hard-core apocalypse" of the period: "another Leda would open her knees to the swan, another Achilles beleaguer Troy" [*Myth*:310]; the harlot gives birth to "the likeness of a unicorn ... most unlike man of all living things, being cold, hard and virginal" [*ibid.*:312]. Some critics, neglecting to compare the several versions, have mistakenly attributed these uncompromising images to the earlier, softer version of the fable.)

The evidence of these stories, together with that of the poems and commentaries, suggests the overthrow of Victorian convention and ethics in favour of no brutal disorder, but of a subversive concept of art and beauty — "torches thrown into a burning city" — distilled from Nietzsche, Pater, Wilde and Gustave Moreau, sponsored by such mystical patrons as Joachim with his "multitudinous influx" and Blake, who wrote of Christ: "His mother should a harlot have been,/ Just such an one as Magdalen"; and Shelley, who announced:

> The world's great age begins anew;
> The golden age returns.

That the Armageddon should be an Irish affair, with Celtic gods and mystic harlot, is consonant with current Renanesque theories of the Celt and with Yeats's current determination to found an Order of Celtic mysteries, and to find, with the help of "A.E." a Celtic Avatar among the hills of Donegal.

After this Armageddon, I would therefore insist, the New Dispensation would be akin to the dream of the Alchemists: a new Golden Age of the kind foretold in Virgil's Eclogue; Joachim's Age of the Holy Spirit; Blake's Golden Age of the Ancients. It is indeed, as Yeats is soon to acknowledge, a "fanciful reverie" which he quickly buries — marking the spot — as the century turns and he enters upon the Iron Age of the Lane controversy and the *Playboy* riots, the world out of which the "hard-core" apocalyptics of his middle age are born.

But these feverish millennial hopes are dramatically revived in 1914 when Mathers' prophecies of "immense wars" become a reality. The poet who can so eloquently despair of sacrificial blood in "September 1913" soon finds himself celebrating the Medusa birth of "a terrible beauty" in "Easter 1916", completing that brilliant triptych with "Nineteen Hundred and Nineteen" which faces the appalling reality that "days are dragon-ridden" while nightmare "rides upon sleep". And in a shrewd reversal of Tennyson's nervous Christian optimism he acknowledges with mingled dread and fascination:

> So the Platonic Year
> Whirls out new right and wrong,
> Whirls in the old instead;
> All men are dancers and their tread
> Goes to the barbarous clangour of a gong.
>
> 						(*CP*:234; *PNE*:213)

This visionary terrorism, born of an apprehension of total war, has drawn upon the poet charges of "hysteria", "brutality", "fascist authoritarianism". The poem used most to indict him is "The Second Coming", written in the midst of Ireland's experience of the Black and Tans, and in the bloody aftermath of the Russian Revolution. The most celebrated of these indictments has come from Harold Bloom in his book *Yeats* (1970) where he levels charges that have often been reiterated, especially in the terminology of Marxism. Having, with a spirited pedantry, upbraided Yeats for switching from an imagology of St Matthew's "second coming of Jesus" in the final text — why can't Yeats have his clinamen? — he concentrates his fire-power at the second stanza:

> With the second stanza, heretofore evaded difficulties crowd upon the detached reader, if he can resist not only Yeats's heroic rhetoric but also the awed piety of the exegetes. The poet (or the poem's speaker) says "surely" revelation, the uncovering of the apocalypse, is at hand, but what in the poem justifies that word surely? Mere anarchy does not always bring on revelation, and we would all of us be scarred with multiple apocalypses by now if every loosing of a blood-dimmed tide had compelled the final reality to appear .... In fact the Second Birth of the sphinx of Egypt, even in the poet's personal apocalypse, is what comes upon him, and us .... In what sense will the rough beast be "born" at Bethlehem? Clearly, not literally, but is it legitimate then to use "born" for what would be a demonic epiphany?

He concludes that Ivor Winters was justified in asserting that

> Yeats's attitude towards the beast is different from ours; we may find the beast terrifying, but Yeats finds him satisfying — he is Yeats's judgment upon all that we regard as civilized. Yeats approves of his kind of brutality.[2]

I have tried so far in this essay to give a context, a sense of continuity and human process to Yeats's dialogue with apocalypse. Therefore I may be forgiven if I point to that quibble with the word "surely" which can be usefully referred to one of Yeats's early annunciation of apocalypse, the final couplet of "The Secret Rose":

> Surely thine hour has come, thy great wind blows,

---

2. Harold Bloom, *Yeats*, London, 1970, 322-23.

Far-off, most secret and inviolate Rose?

(*CP*:78; *PNE*:67)

Exclamations like "surely" are characteristic, and highly effective, gestures of the apocalyptic liturgy. But the assertion I want to refute categorically — and I hope for the last time — is the assumption that the "rough beast", any more than the "savage god" will preside over the new dispensation, or that the poet in any way "approves of this kind of brutality". The rough beast is a portent of change and the violence that accompanies it. When Yeats seems to be saying "let it come down" he is responding as a human being does in the pause before an imminent and inevitable thunder-storm.

It has been the misfortune of his generation to be born into the end of a primary phase, a miserable changing-post in history, marked by the eclipse of the individual personality and the tyranny of systems — Socialism, Capitalism, Communism, Administration, Democracy itself. In a world where "Conduct and work grow coarse, and coarse the soul" the poet, in the expectation of momentous change, utters "that one word 'Rejoice'", it is because the ugliness will soon be over and humanity will run on "that unfashionable gyre again". Out of the violence that accompanies the crumbling of the primary gyre, the end of the millennium, will emerge a new antithetical civilization, reaching its fullness, its new "Unity of Being", around AD 2,500. Like its great predecessors, Athens, Byzantium and Urbino, it will find "Delight in Art whose end is peace". And if Yeats's belief in reincarnation holds good he may be reborn into it, perhaps as a court poet.

Politics

When Yeats died fifty-five years ago, in January 1939, W.H. Auden, perhaps the most excitable political intelligence among English poets, produced an elegy which appeared in the *New Republic*, in March, and an article, "The Public *v* Mr William Butler Yeats", which appeared in the Spring issue of the *Partisan Review* of that year. Both are sharply relevant to the poet's standing today, and to the political controversies that currently centre upon his work. Auden is torn between his admiration for Yeats's poetic accomplishments and alarm at his political attitudes. The poem is contorted with a desire to find excuses for Yeats: "mad Ireland hurt him into poetry". And in the long run "time", that old reliable, having no political conscience, only an adoration of language, will in due course absolve him and his breed:

Time that with this strange excuse

Pardoned Kipling and his views,
And will pardon Paul Claudel,
Pardon him for writing well.

Realizing, correctly, that time might not pardon *him* for writing thus, Auden excluded these lines from subsequent editions of the poem. But other lines remain: to the effect that "poetry makes nothing happen"; "Ireland", after all, "has her madness and her weather still". And, in the article, the Defence Counsel concludes that "art is a product of history, not a cause", that the Prosecution is deluded in thinking that "art makes anything happen".[3] It could be Haines, another troubled Englishman, telling Stephen Dedalus: "It seems history is to blame." It goes without saying that this sort of absolution would have infuriated Yeats, who in his youth would not give a penny for a song unless "the poet sang it with such airs/That one believed he had a sword upstairs", and in his old age could lie awake wondering if "that play of mine sent out/Certain men the English shot".

The decades that followed brought the New Criticism to dominate the academies and for a long period there was little or no interrogation of Yeats's politics. Instead extravagant energies were bent upon exploration of the weird and labyrinthine sources of the thought, exposure of the early drafts and their subsequent revisions, publication of the occasional prose and of the letters, biographical investigation of the Yeats family ("He, she, all of them — yea"), and the perennial homage of the Summer School at Sligo. This could not and did not last.

The reaction set in with Cruise O'Brien's 1965 essay, "Passion and Cunning: Politics of Yeats", in which he asserted that Yeats "expected and hoped, that Ireland 'after the revolution' would be a sort of satellite of a Fascist-dominated Europe". Then came books, largely countervailing, by Elizabeth Cullingford and Grattan Freyer, before the onslaught of the Freudian, Marxist, Feminist, Deconstructionist criticism of the Eighties. These criticisms found their chief Irish platform in the *Crane Bag* magazine and continued among the Field Day pamphleteers, provoking a modicum of healthy controversy.

The Auden dilemma is, for instance, rehearsed, but again left unresolved, by Terry Eagleton when he dismisses "All the values, in short, of the artistically admirable, politically revolting 'Prayer for my Daughter'". But "writing well" does nothing to save the poet from

---

3. W.H. Auden, "The Public *v* the Late Mr William Butler Yeats" (1939), repr. in *W.B. Yeats*, ed. William H. Pritchard, Penguin, 1972, 142. Auden's poem is reprinted in this volume on pages 143-45.

sustained charges of "phallocentric ideology", "swaggering, anarchic Byronic affirmation", and "reactionary political ideology".[4] Tom Paulin is also disturbed by Yeats's "phallocentric vision" and voices a recurrent contrast with Joyce (who is urban, pacifist, modern and "socialist" — therefore favourite of these schoolrooms): "where Yeats often mobilizes some of the most rabid goblins of nationalist emotion, Joyce scorned consciously *volkisch* ideas."[5] Such charges as these are rehearsed with various emphasis by Seamus Deane, Declan Kiberd, Fintan O'Toole and others who see Yeats as an irresistible challenge to a leftist, political — and largely polemical — criticism: his phoney aristocracy and surrender to violence, his promotion of the phoney pastoral at the expense of the authentic urban, and so on.

The charges, however rudely I summarize them, keep reminding me of my first lessons in literary criticism: that I should not rush to moral judgment; that the poem is first a poem and not a homily; that I should get rid of that schoolboy idea instilled by priest and teacher that a poem need be in any way "uplifting"; that it is sharp practice to extract the conceptual meaning from a poem and judge the poem be judging it.

On the other hand "writing well" is not enough. I do not understand how a poem can be "politically revolting" while remaining a good poem, let alone a great one like "Prayer for my Daughter". (Does Terry Eagleton judge it a good poem in its totality? he declines to say.) In other words I declare my prejudice against a criticism that asks the political or the moral questions first or which refuses to see a poem as an integral act.

This having been said it is, it seems, necessary to say again that Yeats's attitude to any of these themes — sex, love, power, violence, class, history — cannot be established by recourse to any single poem. In the first place he was constantly developing, learning and unlearning. The same love poet wrote "The Cloths of Heaven", "The Travail of Passion", "No Second Troy", "Adam's Curse", "Broken Dreams", "The Mermaid", "Solomon and Sheba", "Crazy Jane Talks to the Bishop" and "The Spur". The same political animal wrote "September 1913", corrected it with "Easter 1916", reversed that with "Nineteen Hundred and Nineteen" and cancelled all of them with "The Great Day":

> Hurrah for revolution and more cannon-shot!
> A beggar on horseback lashes a beggar on foot.

---

4. Terry Eagleton, *Crane Bag*, IX/2 (1985).

5. Tom Paulin, *Ireland and the English Crisis*, Newcastle upon Tyne, 1985.

Hurrah for revolutions and cannon come again!
The beggars have changed places, but the lash goes on.
                                        (*CP*:358; *PNE*:343)

So he kept changing, and changing his mind. He believed like every poet
in history that poetry is a privileged mode of thought with the right to
say "this might be how things are, or this, or again this". His astonishing
range, the endless variety of his forms, lyric, epic, elegiac, dramatic,
reflective, and of his moods, is therefore an infallible hallmark of his
genius. His elaborate response to every nuance of contemporary history,
the dialogue between his public and private self, is another.

So he grew and changed. But furthermore his art is not syncretic but
antinomial, dialectical. His method is to state a position with maximum
intensity and draw from that utterance the energy to state its opposite.
Neither statement is essentially "true", far less so can it be held to
represent the poet's settled conviction on the matter. One who knows his
Yeats is therefore outraged to see another seize upon and isolate any
single poem to trap the general conscience of the poet. Especially
outraged to see a *section* of a long symphonic poem like "Meditations in
Time of Civil War" debated as if its status could be other than
provisional in the poem's general economy. That opening movement,
"Ancestral Houses", was a source of controversy between Seamus Deane
and Denis Donoghue (*Irish Review*, Number 5, Winter 1988) where its
statements on aristocracy, violence and greatness are treated as if the
poem ended there and did not embody in its sixth movement, "The
Snare's Nest at my Window", one of the most piercing — and self-
accusing — cries for compassion and peace in all modern literature:

We had fed the heart on fantasies,
The heart's grown brutal from the fare;
More substance in our enmities
Than in our love; O honey-bees,
Come build in the empty house of the stare.
                                        (*CP*:230-31; *PNE*:211)

That poetic sequence, in fact, dramatizes in each of its seven parts a
different apprehension of violence. The first asks, with resonant
impersonality whether man's greatness is somehow indivisible from his
violence. The second records that the tower where he pursues his
peaceful meditations, once built by men-at-arms as a fortress, has
resumed for him its function as a "befitting emblem of adversity". The
third contemplates Sato's sword, symbol of art and war, destruction and

creation, and of apocalypse — "Juno's peacock screamed". The fourth ponders whether his descendants, born between art and violence, will flourish or decline. The fifth finds the poet, a man of words, envying the men of action who appear at his door. The sixth, with mounting personal involvement, prays for peace — "the sweetness that all longed for night and day". In the last the poet, "his wits astray" — imagines himself in a vision of millennial panic almost yielding to the fever of mob violence, before returning to the solitude of his sedentary craft.

The poem in Sidney's purest sense "nothing affirmeth"; but no poet since Shakespeare has confronted the terrible urge to violence that human kind has everywhere in common; our compulsion to murder and create. Nor has any poet, even Shakespeare, so dramatized the rage for order that accompanies our temptation to immerse in the destructive element. This is intrinsic to his greatness. It is easy to condemn violence, war, the lot. It takes especial courage to confront it in oneself and give witness — "What theme had Homer but original sin?" That, I suspect, is why Yeats was so dismissive of Wilfred Owen and the war poets. They had the comfort of being right. Yeats, on the other hand, takes the big risks, and goes at times over the top. But only the most perversely hostile reading would convict his poetry as a whole of sponsoring violence.

As for Fascism: here we must be most scrupulous of all in seeking to indict a conscientious senator of the fledgling state. With the exception of his speech on divorce — an altogether forgivable oratorical *tour de force* — his contributions to the House were sensible and balanced on education, censorship, public order, partition — which he suggested would be solved only by the Free State making its life-style attractive enough for northern Unionists to want a share of it.

He had sought in vain among Mussolini's experiments and Gentile's thought for a model of the "corporate state" applicable to Cosgrave's democratic vision of the nation. He had despaired of conscripting the visions of Swift, Berkeley or of "haughtier-headed Burke who proved the State a tree" to the conditions of de Valera's Ireland. He found himself weary of ideology:

> How can I, that girl standing there
> My attention fix
> On Roman or on Russian
> Or on Spanish politics?

> (*CP*:392-93; *PNE*:374)

Besides, why should I trouble about communism, fascism, liberalism, radicalism, when all, though some bow first and some stern first but all at the same pace, all are going down stream with the artificial unity which ends every civilisation? (*L*:869)

Only the implosion of the cycle will bring back the promise of an organic society, the unity of being implicit in a new dispensation; a world where politics will cohere with culture, to find unity of being and run on "that unfashionable gyre again."

THE DEATH OF CUCHULAIN AND THE POLITICS OF MYTH

ANDREW PARKIN

During his lifetime Yeats was often attacked, as he is sometimes even nowadays, by those who for religious or political reasons perceived his values and attitudes to be dangerous to their own causes. The attacks, of course, continue, politics being what it is, but with this difference: when Yeats was alive critics could treat him as a contemporary rather than as a "great writer". Now his critics are all faced with the awkward fact that he is undoubtedly Ireland's greatest poet and overall writer, when we take into account his drama, his theatre work, and his body of essays and stories. If as rationalists critics deplore his occult side, or as international socialists his "reactionary" attitudes, they still have to account for his literary achievement, unless they are going to take the intellectually bankrupt line that there is no such thing as "great" literature or "great" writers, thus leaving the way open for the thought police to move in and make not literary but merely ideological judgments. Such tactics work only in a class where teachers are controlling grades or in a country where a government is controlling all the publishing.

My own study of Yeats's work over the past thirty years has taught me that the world of party politics, "politics" in one of its more usual senses, is more often than not irrelevant to him. It may occupy many people, arouse them to action, and kill them in great numbers. It thus seems all-important, crucial, and sometimes worth killing for. In a small country like Ireland, politics in this sense becomes particularly urgent and sometimes very squalid. But Yeats had a larger vision; he was European as well as Irish, Asian as well as European. This breadth of vision is still rare, even in our era of multiculturalism. From this wider point of view, those locked in political dispute or struggle can be seen to be pursuing a "myth", the popular myth that party politics alone achieves progress, solutions to social problems, and makes real changes. From this broader view also, political killing can be seen not only as morally inexcusable; it can also be regarded as the result of myths, fantasies used to serve the ends of party politics, or, worse still, politicians, and leading to an odious brutalizing of the heart. Yeats expressed this in "The Stare's Nest By My Window" and "Nineteen Hundred and Nineteen":

> We pieced our thoughts into philosophy,
> And planned to bring the world under a rule,
> Who are but weasels fighting in a hole.
>
> (*CP*:233; *PNE*:213)

Fahmy Farag has ably shown in his *The Opposing Virtues* that critics caught up in the myth of politics promulgated in the newspapers and by political parties very often misread Yeats.[1] Farag acknowledges Yeats's dislike of liberal democracy (a dangerous dislike shared by many of his left and right wing contemporaries, as well as by communist fellow-travellers in academia from say, 1918 to the recent collapse of the Marxist-Leninist empire); nor does Farag ignore Yeats's mistake in having anything to do with the Irish Fascist Blue Shirts.[2] This was an error Yeats himself soon admitted and regretted. But Farag shows convincingly that Yeats was certainly no Fascist. Left wing critics who attack him remember that he inveighed against communism but they ignore his dislike of the Fascists. Farag points out that by 1936 Yeats had lost "faith in any form of modern government".[3] Yeats had asked: "why should I trouble about communism, fascism, liberalism, radicalism, when all ... are going down stream with the artificial unity which ends every civilization? Only dead sticks can be tied into convenient bundles" (*L*:869).

The last remark was an adroit use of the Fascist emblem of the sheaf to point out that people who allowed themselves to be swept into the Fascist or any other bundle were spiritually and imaginatively dead. Yeats rejects earthly politics partly because he has spent a lifetime working out a metaphysical system in which he finds a cyclic pattern to history and within individual human lives, a system which would give him metaphors to express his vision of the life and soul of mankind. Art was the vision of the reality he had come to perceive, and party politics was a far cry from this vision. The pre-Socratic philosophers, the neo-Platonists, the occult writers he read, and his study of oriental thought and art gave him a very different perspective from naive pre-war

---

1. Fahmy Farag, *The Opposing Virtues*, Dublin, 1978.

2. For a more detailed account of this movement than is to be found in any literary scholarship, see Maurice Manning's *The Blueshirts*, Dublin, 1971, rpt. 1987.

3. Farag, 42.

pacifists, murderous Nazis, and Communists. Another part of his rejection of the myth of party or national politics was his horror of its blood-lust: "my horror at the cruelty of governments grows greater.... Communist, Fascist, nationalist, clerical, anti-clerical, are all responsible according to the number of their victims" (*L*:851).

In *Last Poems* Yeats rejects politics in the widely-known lyric of that title. He admits the very real possibility that " '*In our time the destiny of man presents its meaning in political terms*'" (*CP*:392; *PNE*:374). At the same time he sees as more absorbing his own human condition, that of a dying man lusting for life. To the pious and puritanical (political parties and senior common rooms are full of them), this is heresy. Yeats, however, was being true to his own artistic instinct. If the received wisdom of the majority is to see everything in political terms, the artist's task is to resist.

This weariness with politics was something he had naturally felt much earlier — he had remarked to Joseph Holloway, the inveterate Abbey Theatre diarist, "People who do aught for Ireland ever and always have to fight with the waves in the end".[4] His dislike of the deviousness, false bonhomie, and arrogance of politicians came out in the portrait of King Conchubar in the Cuchulain play *On Baile's Strand*, where Cuchulain, lured into political allegiance, tragically ends up killing his own son and, realizing what he has done, goes mad for revenge, but is diverted by Druid magic from attacking Conchubar and instead fights the waves of the sea. Yeats uses myth to bring out a point about the tragedy that politics can cause. We might call this a Yeatsian politics of myth.

The politics of myth emerges very powerfully in Yeats's last play, written on his death-bed, *The Death of Cuchulain*. This play is remarkable for its energy and momentum. Writing in the hills of southern France in the winter of 1938 and the January of 1939, the month in which he died, Yeats completes his cycle of Cuchulain plays with the death of his hero. Mussolini's Italy was not far along the railway track from Monaco. Franco's Spain was quite close. Hitler, although somewhat further away, was quite obviously bent on another war. And his Soviet allies had their most spectacular show trial in 1938.[5] In the same year the "Treaty Ports" were handed over by Britain to the Irish government,

---

4. *Joseph Holloway's Abbey Theatre: A Selection from his Unpublished Journal "Impressions of a Dublin Playgoer"*, eds Robert Hogan and Michael J. O'Neill, Carbondale, 1967, 58.

5. A vividly written account of the 1938 show trial of Bukharin and others may be found in Fitzroy Maclean's *Eastern Approaches* (1964), Chicago, 1980, 78-118.

who, in exchange, promised that their facilities would be closed to foreign powers in the event of war. Without this arrangement Ireland would have been embroiled in the war. Now it was able to remain neutral, if its leadership could stomach neutrality in a war against the Axis. It could, although many Irish citizens could not.

In the face of another World War, Irish national politics seemed less significant; the men of 1916 were acting on a world stage, albeit near the wings. But now the Free State had been established long enough to show that independence in itself did not bring about immediate improvements in Ireland. Yeats's disgust with certain aspects of his country extended to modern Europe itself, poised for another war. For Yeats's generation things were never the same after 1914. An older civilisation was swept away with unprecedented speed for a mechanized age of new technologies accompanied by political upheaval and rampant materialism. Yeats dramatizes a myth which will express his opposition to the reality around him.

The Death of Cuchulain, a dance play, varies the pattern a little from that established in *At the Hawk's Well*, a play more closely affiliated with Japanese Noh. The play was written for the public stage rather than the salon, relying on a theatrical use of light and darkness, an effect ancient Noh drama lacks because it had no stage lighting in a darkened auditorium.

Yeats begins his play not by plunging into the Irish myth itself but by bringing onstage the Old Man, a representative of the mythopoeic imagination. His monologue suggests that he is the artistic director of the play we are about to see. With this metatheatrical device, Yeats rapidly establishes him as the artist as a wild and wicked old man. This gives us a Yeatsian variant on the Romantic myth of artist as hero: the artist as defeated hero, living on, Tithonus-like, into an age with which he has no sympathy. This embodiment of the mythopoeic imagination is the perfect Master of Ceremonies or Chorus for "the antiquated romantic stuff" (*CPl*:693) of the Yeats play we are about to see. He aligns himself with the French tragedian Talma, who lived through the Revolution of 1789, dressed his productions in historical costumes rather than those of mere fantasy, reformed stage diction, wrote *Reflexions sur Lekain et l'art theatral*, and was the favourite actor of a living legend, Napoleon Bonaparte himself. Suddenly, the Abbey Theatre of 1939 seems contemptibly beside the point. Why had it no Talma working on a scale to match events in Europe? An epic imagination could not thrive there. The Old Man therefore shows us the death of the Irish epic imagination.

Even the musicians for the performance are out of phase with the old values. The Old Man will have to teach them, as Irish poets were to be taught in "Under Ben Bulben"; he will teach them "the music of the beggar-man, Homer's music" (*CPl*:694). The greatness of one cycle may survive in some debased form in the outcasts of another cycle. The lost dancer of a previous age could express the wholeness of the tragi-comic view of life, "upon the same neck love and loathing, life and death". Emer will later have to dance with love and loathing, just as the old Irish epics embodied opposing emotions, grotesque comedy and tragic intensity. But the dancer must avoid the balletic style of the tutu. Yeats quickly establishes a myth of the heroic past with which to belabour the present "vile age" with its masses of the half-educated who have no knowledge of the mythic imagination and its epic works. If they know anything it will be "that old maid history" rather than the great defeated epic past, the Ramses of Shelley's "Ozymandias". The Celtic epic world had been swept aside by the rise of modern Europe. That Europe had torn itself apart in 1914-18 and was now poised to finish the job in 1938. In this context Yeats takes the death of Cuchulain as the counterpart of his own death as the last Romantic writer of a crumbling civilization and as an epitaph on the deaths of civilizations, which are born from the energy of the gods but die in decadent squalor. It could well have seemed to the dying Yeats that the new independent Ireland had been born in "terrible beauty" but had already deteriorated and was about to be destroyed in the next world war.

The play begins with the empty space of the imagination; a woman runs on calling the hero by name, "Cuchulain!" The woman is a messenger from Emer, Cuchulain's wife, warning him that he must lose no more time in going out to fight the men of Connacht led by Maeve. Cuchulain thinks the same. Yeats presents the Irish war hero ready to fight to an audience living in an age of appeasement and fashionable pacifism. It was, in fact, the right medicine. But then Cuchulain sees a letter in the messenger's hand; it is from Emer and warns him to wait for reinforcements. Beginning in the middle of a crisis the scene has reached a suspenseful moment of decision within thirty brief lines. Even more rapidly, Yeats links the argument of arms to the sexual theme by surmising that Cuchulain's wife has sent the young woman to sleep with him, further inducing him to resist going to his death. We remember Yeats's *The Only Jealousy of Emer* in which Emer rescued Cuchulain from death by renouncing her right to be loved by him. But Cuchulain makes his heroic and fatal decision to ignore Emer's letter, following his instinct to fight.

At this moment of decision the supernatural force behind the human action appears to the audience in the form of the crow-headed goddess of war, the Morrigu. We are in no doubt that Cuchulain's fate is directed by her just as much as it was by supernatural forces at other crises in his life: when he was led astray at the well of the hawk or when he fought the waves. Cuchulain cannot see the Morrigu but the audience can; the girl messenger is certainly aware of her and is put into a trance by her. Her vision during the trance reveals to the messenger what has happened. She realizes they have been briefly visited by a crow-headed woman; at first she accepts Cuchulain's explanation that it was Morrigu, but then she insists it was Maeve, the warrior queen, grown ugly with "an eye in the middle of her forehead" (*CPl*:696). Human beings are governed by forces they neither perfectly recognize nor understand. These forces Yeats suggests are supernatural; they govern emotions, ideas, and action. Human politics in the so-called "real world" cannot be understood in terms of reason and will alone. The whole being, sexual, emotional, and metaphysical is in fact involved. Yeats's mythic supernatural world impinging on the human world thus proposes a transcendental politics, the supra-rational politics of myth.

Cuchulain responds cynically to the messenger's vision as if it were a deception on her part, as if her message that he must go to fight were not induced by magic but were merely her plan to get him killed so that she might take a new lover. The scene that follows is a lovers' quarrel, it becoming clear to those who know the myth or Yeats's earlier plays about it that the messenger is none other than Cuchulain's young mistress, Eithne Inguba. But his "realistic" interpretation of her behaviour as self-interested is mistaken. Ironically, the mythic hero is reading experience on a cynically materialist level, leaving out the supernatural forces. It is a sign that he now deserves to die, seeing with a merely mortal eye as opposed to that third eye, the spiritual eye in the middle of the forehead that Eithne had glimpsed in her vision. When Eithne, who has seen with the third eye of vision, declares herself ready to die rather than be left as spoil for another warrior, Cuchulain proclaims his devastating lack of trust: "Women have spoken so, plotting a man's death" (*CPl*:698). Has he become at last merely callous, or is he trying to kill her love deliberately that she may take another man willingly, and so survive? It is possible. But the fact that Cuchulain fails to see the Morrigu suggests that he has lost his true vision and is thus in decline.

When Cuchulain goes out to die, Eithne's last words are rhymed couplets, imparting a Shakespearean ring to the end of the scene and an heroic quality to her, as well as suggesting that her lines are a choric commentary on the action. The swift transition by lighting brings us to the next scene, a dying Cuchulain's encounter with Aoife, the mother of his son. Battle (political action) suddenly seems remote. What concerns the dying warrior is his past life and the horror of having killed his own son. The life of the soul now counts for far more than anything else. But Cuchulain finds it hard to understand the crucial personal things Aoife is telling him. She puts it down to the fact that he is weak "Because about to die!" (*CPl*:701). When Aoife hears someone approach she leaves (somewhat unconvincingly); this causes her to miss her revenge, for the Blind Beggar from *On Baile's Strand* appears, identifies himself and Cuchulain, boasts that he will be paid "twelve pennies" for killing the hero, and brings the dramatic action to its crisis, the beheading of Cuchulain. In the manner of Greek tragedy, physical violence is kept off stage, but the scene of the Blind Man preparing to hack off the hero's head is one that works powerfully by suggestion. It captures the full horror of the use of the small knife rather than the sword of battle and the squalor of the killing for money, and not very much money at that. Yeats gives us a version of the myth's climax perfectly attuned to the weasel's tooth view of Irish politics. From myth we can deduce a larger view of politics.

Philip Marcus's study of the manuscripts of the play shows that Yeats had trouble with the ending.[6] After the beheading he had the Old Man coming on with the wooden cube heads; he was to prattle about Lady Gregory's version of the myth, and he was to follow up on Cuchulain's anticipation of bird song (the soul about to sing) by recalling the rhyme "Sing a Song of Sixpence" — "an untrue song & yet immortal".[7] But this idea gave Yeats some difficulty. For one thing, he had used song to follow squalid murder in his previous play, *Purgatory*. His breakthrough was to substitute the Morrigu for the Old Man as choreographer of Emer's dance.[8] It is clear, though, from this draft and from the letter Yeats wrote pointing out that "You can refute Hegel but not the Saint or the Song of Sixpence" (*L*:922) that his concern was to present a dramatic myth without the arguments or explanations of politicians; his task was to make myth the embodiment of his thought and feeling. The Morrigu declares her words are for the dead, that is for the immortal soul — that which endures, generation after generation. What she shows is that the death of the hero was a matter of revenge as much as tribal warfare, of Maeve and her lovers' sexuality as much as revenge. Through myth Yeats could embody earthly wisdom about political action, and even go

---

6. *W.B. Yeats, The Death of Cuchulain: Manuscript Materials, Including the Author's Final Text*, ed. Philip Marcus, Ithaca and London, 1982.

7. Marcus, 93.

8. Marcus, 91.

a step further: by introducing the Morrigu as choreographer Yeats also made the point that although human beings think that they are directing the action (the Old Man at the beginning of the play) supernatural forces may in fact control us. Emer's dance of love and loathing becomes the artistic embodiment of love and grief, sexuality and death. The mythic dimension of human experience is confirmed by the few bird notes, that irrational yet convincing image of the immortality of the soul.

The switch from the heroic age and the mythic action of the play to "some Irish Fair of our day" (*CPl*:704) is swift and effective, using bright lighting effects and pipe and drum music. From a performance point of view I believe that the Singer should be talking as well as singing. Thus in my director's notebook she would introduce her song (perhaps in a Brechtian way) by speaking "The harlot sang to the beggar man" (*CPl*:704) and frame the subsequent lines of the first part of her song at the end by speaking:

> A statue's there to mark the place,
> By Oliver Sheppard done.
> So ends the tale that the harlot
> Sang to the beggar-man.

> > > > > (*CPl*:705)

She might also interrupt her song to confide in the audience (working the crowd at the fair) "Maeve had three in an hour, they say", and introduce the second half of the lyric with a question asked of the crowd: "Are those things that men (with the emphasis on men as opposed to the female) adore and loathe/Their sole reality?" This leaves us with a song that in three lines asserts that the harlot meets the ancient Celtic heroes; another three lines deflate the assertion by regretting she "can get/No grip upon their thighs" (*CPl*:704). The next four lines assert that she meets the legendary horsemen, but deflates it by saying they have long been dead, are merely spirits. The next four lines assert that her love for living men who can deliver the pleasure of the flesh is mixed with loathing, the implication being that the present does not match up to the heroic past. The next part of the song answers the question about man's "sole reality" with three questions challenging the materialistic interpretation of experience. They suggest that the living can at moments of crisis attract to them the spirits of the dead. The men of 1916 were perhaps in the company of the old Celtic warriors. Myth can have a practical political outcome when it inspires or energizes the living. The last part of the song is a quatrain that asserts no modern woman has given birth to a Cuchulain, but an old man (the Old Man at the beginning, and/or Yeats?) observing life imagines such a birth and feels scorn — for Cuchulain? for modern life? It is not clear. Perhaps it is for both:

> No body like his body
> Has modern woman borne,
> But an old man looking on life
> Imagines it in scorn.
>
> (*CPl*:705)

The whole point of the song is that the dreams of the heroic past make the modern world of 1938 seem to be in decline and degenerating. This of course was part of the attraction (for millions of adults in the 1930s) of Fascist and Nazi rhetoric and art, not to mention the larger-than-life heroism of Communist public art. These mass movements of right and left seemed to possess vision and the vital capacity for heroic struggle. But the Old Man of Yeats, and Yeats himself on his death-bed, "imagines it in scorn".

At the end of the play, we are left with a Yeatsian version of the old legendary material that is abbreviated, dramatic, presented on a more human level than the original, but which presents a myth showing that politics and its servant, war, are not rational. Yeats does not lecture, but embodies in the play the supernatural and human springs of action. The politics of myth insists on the history of the soul, a view in which eternity is in love with the productions of time, where desecration and the lover's night are accepted as necessary. The Yeatsian politics of myth refuses to confine itself to "the old maid" history, who knows only the barren chronicle of party politics. The idea that we cannot know historical truth seems just as dangerous in terms of ordinary politics as the Marxist idea that we can know what is historically "inevitable", leaving the way open for cynical manipulation of the population. Yet the advantage of the view that history is a version of events, a myth, is that if the mythopoeic imagination at work on it is powerful and profound enough it can embody in the myth an enduring vision, true to human behaviour and irrefutable by logic.

The last letter of Yeats to be printed in Wade's edition contains the best epigram on the play:

> I am happy, and I think full of an energy, of an energy I had despaired of. It seems to me that I have found what I wanted. When I try to put all into a phrase I say, "Man can embody truth but he cannot know it." I must embody it in the completion of my

life. The abstract is not life and everywhere draws out its contradictions (*L*:922).

In the play, Cuchulain could not know the truth as to whether Eithne was sending him deliberately into a trap; in following his deepest instinct he went out to death and defeat. But the legend made from the ignorant man embodied heroic truth. This gives the politics of myth its enormous power and its very real danger for those trying to deal in the daily politics of negotiation and compromise.

"DISTINGUISHED, INDIRECT AND SYMBOLIC": YEATS AND NOH

C.C. BARFOOT

Accident and purpose both led W.B. Yeats to Noh, for Yeats, like all great and significant artists, was equally the moulder of the aesthetic currents of his time and the moulded. He was made by the artistic modes and movements of the period in which he grew up and matured — the Pre-Raphaelites and the Aesthetic movement — and, possibly as a consequence, this enabled him to shape the course of modern poetry and modern drama. As an Irishman he was also influenced by the national movement, which he encouraged and criticized both in his writing and in his deeds.

Aestheticism and Irish nationalism, then, were part of the air that the young Yeats breathed, and in their different ways both were to prepare the older Yeats for the fruitful reception and creative exploitation of Noh drama when he came upon it, or more accurately, when it came upon him. In the second half of 1913 Ezra Pound met the widow of the Ernest Fenollosa who gave him "about sixteen" of her husband's notebooks "containing", amongst other things "notes on Far Eastern literature, draft translations of Chinese poetry and Noh dramas ...". Pound first began to work on the Noh dramas at Stone Cottage, at Coleman's Hatch in Sussex, which he was sharing with W.B. Yeats, during the winter of 1913-14; and by 31 January 1914 he had finished editing and polishing up Fenollasa's literal translation of *Nishikigi*, which was published in Harriet Monroe's influential Chicago based "Magazine of Verse" *Poetry* in May.[1] Therefore, one might say that through the accident of

---

1. Noel Stock, *The Life of Ezra Pound*, London, 1970, 148-49. Although dated 1916, *"Noh" or Accomplishment*, "a study of the classical stage of Japan by Ernest Fenollosa and Ezra Pound", was published in January 1917 (reprinted in *The Translations of Ezra Pound*, with an introduction by Hugh Kenner, London, 1970, 213-360). This present essay is a shortened and revised version of an article with the same title which first appeared in *Theatre Intercontinental: Forms, Functions, Correspondences*, eds C.C. Barfoot and Cobi Bordewijk, Textxet: Studies in

friendship and an arrangement by which an older poet employed a younger poet as his secretary, Yeats was presented at close domestic quarters with an example of a dramatic style or genre which was to have immediate consequences for his future development as a poetic dramatist. But, as we shall see, perhaps the whole development of Yeats's interest in Noh was not so much of an accident after all.

The aesthetic background

Yeats, with a fashionable painter as a father, grew up in an artistic milieu in London and in Ireland, in which, apart from the inescapable influence of English Romanticism, the two artistic movements that most affected him in his early days were Pre-Raphaelitism, which had begun to lose much of its force when Yeats was born in 1865; and Aestheticism, the which began to develop in the late 1870s and blossomed in the 1880s. Both of these movements, in their different but related ways, were a reaction against basic bourgeois assumptions of academic art. Walter Pater's admonition "to burn always with [a] hard, gemlike flame", and his advocacy of a cult of Beauty and the cult of sensation, was intended and seen as a challenge to the settled moral materialism of Victorian society, with its predilection for sentimental realism.[2]

It had taken more than three decades for *l'art pour l'art* defined by Gautier in his Preface to *Mademoiselle de Maupin* in 1835 to emerge in the final paragraph of Pater's famous essay:

> Of this wisdom, the poetic passion, the desire of beauty, the love of art for art's sake, has most; for art comes to you professing frankly to give nothing but the highest quality to your moments as they pass, and simply for those moments' sake.[3]

On the Continent Aestheticism was soon to transform itself into Symbolism; and for the young Yeats, Aestheticism and Symbolism

---

Comparative Literature 1, Amsterdam and Atlanta: GA, 1993.

2. Pater's "Conclusion" to *The Renaissance*, London, 1873, from which the previous quotation comes, is usually considered to be the text best epitomizing this challenge. Pater felt the need to omit the "Conclusion" in the second edition of the book in 1877, "as [he] conceived it might possibly mislead some of those young men into whose hands it might fall" (the author's own note in later editions of *The Renaissance* which restored the conclusion).

3. See *The Aesthetes: A Sourcebook*, ed. Ian Small, London, 1979, 21 (where the original 1868 version of Pater's "Conclusion" is to be found as a review of "Poems by William Morris" in the *Westminster Review*).

offered a current means of extending his natural inheritance of English Romanticism into recognizably contemporary styles of writing.[4] Most avant-garde art at the end of the nineteenth century — of the kind that one mainly associates with Mallarmé, Verlaine, Rimbaud; dramatists such as Villiers de l'Ilse-Adam (*Axel*, 1890), Maeterlinck (*Pelléas et Mélisande*, 1892); novelists such as Huysmans (*A rebours*, 1884); and painters such as Odilon Redon, Gustave Moreau — was unrealistic, therefore "Symbolist"; non-materialistic, therefore "Spiritualist". So we find that the artistic environment of Yeats's upbringing was not confined to the axis of London and Dublin, but had a Continental credibility that was undoubtedly encouraging to a young artist who was to become increasingly conscious of the demands of Irish nationalism, and wished to assert (like James Joyce later) the broader European affiliations of Irish culture.

What these artists, both at home and abroad, had in common was a desire to render, and to give expression and artistic manifestation to the immaterial, the spiritual, the invisible, the hidden, the esoteric and the exotic. This they attempted to do in works that sought an overall unity of tone, uncontaminated by the physical world, remote, detached, unearthly, in which music and meaning, sense and sensibility, inflection and timbre were blended. Although they often produced small works, even miniatures (so as to remain as pure as possible), the Wagnerian ideal of the *Gesamtkunstwerk* was never far from their thoughts, especially when it came to stage representations, which began to strive for a totality of actions and words, movements and costumes, scenery, movement, delivery, gesture, etc. in the totally designed, totally co-ordinated, coherently patterned work of art. As a consequence, Japanese art, from coloured woodcuts to ceramics, screen-painting, lacquer work, textiles, with its striving for pure expressive beauty that hinted at a vision

---

4. One of the reasons why a self-conscious Aestheticism took some thirty years to begin to influence English art may not be due entirely to the usual defensive insularity of the British: one could argue that the early potent success of the English Romantic poets made the French assertions of artistic independence unnecessary on the other side of the Channel. It could be claimed that Walter Pater's Aestheticism was little more than a shriller reassertion of the Romanticism to be found in such poets as Coleridge and Keats. Yeats admitted in particular the influence of Shelley and Blake, both of whom were seen by him as proto-Symbolists, and, indeed, on the basis of Blake's anticipation of late nineteenth-century mystical notions, was one of the first to recognize his place in the Romantic pantheon: see Yeats's several essays on Shelley and Blake in *E&I*.

of spiritual truth, made a great impact on many Western artists at this time.[5]

Therefore when Yeats was introduced to examples of Noh plays by his friend Ezra Pound in 1913, he was prepared by disposition, by the artists of the era in which he had been brought up and had developed his own artistic practice, and by the kind of poetry and poetic drama he had himself been attempting to create in the theatre from as long ago as *The Countess Cathleen* in 1892, to respond in a characteristically open way. For the reasons already implied here and for others yet to be considered, it is no surprise that "the Noh plays were more to Yeats's taste than to Pound's".[6]

The nationalist background

In a general way, therefore, Yeats was already conditioned by 1913 to be receptive to the accidental incursion of Noh. More particularly, in the ten or eleven plays that he had written between 1892 and 1914, before the first of what were to become his *Plays for Dancers*, *At the Hawk's Well*, was performed "in Lady Cunard's drawing room in London on 2 April 1916",[7] he had moved towards a Noh-like drama, spurred on by his own search for a dramatic form that would cohere with his own evolving poetic style. Realism had not disappeared from the bookshelves or the theatres with the advent of Symbolism: and a major realist, Henrik Ibsen, was one of the dramatists beginning to make the greatest impact on the English stage at the turn of the century. Whether this is a true designation of Ibsen is not important — and certainly his later plays from *Rosmersholm* (1886) onwards, and especially the last, *When We Dead Awaken* (*Naar vi døde vaagner*, 1899) are increasingly symbolic not to say Symbolist — for the plays that first made an impact in England were early realistic plays such as *A Doll's House*. Yeats's attitude to Ibsen was extremely ambivalent:

---

5. The clearest evidence of popular interest in Japanese manners and style in the last two decades of the nineteenth century is the brilliant success of W.S. Gilbert's *The Mikado* in 1885, which was to run for 672 nights, and was both a satire upon and an exploitation of the Victorian cult of *japonaiserie*.

6. Richard Ellmann, "Ez and Old Billyum", in *New Approaches to Ezra Pound*, ed. Eva Hesse, London, 1969, 70 (this essay originally appeared in German in *Ezra Pound: 22 Versuche über einen Dichter*, Frankfurt, 1967; and in English in Richard Ellmann's *Eminent Domain: Yeats among Wilde, Joyce, Pound, Eliot and Auden*, New York, 1967).

7. Masaru Sekine and Christopher Murray, *Yeats and the Noh: A Comparative Study*, Gerrards Cross, 1990, 7.

Two or three years after our return to Bedford Park *A Doll's House* had been played at the Royalty Theatre in Dean Street, the first Ibsen play to be played in England, and somebody had given me a seat for the gallery. In the middle of the first act, while the heroine was asking for macaroons, a middle-aged washerwoman who sat in front of me stood up and said to the little boy at her side, "Tommy, if you promise to go home straight, we will go now"; and at the end of the play, as I wandered through the entrance hall, I heard an elderly critic murmur, "A series of conversations terminated by an accident". I was divided in mind, I hated the play ... I resented being invited to admire dialogue so close to modern educated speech that music and style were impossible.

"Art is art because it is not nature", I kept repeating to myself, but how could I take the same side with critic and washerwoman? As time passed Ibsen became in my eyes the chosen author of very clever young journalists, who, condemned to their treadmill of abstraction, hated music and style; and yet neither I nor my generation could escape him because, though we and he had not the same friends, we had the same enemies (*Au*:279).[8]

Since he wanted "music and style", and therefore needed to avoid "modern educated speech", it is no wonder that Yeats looked for his dramatic substance in historical material; and since he wanted to write plays for an Irish audience he sought for traditional Irish material. In this respect his first play, *The Countess Cathleen* (1892) and *The Land of Heart's Desire* (1894) are perfectly characteristic. But the material upon which Yeats drew for his best plays was the Ulster saga of Cuchulain, which had been "arranged and put into English by Lady Gregory" in a book first published in 1902.[9]

The first of these plays was *On Baile's Strand* written in 1904, telling the tragic tale of how Cuchulain came to kill his own son, and then went mad wrestling with the waves. It is the most effective and powerful of

---

8. Yeats seems to have been mistaken in his facts about early Ibsen productions in England. According to *The Oxford Companion to the Theatre*, 3rd edn, Oxford, 1967, *The Pillars of Society* (under the title of *Quicksands*) was the first Ibsen play to be performed in England in December 1880; *A Doll's House* (entitled *Breaking a Butterfly*) was first performed at the Princess in 1884, and under its usual title at the Novelty in June 1889.

9. Lady Gregory, *Cuchulain of Muirthemne: The Story of the Men of the Red Branch of Ulster ... with a Preface by W.B. Yeats* (1902), 5th edn, Gerrards Cross, 1970.

his early plays. Using the lyrical prose frame of a "blind man" (who knows) and a "fool" (who sings), and the verse-speaking heroic characters of Cuchulain and Conchubar, the high King of Uladh, the appeal of this material is that it is mythic, poetic, mysterious, and deals with basic issues of life and death; of tragic confrontation, and mixed loyalties which leads Cuchulain to the terrible deed. Unlike Nora in *The Doll's House* or Hedda Gabler, these characters of heroic myth and legend hover on the edge of the supernatural; they live in the world of the *Sidhe* (the fairies); and they will be haunted and driven mad by their deeds, with the unrighteous dead never finding rest, and persisting as restless ghosts and disturbed spirits. In this respect the material has similarities with the traditional tales and legends of the divided souls of dead lovers, haunted and haunting villains, unhappy ghosts that one finds in Noh drama.

Therefore when Yeats learned about Noh theatre he immediately recognized it as a style of total theatre which he had been looking for — combining the usual dramatic features of narrative, action and dialogue with music and dancing in a highly conventional stylized manner.[10] The narrative was considerably foreshortened to a single fragment or moment; action was severely restricted to a few significant movements; dialogue was often indirect, allusive, and poetic; and a great deal was to be conveyed by music and dance movement. Frequently characters were spirits or ghosts; and memory of tragic events in the past predominated. The plays were rather ceremonies of remembrance, rituals of tribal re-enactment, liturgies of obeisance and celebration than dramas of secular, material, modern man. The representation of the unseen rather than the seen, the transformation of the ordinary into the supernatural, the concentration on feeling rather than on doing (perhaps even the concern with contemplation rather than with feeling) must have appealed to the Yeats of such earlier plays as *The Shadowy Waters* (1906/1911). It is no wonder that in his edition of Noh plays "Pound refers frequently to parallels furnished him by Yeats".[11]

The staging too allowed him to develop the kind of symbolic representations that he had already been experimenting with under the

---

10. For the dance as an absorbing symbol throughout Yeats's poetic and dramatic carrier, both before and after his discovery of Noh, see ch. 4, "The Dancer", in Frank Kermode's *Romantic Image*, London, 1957, a book which discusses the magnetic appeal of the figure of the dancer in Aestheticism and the earliest phases of Modernism.

11. Ellmann, 69, who cites pages 27, 44, 91, 106 from the original edition of 1916 [1917].

influence of Edward Gordon Craig in recent productions of earlier plays of his: in some respects Yeats longed for a return to Shakespearean simplicities of the "round-O", in this case a "square-O", and an empty acting space, few props, no unnecessary scenery — the essentials of which could be left to the characters themselves — and away from the cluttered naturalism that so appealed to the average Dublin theatre-goer. As Ellmann says:

> The Noh plays, so fortuitously put in his hands, had won without his being aware of it the battle with naturalistic drama which he had himself been fighting in beleaguered fashion. Here was the authorization he needed for leaving probability in the lurch by abolishing scenery so the imagination would be untrammelled, by covering faces with masks, by portraying character in broad strokes — emptied of Ibsen's convincing details — through isolating the moment in which some irrevocable deed separates a man from his fellows. He was also prompted to new and more reckless devices, the symbolic dance as a climax to suggest the impingement of the timeless upon the actual .... Yeats saw how he might focus an entire play, as he had entire poems, on a single metaphor.[12]

"Certain Noble Plays of Japan"

Perhaps it is not at all paradoxical that Yeats was to find his initial audience for his first Noh inspired drama in an aristocratic English drawing-room, since the Japanese original had been "an aristocratic theatre since it was first formalized by two actors, Kan-Ami and Ze-Ami, in the late fourteenth century".[13] Yeats's attempt to draw upon the substance of traditional Irish history and legend for three of his *Four Plays for Dancers* (first published together in 1921) — *At the Hawk's Well* (1917), *The Only Jealousy of Emer* (1919), and *The Dreaming of the Bones* (1919) — and material from the Gospels (admittedly treated in an eccentric way) for the fourth — *Calvary* (1920) — indicates that in theory at least the plays should have been immediately attractive to a

---

12. Ellmann, 70-71: for the last phrase Ellmann gives a reference to Yeats's own statement in "Certain Noble Plays of Japan": "I wonder whether I am fanciful in discovering in the plays themselves (few examples have as yet been translated and I may be misled by accident or the idiosyncrasy of some poet) a playing upon a single metaphor, as deliberate as the echoing rhythm of line in Chinese and Japanese painting" (*E&I*:233-34).

13. Sekine and Murray, 22 (see also Erika de Poorter, "Japanese Theatre: In Search of the Beautiful and the Spectacular", in *Theatre Intercontinental*, 44 ff.).

Dublin audience (especially since the third play of the cycle made obvious appeals to nationalist sentiment).

Yeats had always stressed the alliance between peasant and aristocrat against "our old Paudeen in his shop", the middle-class shopkeepers of Dublin who were destroying the spirit of "Romantic Ireland"[14] — all part of his Aesthetic anti-bourgeois inheritance. Nevertheless although a few aristocrats of spirit and blood may have followed Lady Gregory in associating themselves with Yeats's Abbey Theatre, the bulk of the audience were undoubtedly those "common people" for whom "Realism [was] created ... and was always their peculiar delight" and "is the delight to-day of all those whose minds, educated alone by schoolmasters and newspapers, are without the memory of beauty and emotional subtlety" (*E&I*:227).[15]

Therefore, from the beginning Yeats was aware that the play that he had written "with the help of Japanese plays 'translated by Ernest Fenollosa and finished by Ezra Pound'" was unlikely to be popular: "I have invented a form of drama", he says in "Certain Noble Plays of Japan", written in April 1916, "distinguished, indirect, and symbolic, and having no need of mob or Press to pay its way — an aristocratic form":

> All imaginative art remains at a distance and this distance, once chosen, must be firmly held against a pushing world. Verse, ritual, music, and dance in association with action require that gesture, costume, facial expression, stage arrangement must help in keeping the door. Our unimaginative arts are content to set a piece of the world as we know it in a place by itself, to put their photographs as it were in a plush or a plain frame, but the arts which interest me, while seeming to separate from the world and us a group of figures, images, symbols, enable us to pass for a few moments into a deep of the mind that had hitherto been too subtle for our habitation ....
> Therefore it is natural that I go to Asia for a stage convention, for more formal faces, for a chorus that has no part in the action,

---

14. See "To a Wealthy Man Who Promised a Second Subscription to the Dublin Municipal Gallery if It Were Proved the People Wanted Pictures", "September 1913", and "Paudeen" published in his 1914 volume *Responsibilities* (*CP*:119-22).

15. It may be that Yeats is here implying a distinction between "the common people" of the past, whose delight in realism he approves of, and the mass of theatre audiences of his own day, whose artistic taste has been deformed by the prejudices of mediocre education and journalism.

and perhaps for those movements of the body copied from the marionette shows of the fourteenth century.

This brings him to consider the advantage of the use of masks in the theatre, which "will enable me to substitute for the face of some commonplace player, or for that face repainted to suit his own vulgar fancy, the fine invention of a sculptor":

> A mask never seems but a dirty face, and no matter how close you go is yet a work of art; nor shall we lose by stilling the movement of the features, for deep feeling is expressed by a movement of the whole body. In poetical painting and in sculpture the face seems the nobler for lacking curiosity, alert attention, all that we sum up under the famous word of the realists, "vitality." It is even possible that being is only possessed completely by the dead, and that it some knowledge of this that makes us gaze with so much emotion upon the face of the Sphinx or of Buddha (*E&I*:224-26).

Yeats is seeking and appears to have found in Noh theatre an indication of the means of returning to a viable poetic theatre "where there is nothing ostentatious, nothing crude, no breath of parvenu or journalist" (the latter indicating those familiar targets of Yeats's scorn since the row at the Abbey Theatre following the first performance of J.M. Synge's *The Playboy of the Western World* in January 1907):

> Let us press the popular arts on to a more complete realism — that would be their honesty — for the commercial arts demoralise by their compromise, their incompleteness, their idealism without sincerity or elegance, their pretence that ignorance can understand beauty. In the studio and in the drawing-room we can found a true theatre of beauty. Poets from the time of Keats and Blake have derived their descent only through what is least declamatory, least popular in the art of Shakespeare, and in such a theatre they will find their habitual audience and keep their freedom. Europe is very old and has seen many arts run through the circle and has learned the fruit of every flower and known what this fruit sends up, and it is now time to copy the East and live deliberately (*E&I*:228).

From the tone and style of these remarks not only is the excitement of Yeats's discovery of Noh evident, but also the extent to which the essay they come from is intended as a manifesto proclaimed in the teeth of the admitted preferences and prejudices of regular theatre audiences both in Dublin at the Abbey and elsewhere. Yeats's embrace of Eastern deliberation consciously affirms values that he prizes and equally intentionally repudiates tastes that he despises, not without a calculated degree of arrogance, perhaps even towards Noh itself. As Ellmann says:

> That the Noh plays were often blurred in effect did not ruffle him; the form, he saw, could be improved. He kept the strangeness and increased the dramatic tension, splicing natural with preternatural in order, unpredictably, to heighten the human dilemma. The Yeatsian paradox was to disintegrate verisimilitude by miracle for the purposes of a more ultimate realism.[16]

Yeats's *Four Plays for Dancers*

So far we have seen some of the reasons why Noh theatre appealed to Yeats as a model for his own drama. What we should finally consider briefly is the extent to which he properly understood Noh, and successfully imitated or effectively modified it for his own ends in his *Four Plays for Dancers*, beginning with his first attempt at inventing a "distinguished, indirect, and symbolic ... aristocratic form" of drama, *At the Hawk's Well*. But first we need to remind ourselves of some of the features of Noh drama not so far touched upon:

> There are only two important roles in most Nō plays: the *shite*, the principal character, and the *waki*, the secondary one. Each of these may have followers (*tsure*), but such characters are usually not in themselves individuals, but vocal and physical extensions of the principal characters. Dramatically, the Nō play tends to be a two-character play, and structurally it comes close to being a one-character play. The *waki* and the *shite* are not protagonist and antagonist, for there is seldom any conflict between them. And even when conflict exists, the sense of conflict is diminished by substituting at this point a dance by the *shite*. The importance of the *shite* is further increased by his being given the best lines, the most poetic passages. Nevertheless, the *shite* does not emerge as a three-dimensional, complex character, for he is subject to the same artistic reduction as the other elements of the Nō theatre. The plays themselves in their subject matter, in their characters, are a similar distillation of human experience to its essence, as this essence is reflected in Buddhist philosophy.[17]

---

16. Ellmann, 71.

17. Earle Ernst, *Three Japanese Plays from the Traditional Theatre*, London, New York and Toronto, 1959, 5.

In most respects Yeats's "plays for dancers" reflect the number and nature of the characters of Noh theatre: all the plays demand "Three Musicians" who Yeats hoped would supply the want of scenery by describing "place and weather, and at moments action", accompanied "by drum and gong or flute and dulcimer", and "whose seeming sunburned faces will ... suggest that they have wandered from village to village in some country of our dreams". In all four plays, as the collective title indicates, dance is required, towards the culmination of the action, although the character who dances is not invariably the one to be described as the *shite*: in *At the Hawk's Well*, it is the Guardian of the Well who dances, and neither the Old Man nor the Young Man;[18] in *The Only Jealousy of Emer*, the Woman of the Sidhe dances;[19] in *The Dreaming of the Bones*, the Stranger and the Young Girl, the ghosts of Diarmuid and Dervorgilla, to be compared to the *shite* and *tsure* of the Noh play, *Nishikigi*, that Yeats comments on in "Certain Noble Plays of Japan", drift "in the dance from rock to rock" (*CPl*:444); and in *Calvary*, it is the Three Roman Soldiers who dance.

Nor could one describe Yeats as diminishing the conflict between characters by dance, in fact, on the contrary in both *At the Hawk's Well* and *The Only Jealousy of Emer* the dance seems to lead to a culmination of dramatic conflict. Altogether Yeats seems unable to avoid the usual Western expectation of conflict between dramatic characters. In *At the Hawk's Well*, if the Old Man and the Young Man are indeed to be regarded as dividing the roles of *shite* and *tsure* between them, then in Noh terms there is an illegitimate amount of actual and potential conflict between them; while in *The Dreaming of the Bones*, the *waki* (the Young Man) and the *shite* and *tsure* (the ghosts of the lovers) remain as antagonist and protagonists with an unresolved conflict left between them at the end. As a result, although in a general way Yeats conforms to the indirections and restrictions of Noh, he cannot entirely escape the habits of the theatrical traditions he was trying to remould. As Earle Ernst tells

18. Sekine and Murray refer to Richard Taylor's observation in *The Drama of W.B. Yeats: Irish Myth and the Japanese Nō*, New Haven and London, 1976, 129, that Yeats has "divided the role of the *shite* and *tsure* between the Old Man and the Young Man" (47).

19. Comparing Yeats's stage directions both for this play and his later version, *Fighting the Waves* (1929) — described by Yeats himself as "a prose version of *The Only Jealousy of Emer* so arranged as to admit of many dancers and to be immediately intelligible to an average theatrical audience ("Preface to the First Edition", *CPl*:v) — Sekine and Murray deplore "Yeats's general imprecision over the directions for the dances in his plays" (88).

us, "if the entire past of the Nō play is reconstructed, it frequently reveals all the conflict, struggle, pain, and bloodshed of the most agitated and lurid melodrama"; and this is true of all four of Yeats's "plays for dancers" (in *At the Hawk's Well* in prospect, and in the other three mainly in retrospect). But whereas in Noh "none of this appears in the theatre", in Yeats's "plays for dancers" less of the agitation is resolved in memory and retrospection, as we can see particularly in the climax to *The Only Jealousy of Emer*:

> *Figure of Cuchulain.*   Fool, fool!
> I am Fand's enemy come to thwart her will,
> And you stand gaping there. There is still time.
> Hear how the horses trample on the shore,
> Hear how they trample! She has mounted up.
> Cuchulain's not beside her in the chariot.
> There is still a moment left; cry out, cry out!
> Renounce him, and her power is at an end.
> Cuchulain's foot is on the chariot-step.
> Cry ——
> *Emer.*
> I renounce Cuchulain's love for ever.
>
> (*CPl*:294)

The openings of Yeats's "plays for dancers" in general conform to the description of the first part of the Noh play given by Ernst, in which "the *waki*, often a monk or priest, meets the *shite* at a place of special significance", where "they speak of what happened there in the past, and the *shite*, appearing first to be an ordinary, even innocuous, person, displays a rather unusual knowledge of the event". But the exit of the *shite*, and the "short interlude (confusingly called *kyōgen*, although there is usually nothing comic about it)" during which "he changes costume and mask and reappears for the second part in what might be said to be his basic identity" (11) does not discernably occur in Yeats's plays, although the character of the Guardian of the Well and the true characters of the lovers is revealed in the latter parts of *At the Hawk's Well* and *The Dreaming of the Bones* respectively.

But there is no reason why Yeats had to exactly imitate the dramas which had so impressed him on his first acquaintance with them. It may be the case that the Japanese dancer, Michio Ito, who so encouraged Yeats to develop the dancing part of the Guardian of the Well for him, "was not actually a trained Noh performer and, apparently, held no very high opinion of the Noh arts",[20] and maybe all the ritual of the unfolding and the folding of the cloth that Yeats introduced at the beginnings and ends of the plays had no precedent in Noh, but ultimately since Yeats was engaged essentially in creating his own drama and not in recreating Noh theatre, his lack of deep knowledge and his failures of understanding are of more interest to the scholar than to any theatre audience, past, present or future.

The conclusion that Masaru Sekine and Christopher Murray reach in their detailed "comparative study" of *Yeats and the Noh* is rather dispiriting, and leads one to wonder why they ever bothered to embark on the venture in the first place:

> there is a lack of finish in the plays, a failure to follow up inspiration and to complete the promise inherent in the material. In particular, the lack of consideration given to the dance itself, its nature, timing, and relation to the style of each play, is disappointing. So, too, is the seeming indifference to unity of design: the ideas on mask, scenery, costume and staging never actually cohere into a realized *praxis*.

Of course, there are mitigating circumstances, "a lack of a theatre in which to try out ideas with actors and designers", and his alienation from the Abbey Theatre during this period "paralyzed his efforts to create a new dramatic style": "his attitude towards these dance plays was, it must be said, too aristocratic, too amateur, to achieve their full potential".[21] But perhaps less sensitive to the finer shades of Noh tradition than Masaru Sekine, who is a trained Noh actor, Katharine Worth has stressed Yeats's achievement of a modern theatrical syntax in his Noh plays which enabled him eventually to create "a new kind of dramatic mirror, as complex as any novel or poetry could offer, to reflect complex modern states of self-consciousness", and in so doing making the contemporary theatre.[22] The finer points of comparison between Yeats's plays and specific Noh examples can be considered in Sekine and Murray's fascinating book; and their critical conclusions about the artistic

---

20. Sekine and Murray, 86.

21. *Ibid.*, 119.

22. Katharine Worth, *The Irish Drama of Europe from Yeats to Beckett*, London, 193 and 194. In the absence of regular professional performances of Yeats's plays it is difficult to judge these claims: indeed the only performances of Yeats plays that I have seen are student performances on videos kindly supplied by Professor Worth, to whom I am most grateful, which certainly whet one's appetite.

value of Yeats's Noh dramas weighed against Katherine Worth's. My own conclusions about the success of Yeats's *Four Plays for Dancers* as imitations of Noh would dwell rather on the contrasting nature of narrative in Western and in Oriental fiction, including drama.

The point has often been made about Western art that its mode of thought is essentially lineal and sequential, that traditionally Western narrative makes explicit and implicit claims to Beginnings, Middles and Ends — the most prominent exemplar of this tradition being the Bible, which starts with Genesis (proclaiming a beginning) and closes with Revelations or the Apocalypse (asserting an anticipated end of all things).[23] At the end of the nineteenth century with the increasing interest amongst intellectuals in oriental religious concepts (signalled at one level by the involvement of Yeats and other writers in Theosophy, and their fascination with such concepts as reincarnation) a forceful attack was mounted on the linear mode of Western thought. Consequently, one could argue that the fragmentation and abstraction of modern art and of modern literature in the first two decades of the twentieth century was a means of attempting to frustrate the conventional expectations of Western narrative.[24]

---

23. The classic exploration of the complexities of this mode of Western thought, its conditions and contradictions, is Frank Kermode's *A Sense of an Ending*, New York, 1967: see especially ch. 3, "World Without End or Beginning".

24. Nineteenth-century academic art, like most painting of historical subjects before it, was, by Modernist lights, notoriously narrative; and so even were the Pre-Raphaelites. Nor did the French Impressionists escape entirely from the narrative possibilities of their subjects. Therefore perhaps it was inevitable that in the initial surge of Modernism painting was the first of the narrative arts to attempt to escape what were considered to be the bonds of story-telling by experiments with various kinds of abstraction (in artists like Malevich and Kandinsky often in pursuit of mystical goals). In the late nineteenth century, orchestral music too had become increasingly bound to narrative: and one could argue that the movement towards atonality by composers such as Schönberg previously wedded to programme music was an attempt to frustrate the linear harmonic expectations which the classical composers had developed and dramatically exploited even in what is usually described as "pure" music. Naturally it was always more difficult for literature to evade narrative sequence: but E.M. Forster's famous though muted lament that "Yes — oh dear yes — the novel tells a story" (*Aspects of the Novel*, Penguin, 1962, 34), is a symptom of the novelist's longing to evade narrative, which was, of course, much easier for poets such as T.S. Eliot (even as early as such poems as "A Portrait of a Lady" and "The Love Song of J. Alfred Prufrock", and culminating in *The Waste Land*), and Ezra Pound (particularly in the *Cantos*). Characteristic of this aspect of Modernism is the comment, often made, that while Yeats never wrote the long poem expected of a major poet, his *Collected Poems* should be regarded as a

However, perhaps it has never really been possible for Western writers, even those most captivated by Buddhist and related ideas, to be entirely convinced by the concept of nirvana. Linear narrative has thrived on an over-assertive claim for beginnings — "Once upon a time ...", "Es war einmal ...", "In the beginning ..." — which, paradoxically, has the effect of alerting the reader to the truth that the beginning the story about to be told was not really *the* beginning at all: naturally, as we come to realize in the course of the story, the frog prince had a previous history, as did Cinderella and as must Goldilocks. All stories, even stories starting with "Once upon a time ..." (*particularly*, one might say, stories beginning with that familiar phrase), are actually starting *in medias res*, as we have been led to expect from time-honoured classical tradition. Even the existence of a creative God presupposes an earlier creation myth which we are not supposed to ask questions about.

Likewise endings, however apocalyptic, are to be regarded only as convenient fictional finales. Christian theology fudges the issue by leading the faithful to believe that all good people go to Heaven or if already dead are in Heaven, yet are at the same time awaiting the Last Judgement which will decide whether or not they are to go to Heaven. But then not even the Last Judgement is the end of story since Heaven as an end station itself promises eternal life, which may be short on further dramatic narrative but effectively foils any attempt to foist a quittance on the virtuous believer. "They lived happily ever after" is, as most adults realize, an evasion of the rest of the story, which may be more difficult to tell. As modern critics have suggested all Victorian novels end in death even when the hero and heroine marry, since there appears to be no life after marriage.[25] But this too, we realize, is a convention resorted to as a means of at least temporally closing the unending line of Western narratives, which in fact close, just as they began, *in medias res*.

Modern Western concerns about the environment indicate this presupposition of unending life. Environmentalists in Europe and the USA are scandalized by the possibility that the life of the species is not guaranteed to last forever. Modern secular man may no longer believe in his own personal survival beyond death, but he does want to assume

---

single work with the desired epic length, whose modernist fragmentation, by design or accident, helps to thwart narrative unity.

25. For a discussion of the relations between marriage and death, see Alexander Welsh, *The City of Dickens*, Oxford, 1971, esp. ch. 13, "The Novel and the End of Life".

that the eternal life of the human species is guaranteed. The contemporary appeal of the picturesque myth of Gaea is that it posits an unspecified scientific beginning to the life of a planet whose end is equally unspecified, and probably indefinitely postponed, unless it is inadvertently cut short by human rapacity. From God and Empire and Duty to Freedom and the secular Rights of men, women, children and dogs and ultimately to universal prosperity, so the political narrative is formulated and projected onto the history of the world, as it has been and will be. The Whig myth of history is the best known label for such a linear narrative, and although that particular local British version may now be derided as hopelessly optimistic and old-fashioned, nevertheless it continues to flourish as a history of progress in the Western world. This progress may be subject to occasional unnecessarily atavistic steps backwards and economic hiccups, but it is considered to be the essential law of our expanding galaxy: there shall be no end, a life in a spiritual eternity beyond death will not be inaugurated, nor will nirvana be achieved, but scientific and material progress as initiated by the Enlightenment will continue until the sun burns out (and even that eventual catastrophe may be averted by careful conservation and sensible alternative fuel policies). There is to be no end to history, but just an occasional shift of emphasis and focus from time to time. Western narrative is predicated on such a premise.

My understanding of Noh is that these plays are genuine resolutions of stories, and more often than not indicate a release into nirvana: they are beautiful memorials of moments of ritualized escape from the painful physical and psychological bonds of human narrative. Perhaps this memorializing of such escapes have always been impossible for Western artists, since the story, whether we like it or not, goes on.[26] But it is Yeats's most notable failure as the writer of Noh dramas that he is characteristically committed to and involved in an ongoing narrative: *At the Hawk's Well* is an initiating drama written a dozen years after what should be its narrative sequence, *On Baile's Strand*, which reveals in a haunting way the tragic outcome of the encounter of Cuchulain and the dancer; while the second Noh play, *The Only Jealousy of Emer*, only partly resolves the consequences of Cuchulain's breakdown following his murder of his son. Ostensibly, Yeats's final play, *The Death of Cuchulain* (1939), completes the cycle, appropriately with a dancer and

---

26. Even in Beckett? Cf. Carol Fisher Sorgenfrei's consideration of the attempts of Samuel Beckett's characters to achieve "Zen-like self-obliteration" in her article "Broken Bodies: Comic Deformity in the Plays of Samuel Beckett, Kyōgen, and Contemporary Japanese Theatre", in *Theatre Intercontinental*, 83-100.

a singer, taking Yeats's particular and peculiar version of Noh to the very end of his life and his career. But as that final song in *The Death of Cuchulain* intimates even the death of the hero from "six mortal wounds" and his final beheading, does not conclude the story:

> What stood in the Post Office
> With Pearse and Connolly?
> What comes out of the mountain
> Where men first shed their blood?
> Who thought Cuchulain till it seemed
> He stood where they had stood?

*(CPl:*704-705)[27]

The interweaving of Irish myth and legend, Irish history and Irish politics even to the present day ensures that, so far, no final ritual cleansing has been achieved. The ghosts are not allayed; the living continue to be haunted and moved by the past (even in debased propagandist versions, which Yeats was aware of); and one could say that his third Noh play, *The Dreaming of the Bones*, explores that very situation, poignantly but without resolution. The ghosts of the lovers are unforgiven and unappeased; the Young Man, escaping from pursuit after the 1916 Easter Rising, remains resolutely vengeful, seeing off the lovers and their drifting dance:

> I had almost yielded and forgiven it all —
> Terrible the temptation and the place!

*(CPl:*444)

The last Noh play, *Calvary*, is essentially a dialectical debate in the tradition of such works as Marvell's "A Dialogue between the Soul and Body", and many poems of Yeats himself such as "Ego Dominus Tuus" (*CP*:180-83). Such poems are by their nature not intended to lead to harmonious conclusions, but are designed as celebrations of difference. *Calvary* ends on an unreconciled note comparable to *The Dreaming of the Bones*: Christ is left crying "My Father, why hast Thou forsaken Me?", and the Second Musician singing "God has not appeared to the birds"

---

27. Earlier his encounter with Aoife prompts Cuchulain to a fitting summary of the whole tragic subject matter of the cycle: "And now I know your name,/Aoife, the mother of my son. We met/At the Hawk's Well under the withered trees./I killed him upon Baile's Strand, that is why/Maeve parted ranks that she might let you through./You have a right to kill me" (*CPl*:699).

(*CPl*:456-57); while Lazarus and Judas are equally set in their quite different ways in their opposition to Christ's actions and claims.

All of these plays, whatever their recognition of Noh practices and their attempts to incorporate Noh manners and traditions within their structures and styles of performance, are resolutely Western in their saturation with narrative. Every character with his or her own point of view is involved in a nexus of narratives, some of which are realized in the drama itself, many of which remain latent. Competing to place their stories at the centre of the stage, threatening to take over the direction of the narrative, implying that they may easily return in some future version of the story and turn it on its head and that, above all, the story is not to be resolved with a single version or a single performance, the characters in *Four Plays for Dancers* indicate the extent to which Yeats's Noh plays are well within the Western tradition, dramatically, philosophically and politically, and do not really conform to the spiritual expectations of the aristocratic Noh theatre.

SOME WESTERN PRODUCTIONS OF *AT THE HAWK'S WELL*, WITH A MYTHOLOGICAL FOOTNOTE

MAUREEN MURPHY

If we discount as performance Joseph Hone's report of W.B. Yeats and the Japanese dancer Michiko Ito flapping their arms in imitation of hawks at the London Zoo, the first production of Yeats's *At the Hawk's Well, or Waters of Immortality* was held in Lady Nancy Cunard's drawing room in Cavendish Square in London, on 2 April 1916.[1] The play was the second of what would be five plays about Cuchulain. Yeats wrote *At the Hawk's Well* in his version of the Japanese Noh style. He had been introduced to Japanese theatre in 1913 through his friendship with Ezra Pound, who published four Noh plays, *Certain Noble Plays of Japan*, with an introduction by Yeats, with the Cuala Press in 1916.

The most important play in Pound's collection was *Hagoromo*, the beloved Japanese legend of the *tennin* (angel/maiden) who comes to earth dressed in a feather robe. Her robe is taken by a fisherman who demands that she dance for its return. She dances and as she performs the intricate pattern of steps — some say the symbolic waxing and waning of the moon — she ascends to heaven. It was a play that struck a familiar chord in Yeats's folk memory, for it is very like a mermaid legend widely collected in the west of Ireland. What is more, Yeats saw an amateur *Hagoromo* in London,[2] and was clearly impressed by its most essential feature — the symbolic dance by the play's main character or *shite*.

While Yeats remade the Noh in many respects, the dance of the Hawk/woman remained the play's central episode; however, unlike the Noh tradition, she was not the play's central character. Professor Ishibashi in *Yeats and the Noh* has pointed out that "if Yeats had strictly

---

1. Joseph Hone, *W.B. Yeats*, 2nd edn, London, 1962, 289, 297.

2. Hiro Ishibashi, *Yeats and the Noh: Types of Japanese Beauty and Their Reflection on Yeats's Plays*, ed. Anthony Kerrigan, Dublin, 1965, 164.

adapted the Noh form in *At the Hawk's Well*, the hawk would have been the main player".[3]

At the first performance of *At the Hawk's Well*, it was Ito's dancing, in black wings, red tights and mask and Edmund Dulac's designs, music and masks that seem to have been most memorable to the audience.[4] Yeats wrote to Lady Gregory on 10 April 1916, after a second performance of the play to benefit the Socal Institute Union that was held in Lady Islington's drawing room at 8 Chesterfield Gardens: "The form is a discovery and the dancing and masks wonderful" (*L*:611).

In fact, for the most part, western productions have been a matter of masks and music with great attention paid to the style of each. As usual, not the least aspect of Yeats's genius, was his ability to recognize and to engage people of remarkable talent: the Fay brothers for the Abbey, and for his Noh venture, Ito and Edmund Dulac (1882-1953) the French born illustrator, painter and designer who provided the design for the set, the costumes, the masks as well as the music.

Dulac's black cloth with its gold Art Nouveau hawk supplied the prop for the Yeatsian innovation — the ritual unfolding and folding of the cloth that opened and closed the play which was a visual metaphor for the formulaic begenings and endings of folktales that enabled the "suspension of disbelief" necesary to engage the audience. Liam Miller directs us to the prompt book for the first production to suggest how seriously Yeats considered this detail of the play.[5]

Yeats decided to mask the Old Man and Cuchulain and to have the musicians and the hawk made up to resemble masked faces. He wrote, "A mask will enable me to substitute for the face of some commonplace player, or for that face repainted to suit his own vulgar fancy, the fine invention of a sculptor, and to bring the audience close enough to the play to hear every inflection of the voice" (*E&I*:226).

Dulac's masks merged East with West. Yeats opened his "Certain Noble Plays of Japan" describing the Cuchulain mask as "half-Greek, half-Asiatic" (*E&I*:221); however, it was the Greek aspect he emphasized in a letter to John Quinn on the day of the performance at Lady Cunard's (*L*:610).

Dulac supplied the costumes for the performance and he composed the music. While the designs were a success, the music was more problematic. Edward Mallins describes Dulac's impressionistic score for

---

3. *Ibid.*, 145.

4. *Ibid.*, 131.

5. Liam Miller, *The Noble Drama of W.B. Yeats*, Dublin, 1977, 220.

drum, song and zither as "tedious" and "sometimes so insensitive to the
rhythm of the words which are strait-jacketed against their natural
accents".[6] William Worthen also notices the incompatible rhythms of
speech and song: "While the repeated triplets in Dulac's score embed a
trimeter rhythm in the lyric passage, the spoken descriptions tend toward
a more pronounced tetrameter."[7]

Not only was the music at odds with the words, the musicians
apparently were reluctant to subordinate their music to the speech of the
actors. Yeats complained to Lady Gregory as well as to Quinn that the
musicians were troublesome (*L*:609-11). They were playing western
instruments (drum, song and zither) not the traditional flute, tsuzumi and
taiko drums,[8] but the most serious difference between Dulac's music and
the music of the traditional Noh was Dulac's use of improvisation in
contrast to the strict conventions of the music of the Noh which Ishibashi
decribes as "constructed from a combination of established patterns".[9]

Dulac's designs and music were not only featured in Irish productions
into the 1930s, the masks were used in two New York productions. At
the Greenwich Village Theatre in November 1916, Miticho Ito danced
the part of the Hawk. Two years later, while Dulac's masks were on
display at the Scott and Fowles Gallery, there was a second performance
at the Greenwich Village Theatre. Once again Ito danced the Hawk and
the Dulac masks were used; however, the Japanese composer Kosaku
Yamada provided the music.

Yeats recovered the Dulac masks from New York early in 1924, in
time for the Dublin Drama League "At Home" held at Yeats's home in
Merrion Square on March 23, 1924. Abbey actors appeared; Mick Dolan
played Cuchulain and Lennox Robinson was co-opted to play one of the
musicians. While O'Casey confided to Joseph Holloway that he did not
understand the play,[10] it did not prevent him from judging it "charming

---

6. Miller, 228.

7. William Worthen, "The Discipline of the Theatrical Sense: *At the Hawk's
Well* and the Rhetoric of the Stage", *Modern Drama*, 30 (1987), 101.

8. Ishibashi, 109.

9. *Ibid.*, 139.

10. *Joseph Holloway's Abbey Theatre: A Selection from his Unpublished
Journal. Impressions of a Dublin Playgoer*, eds Robert Hogan and Michael J.
O'Neill, Carbondale, 1967, 229.

and amiable", but "it wasn't a Noh play", "because a Japanese spirit had failed to climb into the soul of a Kelt".[11]

We have another account of the play from a more appreciative member of the audience, one of Lily Yeats's senior embroidery girls invited to the evening. Sarah Hyland recalled that the play

> took place upstairs in the two large rooms, opened into one room by folding back the dividing doors. The audience was seated on the floor in darkness when we entered, and some on the players were already in their places under a very subdued greenish light, at an imaginary stage or corner of the room, farthest away from the audience. My recollection is of shadowy figures moving about singing or speaking their various verses. The first player recited, "I call to the eye of the mind, a well long choked and the bough long stripped by the wind." After a very short time another masked player entered the room from the landing outside, and he moved through the players, where he became one of them. It was easy to recognize him from his great height, even if Dr. Oliver Gogarty had not said, in an audible whisper, "Lennox is in great form tonight."[12]

Gogarty claimed in *It Isn't This Time of the Year at All* (1954) not to have seen *At the Hawk's Well* until it was presented to about forty people in his drawing room at Renvyle while the Yeatses were staying with the Gogartys and Augustus John was working on his second and last portrait of Yeats. The poet proposed a performance of the play with Abbey actors brought down to Galway and with Dulac's masks, costumes and music.

Gogarty recalls that Yeats concluded his introductory remarks with this description:

> The well is guarded by a woman who is possessed by a hawk; call this woman intellect. She dances a magic dance which draws the hero off in pursuit and sheds sleep upon the old man. The song I have written for this play would suggest that the hero is Cuchulain. I know well that you would not have me be explicit. Let it rest at that.

Gogarty himself was moved by the presentation:

---

11. Sean O'Casey, *Inishfallen, Fare Thee Well*, New York, 1949, 289.

12. Sara Hyland, "'I Call to the Eye of the Mind'", unpublished memoir MS, 125.

I know nothing of Japan, but they could not have produced anything as satisfying and as moving for Europeans as "The Hawk's Well". The crisis faded into a magical dance. What a lovely thing Dulac made out of the human hawk woman.[13]

Liam Miller notes two more productions of *At the Hawk's Well* in the 1930s at the Abbey which were not official Abbey productions: the production on 18 November 1930 at the Peacock by the Abbey School of Acting and the Dulac music, costumes and masks, and a production on 25 July 1933 by the Irish National Theatre, directed by Arthur Shields and featuring Ninette de Valois dancing the part of the hawk. They too used the Dulac costumes, mass and music.[14]

After nearly twenty years, *At the Hawk's Well* enjoyed a revival with the founding of the Lyric Players Theatre in Belfast, a theatre whose Articles of Association require the company to present at least one Yeats play per year.[15] The Lyric lists productions of *At the Hawk's Well* in 1951 (its only Yeats offering), in 1956, in 1960 (with four of the five Cuchulain cycle plays) and 1961, at the Dublin Theatre, in 1960 and 1961 and at the Yeats International Summer School the same years.

In 1965, to commemorate the centenary of Yeats, there were several productions of *At the Hawk's Well*: the Belfast Lyric, the Dublin University Players' production that ran for three weeks in Dublin and for three weeks in Belfast, and a North American production at the University of Winnipeg directed by Reg Skene.

John Jay who directed the Dublin University Players described the production in the Yeats Special Issue of *Threshold*. He produced *At the Hawk's Well* as part of the Cuchulain cycle with a set of two "T blocks", one of which had a hawk-like shape.[16] He abandoned masks, reduced the musicians to two and had them speak, not sing, from the wings (Jay 1965:34). George Hodnett's "Wagnerian" score was pre-recorded; however, there was live music each night: woodwind, zither and percussion.

The same year as Hodnett's Wagnerian *Hawk's Well*, Gerard Victory wrote a score for flute, bass clarinet and percussion that Charles Acton

---

13. Oliver St. John Gogarty, *It Isn't This Time of the Year at All*, New York, 1954, 245, and 246-47.

14. Miller, 232-33.

15. Mary O'Malley, "The Dream Itself", *Threshold*, 19 (1965), 58.

16. John Jay, "'What Stood in the Post Office?'", *Threshold*, 19 (1965), 33.

described as "post-Schönberg".[17] The music was not for a stage production but for an Argo recording of "Four Plays by Yeats". (There was no Hawk of course so the result was a bit like *Hamlet* without the Prince.)

On 30 November 1978, as part of the Dublin Theatre Festival, *At the Hawk's Well* was produced at the Peacock Theatre. It was unique for two reasons: it was the first official Abbey production of the play and it was directed by Hideo Kanze "whose family has been associated with the Noh theatre since its foundation in the fourteenth century".[18] The Noh style was largely a visual one. The Peacock foyer was decorated with Japanese prints, posters and floral arrangements; the actors wearing "elegantly textured" costumes and "sculpted" masks by Wendy Shea moved slowly and formally faithful to traditional Noh technique.[19] The music, on the other hand, was not constrained by Noh tradition. There was Irish music with the Japanese graphics outside and an ensemble of gong, cymbal, ivory and stone along with what reviewer David Nowlan described as "Jolyon Jackson's Celtic Oriental one-man electronic band". Nowlan pronounced the performance and admirable experiment but concluded "Entertainment? Noh." Perhaps not, but it was a pause in a production style that was turning *Four Plays for Dancers* into the Cuchulain cycle.

The most vigorous proponent of the Cuchulain cycle approach to Yeats's plays and the director of the most ambitious — and accessible — *Hawk's Well* to date is James Flannery who produced the Cycle for the first Yeats International Theatre Festival at the Abbey in 1989. Flannery's interest in directing Yeats began in 1965, when he was a graduate student at Trinity writing a thesis on the early Abbey. That year he directed *Calvary* and *The Resurrection* for the 1965 Dublin Theatre Festival. He first articulated his vision of a Yeats drama festival in his article "Action and Reaction at the Dublin Theatre Festival". He said: "I should like to see *The Countess Cathleen* and *The Shadowy Waters* staged with all the theatricality of a Wieland Wagner Bayreuth production as

17. Charles Acton, rev. of *Four Plays by Yeats*, Argo Recordings 2RG 5468-9: RG 468-9. *The Irish Times*, March 1966, 7.

18. Hugh Hunt, *The Abbey: Ireland's National Theatre, 1904-1979*, New York, 1979, 231.

19. David Nowlan, "Yeats' Plays in Noh Tradition at the Peacock", *Irish Times*, 1 December 1978, 5.

Yeats certainly dreamed of having them done when he first wrote them."[20]

Over the twenty-four years that included 60 Yeats productions in Ireland, Canada and the United States, Flannery directed *At the Hawk's Well* at the Centaur Theatre in Montreal in 1972, and at the University of Toronto as art of a production of the Cycle for the 1978 Celtic Conference under the general chairmanship of Robert O'Driscoll. In his remarks about the production, Flannery outlined his two major directorial concerns: that the production "express essential humanity and vast mythopoeic resonances" and that each artist be encouraged "to express himself freely and at the same time remain fully responsive to the overall dramatic and theatrical intentions of Yeats".[21]

There were some very specific Yeatsian associations: Gráinne Yeats played one of the musicians (and later a ballad singer in *The Death of Cuchulain*) and Mitchio Ito's daughter-in-law Wakano Ito danced the part of the hawk. Robert Aitken's music combined Irish and Japanese elements — Japanese instruments played in non-traditional ways, Irish folk songs and experiments with combinations of Eastern and Western scales, pitches and rhythms. Aitken followed Dulac and Flannery's "artistic expression" in his providing his musicians the opportunity to improvise "for the flexibility of sound that could vary from one performance to another". While there were ties to Yeats, to past productions and to Irish tradition, Flannery was determined to open wider mythic possibilities for the plays. For one thing, Sorel Etrog dressed Cuchulain in tights and a sort of football helmet and jersey emblazoned with a stylized hawk and spiral motif on the trunks to try to create "a ritualistic man, an ancient hero yet also a contemporary one".[22] For the hawk, Etrog abandoned stylized wings and hawk's hood/bill for a kimono-style robe and an elaborate headdress. Neither player was masked, nor was Wakano Ito's face made up to resemble a hawk. (Flannery's Centaur Theatre production had included striking masks by Felix Mirbt.)

Flannery's most significant change was introducing Aoife and a sudden embrace between Aoife and Cuchulain, a Jungian symbol of the meeting of male and female. It was a vision of Yeats that he continued

---

20. James Flannery, "Action and Reaction at the Dublin Theatre Festival", *Theatre Journal*, 19 (1967), 79-80.

21. Robert O'Driscoll, "Epilogue: The Celtic Hero", *The Celtic Consciousness*, ed. R. O'Driscoll, Dublin, 1981, 673.

22. *Ibid.*, 670.

to pursue in the 1989 production. The Festival title "Poet with a Thousand Faces" and the Cycle's sub-title "Heroic Journey in Five Episodes" are pure Joseph Campbell and Flannery's summary of *At the Hawk's Well*, "Cuchulain meets the unappeasable shadow and is initiated into the life of the hero", placed Cuchulain at Campbell's threshold of adventure.

But this was a more consciously Irish Cuchulain. In part it was the politics of the Yeats Drama Foundation whose mission, a series of five annual festivals to produce the entire Yeats canon of twenty-six plays, realizes Flannery's vision of creating a Yeatsian Bayreuth with the Cuchulain Cycle as its Ring. To restore Yeats to the national theatre required, at some level, an Irish Cuchulain and to that end, Flannery argues a particular historical interpretation of the plays. For example, he has suggested that the dry well and withered leaves represent Ireland before Yeats and that the spirit of Cuchulain is in the eye of the mind of modern Ireland.[23]

Flannery's metaphor for the Cuchulain cycle is a symphony in five movements, a parts-to-whole relationship that is slightly at odds with critic Fintan O'Toole's observation that:

> Doing the cycle of the plays together means that instead of having the curve of action and intensity moving through a single play, that curve has to be bigger and looser. And that means going for coherence rather than concentration, for a longer, less passionate line of action, for something that is closer to narrative than to ritual.[24]

Part of the strategy of coherence — whether musical theme or narrative episode — was Flannery's decision to use Aoife as the unifying factor enlarging on Yeats's suggestions of her presence and power. Reviewers agree that the choice of Olwen Fouere, a consummate Yeatsian actress, was inspired and her Aoife stalked Cuchulain like the Hound of Heaven.

The Cuchulain-Aoife encounter comes during the last chorus. Rather than have Cuchulain exit before the folding of the cloth, he moves downstage as the musicians sing "Folly alone I cherish". From behind the metallic tree designed by Bronwen Casson (with its association with *Purgatory* and Beckett's *Waiting for Godot*), Aoife appears and moves

---

23. James Flannery, "Yeats's Total Theatre", American Conference for Irish Studies, Madison, WI, 12 April 1991.

24. Fintan O'Toole, "Coca-Cola Yeats Could Be the Real Thing", *The Irish Times*, 16 September 1989, 6.

menacingly toward Cuchulain. His spear goes up in defense; then he pulls back and for a moment looks into her eyes, recognizes the look in his own eyes, his destiny, his *anima*.[25]

There are some similarities to Flannery's Toronto productions. He used no masks, and the costumes, while more military than mythological, were timeless. Rather than try for a fusion of Japanese and Irish music, Flannery engaged Bill Whelan, the classically-trained producer of U2 and Moving Hearts, who produced an accessible, lyric, light rock score. The old problems with balance persisted. O'Toole, who generally liked the music, said "music threatens at times to overwhelm the words, but words are not primarily what this production is about". A very stylish production that demonstrated the Yeats's Cuchulain cycle can be exciting theatre; however, some have asked "but is it Yeats?"

Whatever it is, *At the Hawk's Well* is certainly Cuchulain and his clash with the Hawk (or with Aoife) while a most un-Noh phenomenon, is at the heart of the play and part of Yeats's meditation on the heroic. For that reason, one might consider, by way of conclusion, another mythological source for *At the Hawk's Well*.

Several scholars have investigated the sources for the play. All conclude that the central episode in the play cannot be traced to a corresponding episode in the Cuchulain literature.[26] If, as Anthony Bradley has suggested, the episode is an initiatory rite,[27] it cannot be traced to the Táin where Cuchulain takes arms as a boy on the day that it is prophesied that the hero who arms will have a short life but will achieve immortality.[28] Bradley argues that Cuchulain's initiation rite in the play is the act of looking into the eye of the hawk who distracts him for his quest for the waters of immortality but offers instead a life which will confer immortality based on his heroic acts.[29]

F.A.C. Wilson identified diverse Irish sources for *At the Hawk's Well* including visions Yeats shared with the Golden Dawn, the magic well of Connla, the story of Connla and Slieve Gullion and Niall and his

---

25. James Flannery, "Total Theatre" (see note 23 above).

26. F.A.C. Wilson, *Yeats's Iconography*, New York, 1960, 41. A.N. Jeffares, *A Commentary on the Collected Plays of W.B. Yeats*, Stanford, 1975, 87; Anthony Bradley, *William Butler Yeats*, New York, 1979, 140.

27. Bradley, 141.

28. Thomas Kinsella, *The Táin*, London, 1969, 85.

29. Bradley, 141.

Brothers in Search of the Well.[30] Wilson argues that Yeats's chief
mythological source was the Grail myth, especially William Morris's
retelling in *The Well at the World's End*.[31] Later scholars have generally
accepted Wilson's conclusions and the matter has rested there.

There is still another mythological reading — one more local than the
others and one that in its embodiment of the heroic has an important
Cuchulain connection. The tradition surrounds Tullaghan Well in the Ox
Mountains southwest of Sligo town near the village of Coolaney and not
far from the village of Ballysodare where Yeats, visiting his Middleton
relatives, first heard fairy stories.[32] The Well is mentioned in Sheelah
Kirby's *Yeats Country* and in James McGarry's *Placenames in the Work
of W.B. Yeats*.[33] Both authors link the Well with the nearby Carraig-an-
Seabhac or the Hawks' Rock. Kirby and McGarry relied on the work of
the nineteenth-century local historian and antiquarian Archdeacon
Terence O'Rorke who descibed the hawks around the rocks in terms very
like those spoken by Cuchulain early in *At the Hawk's Well*: "As I came
hither/A great grey hawk swept down out of the sky" (*CPl*:214).
O'Rorke wrote:

> Hawks are diminishing greatly in numbers and abandoning their
> haunts, though some of them still retain possession of Carrig-na-
> Shouck — the hawk's rock — near Coolany; and if a man or boy
> comes near the rock, they are sure to sally forth from their eyrie
> on the face of the precipice and to keep whirling round high up in
> the air, screaming and clattering till the intruder has taken himself
> away out of their sight and left them again in quiet occupation of
> their immemorial retreat.[34]

It is an easy move to shift the hawks' preserve from their rock to the
nearby well, esecially one so renowned for its holy association and its
cures. Tullaghan Well appears in early Irish literature where it is
reckoned one of the *Mirabiles Hiberniae*. It is mentioned also in
Nennius, in Geraldus Cambrensis and in O'Flaherty's *Oygia*:

---

30. Wilson, 35.

31. *Ibid.*, 52.

32. Hone, 21.

33. Sheelah Kirby, *The Yeats Country*, Dublin, 1963, 53-54. James McGarry,
Placenames in the Work of W.B. Yeats, Toronto, 1976, 52.

34. Terence O'Rorke, *The History of Sligo: Town and County*, I, Dublin, n.d.,
18.

> In Sligo district, on Mount Gam's high side
> A fountain lies, not washed by ocean's tide
> Each circling day, its different waters brings
> The fresh — the salt — from its alternate springs.[35]

In the *Dindshenchas* the well is associated with the legend of Gamh, Eremon's servant, who gave his name to the mountains that are called the Ox Mountains today. Gamh was beheaded beside the well and his head was kept in the well for a while. As a result, according to tradition, the water turned bitter and ever since the well alternates between fresh and bitter water.[36]

Given its local reputation, Yeats certainly would have heard of the well of Tullaghan and may have had its essential feature — its ebbing and flowing — in the back of his mind when he was writing *At the Hawk's Well*. Descriptions of this marvelous phenomenon appear as early as the *Book of Ballymote* (1384-1406) and O'Rorke described it fully in his parish history of Ballysodare:

> There was no doubt that the water in the well rose and subsided from time to time to wet-water mark, and this natural phenomenon gave rise to the belief of tidal ebbing and flowing. The water in the well was brackish so it was understandable that it had been supposed to come from the sea, it was heavy and dark as if holding a muddy substance in solution and nurtured beside a slimy thread — like an acquatic plant.[37]

Given the importance of the miraculous rising and falling of the well in local tradition and Yeats's appropriation of it for the play, is there any significance for Yeats in the traditional explanation for the rising and the falling of the well water?

Tradition explains the phenomenon and the sanctity that it confers on the Well by a legend that ties the Well to St Patrick in a wider corpus of stories that connects St Patrick to Croagh Patrick, Ireland's holy mountain that bears his name. These legends are, in turn, associated with the ancient, pre-Christian harvest festival, the Festival of Lughnasa, and we are fortunate to have Máire MacNeill's classic study of that festival to illuminate the way local tradition may have informed aspects of *At the Hawk's Well*.

---

35. Kirby, 54.

36. Máire MacNeill, *The Festival of Lughnasa*, London, 1962, 113.

37. MacNeill, 115.

In Irish mythology, Lugh the leader of the Tuatha Dé Danaan, the Irish Apollo, is also Cuchulain's father. While Cuchulain identifies himself in the play saying "I am named Cuchulain, I am Sualtim's son" (*CPl*:211), his parents are Lugh and Dechtire, sister of Conchor mac Nessa.[38] Yeats seems to suggest the solar myth-hero theory of his day in his description of Cuchulain when the old man says:

> ... If I may judge by the gold
> On your head and feet and glittering in your coat,
> You are not of those who hate the living world.

(CPl:211)

Readers of the *Táin* will remember that Lugh appears after the "great carnage" when Cuchulain, trapped by Maeve's false peace offer, slays fourteen warriors. Lugh offers to stand guard while Cuchulain rests and he brings the sídhe with him and they drop healing herbs over the sleeping hero.[39]

Lugh's most celebrated victory was his defeat of Balor of the Evil Eye, leader of the Fomorians, at the Battle of Moytura. The event is commemorated in the gathering at heights and by rivers and holy wells including the patron at Tullaghan, gatherings that date to pre-Christian times. Christian syncretism transformed this festival, one of the most famous of the gatherings, into the annual pilgrimage to Croagh Patrick on the last Sunday of July which marks the occasion of St Patrick driving the demons from the summit of the mountain. One can see in the Christian tradition traces of the earlier myth: the clever newcomer who routs out the old goddess or a newcomer god driving out blight.[40]

The most popular legend associated with the pilgrimage is the one which describes the Saint overcoming a female fiend, often in serpent form. MacNeill, who found some forty versions of this legend, speculates that it might be responsible for the story that St Patrick banished the snakes from Ireland. Earliest versions of the legend describe not demon serpents but demon birds.

The story continues with another Patrick demon episode at the Well of Tullaghan. Macneill cites the 1836 Sligo Ordnance Survey letters for her account of the legend:

38. Kinsella, 78.

39. *Ibid.*, 142

40. MacNeill, 416.

After Patrick banished the demons from Cruach Patrick he pursued one of them, the Caorthannach (Devil's Mother) across country to Tullaghan. On her way, she polluted all the waters. At Tullaghan, overcome with thirst, Patrick prayed for a drink and the well sprang up beneath him. It has been venerated ever since, and many cures have been effected by it. It was also said to rise and fall with the tide.[41]

Keeping the legend of the Well of Tullaghan in mind, it is possible to read *At the Hawk's Well* as a Lughnasa legend. A young man who has identified himself as Cuchulain travels to a dry well on a mountain top, a well with magical associations. He reports being threatened en route by a demon bird — a hawk. The old man he meets at the well links the hawk with a supernatural female, a woman of the Sidhe, who has taken the shape of a hawk and he warns the young man that a curse awaiting any who gaze "in her unmoistened eyes".

While he is warned that no man is a match for her, the young man/Cuchulain faces her hawk's eyes fearlessly with a hero's steady gaze. While they gaze intently, the water comes and disappears again. The Hawk/woman disappears. Cuchulain tells us she has taken refuge in the rocks. She is not the Caorthannach of local tradition but Aoife, Cuchulain's *nemesis*. Having gazed in the eye of the hawk, Cuchulain goes to confront his hero's destiny with a reassertion of his own identity, "He comes! Cuchulain, son of Saltim, comes!" (*CPl*:218).

A Lughnasa reading does not disqualify other interpretations. The Grail myth reading is strengthened by the identification of Caorthannach as "blight", another image of sterility, and the general Christian Patrician reading offers an Irish version of the myth as does the traditional gatherings at the site and the association of the well with cures that date to medieval times.

At the Hawk's Well read as a Lughnasa legend also supports a Jungian/Campbellian interpretation: the Hero's initiation at the "threshold of adventure"; however, the Campbellian hero undertakes his journey on behalf of his people while the Yeatsain hero obeys only his "lonely impulse of delight". One might go so far as to call it an archetype, for consider that a few centuries of stony sleep later and thirty miles to the west, another young man decides against the "pleasant life/Among indolent meadows" in order to follow his destiny — in the form of a mysterious and compelling woman — to immortality, and to be spoken of forever.

---

41. *Ibid.*, 114.

The essential thing about *At the Hawk's Well* as a Lughnasa legend is that the reading binds play to place and securely to Irish tradition. For now we might leave the last word to Yeats and salute his self-prophecy, for if we read the play as a Lughnasa legend, we acknowledge that Yeats realized his ambition, the ambition expressed in the conclusion to his Introduction to *Certain Noble Plays of Japan* (1916) that his new style of drama be linked to local tradition:

> Perhaps someday a play in the form I am adapting for European purposes may excite once more, whether in Gaelic or in English, under the slope of Slieve-na-mon or Croagh Patrick, ancient memories (*E&I*:236).

SEXUAL AND TEXTUAL POLITICS IN YEATS'S
THE PLAYER QUEEN

HEDWIG SCHWALL

W.B. Yeats divided his protagonists into three categories: the man of action, the poet and the saint. As the last type does not occur frequently — he was more often used as a foil to the others — we will concentrate on the hero and the poet. The doctrine of the Mask is prominent in descriptions of these men, since both the active and the meditative man must assume their typical role through identification with a lofty example. This imitative energy is something we recognize from the hysteric's structuring of his desire. This type of person first wants to idealize every aspect of his daily surroundings, and then to identify with this sublimated reality. According to Yeats, Masks could be found in Irish myths and legends, in the Renaissance universal man, and in such historical heroes as Wolfe Tone, Thomas Davis and Charles Stewart Parnell. All these types and figures have reached Unity of Being, a harmonious state in which all aspects of the personality are unified.

Unity of Being, the expression of a strong individual who has assimilated his ideal image, is paralleled on the national level in Unity of Culture. This is reached when a whole nation strives towards the same ideal, the Unity of Image. In his politics of the imagination, Yeats sees a vital role for "'the applied arts of literature', the association of literature, that is, with music, speech, and dance", as they would "deepen the political passion of the nation that all, artist and poet, craftsman and day-labourer would accept a common design" (*Au*:194).

The Cuchulain plays were to serve this ideal and offer a Unity of Image to the poet's countrymen. Lady Gregory provided the playwright with a hero figure who defended Ulster single-handed, and was admired by all for both his physical prowess and his love of the arts — the *uomo universale* Yeats wanted to focus on in the Abbey Theatre. Cuchulain's noble fights would offer all Irishmen "the fascination of what's difficult", and thus help to unify the divided parties of Irish politics into a common ideal. But it was not only the theatre project which was to unify the Irish intellect and imagination, for the Irish Literary Society and the National Literary Society, which Yeats had founded in London and Dublin respectively, were to serve the same purpose.

Yeats's first Cuchulain play, *On Baile's Strand*, is all about a hero who states explicitly that he wants to be the ideal who will keep all factions together. Moreover, he wants to write his own myth or mythical autobiography: he wants to "leave names upon the harp". He will do so, but for a reason different than the one he had intended, as it is not he himself who is to preside over the realization of his own design, but "the witches of the air". Instead of becoming famous for the protection of his "chicks", his kings, he becomes more than ever feared for the killing of his own son. In *The Player Queen* a witch-queen confronts two men, a poet and a man of action. Again, it seems to be the woman who decides the course of things.

Yeats's problem: the hysteric woman

It is striking that in Yeats's prose texts, especially the essays, women are omitted from the threefold division of types, although they take an active part in his poems and plays. In the essays, women appear as a means of enabling man to situate himself between two poles. On the one hand, women either symbolize the woe done to man, by making him incomplete, or irritate him by their refusal to fit into his schemes and desires. On the other hand, women can be sublime — as *dominae*, Muses and fosterers of self-idealizing lovers in the Petrarchan tradition, they are servants to the man's cause. These are the "good women", but in Yeats's essays about self-ennobling disciplines they remain in the background.

However, both categories of women have one thing in common: they are all hysterics in the sense of the word used by Freud and contemporary psychoanalysts such as Jacques Lacan, Antoine Vergote, Lucien Israël, Paul Moyaert and Paul Verhaeghe, who distinguish three kinds of hysteria — the pathological, the healthy and the abyssal. Yeats himself uses the word too, but in his work, the hysteric is nearly always pathological. Two kinds of women can be found in Yeats: the first are politically active, anarchic women, who are independent from his or any other friend's leadership, and the second are women immersed in immediacy, that is to say their momentary interest makes them obliterate the aesthetic aspect of life. Yeats's "good", non-hysteric, women (the "healthy hysterics" in modern terms) are rather like the poet himself: a fear of sexuality is covered with "the applied arts of literature" — continually varying tall tales. The tendency to idealize is balanced by a sense of humour, and histrionic behaviour tends to develop into a pronounced aesthetic sense and a theatricality that is used for the benefit of one's community. The healthy hysteric's desires may look chameleon-like, but they aim at a wide-ranging search for truth, for they are not just expressions of a wild, aimless desire.

In *Autobiographies*, we find a protagonist who calls himself histrionic in his child's play: at one moment he is Manfred on the glacier, at another he is sorry his tie cannot be blown about by the wind, as in the picture of Byron. Yet, there is one instance in which the poet speaks of "a magnificent hysteria",[1] when he talks about woman actresses who inspire, sustain and obey the poet. Mrs Campbell, for whom Yeats wrote *The Player Queen*, is one, and Florence Farr is another since she offered the poet examples for his theory of the Mask. In his most important treatise on this subject, *Per Amica Silentia Lunae*, Yeats maintains that life and art are always opposed to each other: when Florence Farr is on the stage, she is best as one of Maeterlinck's "young queens", with "so little will, so little self, that they are like shadows sighing at the edge of the world" who "stir to pity and to desire because they need our protection"; whereas, in private life, she "is like the captain of a buccaneer ship holding his crew to good behaviour at the mouth of a blunderbuss" (*Myth*:326-27). Yeats is always interested in "the fatal transfiguration of the footlights, in which reality and the artificial change places with so fantastic a regularity".[2] He loves theatre in life, and life in the theatre, but only in so far as the poet can dictate the "man of action": the instinctive man must learn from the theatre's stylized, idealized model: "[Lionel] Johnson's favourite phrase, that life is ritual, expressed something that was in some degree in all our thoughts, and how could life be ritual if woman had not her symbolical place?" (*Au*:302).

Yeats loves ritual if he can prescribe it. Yet this privilege does not come his way very often. There are three factors which thwart his plans. First, we find the poet angry with his "Muse", Maud Gonne — when she refuses to play the role he had wanted her to play in his life, he has to look for inspiration among dead old symbols.[3] Secondly, he is enraged with the Abbey Theatre public, who misunderstand his symbols and

---

1. C. Laity, "W.B. Yeats and Florence Farr: the Influence of the 'New Woman', Actress, on Yeats's Changing Images of Women", *Modern Drama*, XXVIII/4 (December 1985), 622.

2. Arthur Symons, *The Symbolist Movement in Literature*, London, 1908, 19-20.

3. Yeats wrote in "Reconciliation": "... you went from me, and I could find/Nothing to make a song about but kings,/Helmets, and swords, and half-forgotten things/That were like memories of you— ..." (*CP*:102; *PNE*:95).

cannot form a Unity of Culture around the ideals he offers them on the Abbey stage. Finally, there is the playwright's fight with the style, the text, as we can see in *The Player Queen*, a play where his misunderstanding of, and exasperating fascination with, his own symbols made him waste "the best working months of several years in an attempt to write a poetical play where every character became an example of the finding or not finding of what I have called the Antithetical Self" (*VPl*:761).

So it seems that the woman's anarchic position in the poet's male cosmos creates a serious problem. In fact, two problems come to the fore. First, Yeats's cosmos (whether described in his autobiographical or other more creative writings) hinges on theatricality; secondly, this phenomenon is tightly linked with the peculiar relation between difficult women and the symbolical values of unwieldy signifiers. Or, to put it in another way: in so far as theatricality is problematical, it has something to do with elusive women and comparable symbols, that is with women who refuse to take a definable symbolical place. Especially in the autobiographical prose work written between 1907 and 1917 (mainly *Autobiographies*, *Per Amica Silentia Lunae*, and *The Poet and the Actress*), Yeats's problems with the women he created in his writing and those who performed his texts appear only as an alibi for the problems he was experiencing in his conception of a perfect theory of the Mask. As far as men are concerned there is no problem:

> Men are dominated by self-conquest .... The self-conquest of the writer who is not a man of action is style .... The element which in men of action corresponds to style in literature is the moral element (*Au*:515-16).

Women, however, constitute the unthematizable element in this theory. They cause man to fail in "the moral element" in life, or in its equivalent, the aspect of style in writing. When Yeats describes the signifiers which refuse to do his will — either because his public misunderstood them, like *The Countess Cathleen*, or because he himself did so (he could not fashion Decima in *The Player Queen*) — they are often connected with horse-imagery, especially with the unicorn. They are very unlike the well-trained horses that run in his ideal theatre in the poem "At Galway Races". They are more akin to those conceived by a Japanese animal painter, "so remarkable that horses he had painted upon a temple wall had slipped down after dark and trampled the neighbours' fields of rice" (*Au*:186). Yeats's metaphors lead him, not onto a well-designed racecourse, but into *Hodos Chameliontos*, in a boggy land where literal and figurative meaning cannot be clearly distinguished. Yet he is fascinated with what is difficult, especially with women figures whose development made him write and rewrite *On Baile's Strand* and *The Player Queen*. Since the women in the first play are only present in their absence, they will be discussed only briefly, by way of introduction to the main piece, *The Player Queen*.

On Baile's Strand

The High King of Ulster, Conchubar, wants to rebuild Emain Macha and to reorganize the whole community. In order to do that, he must subdue Cuchulain. He needs this champion's wild strength and fame to defend the town (*pars pro toto* for their nation, and their culture), but at the same time he is afraid of that hero's unbridled passion. Cuchulain's psyche shows a hysteric structure when he refuses the ties and duties of a regulated family life. Since he considers himself the favourite of the divine powers, he is also highly narcissistic. In order to cultivate his desire of desire (rather than aiming at easy fulfilment) he nurses a kind of courtly love for Aoife, who lives "high up on the mountains in high hungry Scotland" (*CPl*:253). Since she is also the arch-enemy of his people, Cuchulain is Romeo-like in his embrace of a family adversary, and so figures as the epitome of Yeats's man of action.

As Conchubar wants to settle his kingship firmly, to institutionalize it, he takes an oath from Cuchulain that he will uphold the High King's children and therefore fight all their enemies. The hero accepts, because the Little Kings ask him to do so — one of the hysteric's foremost values is his desire for popularity. Yet, just after taking the oath, Cuchulain breaks it. A Young Man, sent by Aoife, challenges him to battle. The hero refuses, because he feels a kind of paternal love and wants to adopt the Young Champion as his son. Thus, after his pledge to Conchubar's ideal of regulated family life, Cuchulain turns from his original refusal to glad acceptance. Yet Conchubar cannot have the arch-enemy adopted by his foremost defender, and ascribes the hero's sharp psychological turn to the influence of the witches, who seem to be the only ones who can overcome Cuchulain. As the latter cannot bear his pride of self-dominance being questioned, he fights the Young Man, "messenger of the witches", and kills him. Afterwards, he hears from two beggars, a Fool and a Blind Man, that it was his own son.

The tragedy hinges on several paradoxes, symbolized in Cuchulain, the sea, and the ideals of the Little Kings. These reveal three enigmatic relations, between identity and difference, between the witches and the signifiers of a culture, and finally between the law — the nation's most important signifier — and the women, guardians of desire.

Let us start with Conchubar's need of charm. Cuchulain is fascinating because he is fascinated (by what is "almost impossible"). That means that the stronghold of Emain Macha is also its weak spot: fascination always entails a dependence upon something outside oneself. This outside is the sea, Aoife who lives beyond it, and the witches who twist men's wits. The danger for the men in *On Baile's Strand* comes from the "women of the ungovernable sea". Both the beggars, at the play's opening, and the kings in their ensuing discussion had considered the power of the witches. They, rather than Cuchulain, are Conchubar's worst enemies:

> ... shut the outer door ...
> ... and sing rhyme
> *That has come down from the old law-makers*
> To blow the witches out. Considering
> That the wild will of man could be oath-bound,
> But that a woman's could not, they bid us sing
> Against *the will of woman at its wildest*
> *In the Shape-Changers* that run upon the wind.
>
> (*CPl*:261; my italics)

But the old law-makers were unable to ward the witches off: the male law cannot conquer and cultivate that which gave birth to it. The problem of Cuchulain as both a shielding and a threatening power, as both a prototype and a foreigner to his own people, is repeated in the function of the sea: it is due only to the division between Aoife and Conchubar that Ulster, or the nation, can find its identity — in difference. That difference, however, is shifting, as living beings constantly change in their interaction. But if difference is the ultimately shaping power, this has weighty consequences if it prevails on identity. Whereas Yeats had maintained that the nation is not a crowd of "chance-comers", it turns out here that it is mainly that. Identity or nationality is an enigma, a complex symbol, a puzzling piece of textile, as Cuchulain shows. When he wants to settle the adoption with his "son" with the giving of a coat he had received from his father, the ritual of acceptance is interrupted by others who, in a further paradox, defend the common good, but can only believe in their own family-structure, that formed with one's "own" children only, not with those that might be adopted. Cuchulain's ways, and all that is irregular is called "woman's will", which is symbolized by "the shape-changers".

The witches, bringing about processes which escape the inculturating forms the men have conceived, are a real and vital danger, as they hit a society in its oaths and rituals, in its most sanctified signs. In the case of signs, logic follows chameleon-like ways, because male, that is, clear-cut logic, leaves out all matters of sensibility, which float and thicken in atmosphere, the fictional power that turns out to be decisive about facts. In *On Baile's Strand*, it is the very ritualization of an oath of obedience that leads to the destruction of the political order: the law of the female powers overrules the male ways of institutionalizing.

That intimidating, unprescribable female power comes from "the ungovernable sea": the seat of the queens of the Country-under-Wave, the invisible women who

> ... anoint
> All their bodies, joint by joint,
> With a miracle-working juice
> That is made out of the grease
> Of the ungoverned unicorn.
>
> (*CPl*:262)

The unicorn who is always chased but never caught (except by women), is the sign of desire that never materializes. Its phallic aspect shows how desire is the driving power that makes men make laws; but the laws cannot "catch", foresee, fulfil or regulate all desires. Conchubar, symbol of wisdom, must acknowledge this: his sceptre is now called an "old rod", "a stolen spoon" (*CPl*: 277) with which he wants to eat the world. The first metaphor shows how the lawmaker has to maintain a desire, to keep trying to make a "just law", which implies that he has to forget that he can never reach his aim; but the second metaphor shows the danger of forgetting that a law is only an instrument, constituted with elements borrowed from different traditions, and not an ultimate truth with which to colonize or incorporate the world.

Not only Conchubar, but Cuchulain too is symbolically castrated: the hero who, thanks to his divine father's authority, had thought himself all-powerful, forgets his father's lesson of non-violence, and kills his son; he goes mad and starts to fight the waves, the ever-changing, ever-differing element that allows the nation to situate itself. Thus the hero is drawn into the seat of the Women-under-Wave. There, they had woven the coat Cuchulain wanted to give his son as a sign that the newcomer would be accepted into that complex piece of textile that symbolized the nation he wanted to defend.

None of the figures in the play could avoid the tragedy: the visionary ones were too frightened to intervene, the powerful ones too blind. The authority of those who used weighty symbols, be it the old law-makers' text, the silver sceptre or the coat of Cuchulain's divine father, did not

rest with those who used these signifiers, and so all the men failed in
their intentions. As the enigma of the differing values, which must lead
the politician in his tentative endeavours to settle a country's identity, is
guarded by the invisible, coat-weaving women, the whole conflict of
Cuchulain's society appears here as a problem where sexual and textual
aspects seem densely interwoven. This will be even more pronounced in
the play which preoccupied Yeats in the years when he wrote the bulk of
autobiographies gathered under the title *The Trembling of the Veil: The
Player Queen*.

Mask *versus* face in *The Player Queen*

The title of *The Player Queen* already gives us the full programme: the
poet will deal with women and theatricality. The player queen herself
will progress through the three stages of hysteria: from the pathological
to a healthy form, in which the abyssal foundation of man's and woman's
existence will gradually reveal itself. As the protagonist moves from the
position of a headstrong, cruel female-tyrant to that of a displaced
person, she illustrates how a human being can never have a room of
one's own, as one's signifiers constantly chase one from the illusion that
one has found at last a fixed and fitting reality. As in *On Baile's Strand*,
animal (especially the horse/unicorn) and textile metaphors
(misunderstandings about written texts and pieces of cloth) abound, as
well as that of drowning waves. The fact that a fabulous animal and the
text/textile images are used suggests that the poet will again be
preoccupied with problems about the distinction between the figurative
and the literal (as with the painted Japanese horses) and with the
difficulty that the most important symbols are the most complex (woven,
as it were, by the Women-under-Wave) and the most disputable ones.
The ordinal number metaphor is also used insistently. Like that of the
Flood, it will bear on the hazardous notion of individuality.

The theme of *The Player Queen* is prefigured in the discussion
between "The Poet and the Actress".[4] Chronologically as well as
thematically, this text forms the bridge between the theory of the mask
as expounded in *Per Amica Silentia Lunae*, and the play that was planned
to be the theory's crowning illustration, *The Player Queen*. Central in the
dialogue between "The Poet and the Actress" is the question of the
division between the "unreal theatre" and "circumstantial realism". The
Poet rejects the latter because the playwright who through some striking

4. "'The Poet and the Actress': An Unpublished Dialogue by W.B. Yeats", ed.
David R. Clark, in *The Yeats Annual*, 8, ed. Warwick Gould, London, 1991, 123-
43.

stylization cannot create his own world, is nothing but a slave to perception, to the obvious and subordinate reality of the senses. Following his imagination, itself a divine faculty, the poet will be raised, or transcend himself, to reach higher levels of existence. The Actress, accustomed to interpreting texts rather than writing them, has a more humble and down-to-earth stance: she does not see the difference between face and mask so clearly, because expression, she says, is a much trickier thing than the poet-theorist thinks. From her experience of acting his plays, she accuses him even of thinking too purely in terms of himself: "you are such a realist in spite of your principles." He is even tyrannical, as he tries to impose his own views on others: "So you take away with one hand what you give with the other."[5] Women — both the women in the text and the actresses who perform it — must run on his course. This is exactly what the Player Queen refuses to do.

At sunrise, a Prime Minister orders a group of itinerant players to perform "'The Tragical History of Noah's Deluge' because when Noah beats his wife to make her go into the Ark everybody ... recognizes the mulish obstinacy of their own wives, sweethearts, sisters" (*CPl*:403). In the frame play there are two main strands: first, Decima, the leading actress of the group, refuses to play the servile wife of Noah, as she accepts only grand roles. Nona, a fellow player who wants to break the stranglehold of the leading lady, reveals that Septimus, the husband with whom Decima refuses to sleep, hoping that he will long for her so much that he will write about her, has been unfaithful to her. Nona can prove it — she knows the text which Decima carries on her bodice, since the verses, she tells her rival, have been "made upon my shoulder" and "down along my spine in the small hours of the morning; so many beats a line, and for every beat a tap of the fingers". This treachery hurts Decima so much that she is driven to insanity. In a trance she starts to dance and invites the animals of the Noah-play to dance around her; so, she unwittingly stages a parallel version of the Noah-play that the Prime Minister had ordered, in which woman is the protagonist. Septimus enters, drunk, and full of speeches about unicorns — fragments of stories he has heard from the revolutionaries in town, which inspire him to further texts.

The second strand involves the people, who are organizing a revolution against their Queen, whom they have never seen, but who is reputed to be a witch who copulates with a unicorn. When the Queen hears the angry crowds coming to the castle, she does not dare to stay in

---

5. "The Poet and the Actress", 132.

the throne room, although the Prime Minister had asked her to do so. She chances on Decima, who is willing to take the Queen's role: although she thinks she will be killed by the mob, that will enable her to revenge herself on her husband, and make an old dream of hers — to play a real queen's role for a short while — come true. But when the people come in, they greet the alleged queen with reverence, as they have just heard from the Prime Minister that she is not a witch at all but wants to marry him; when the latter comes in, he is aghast to find a bride on the throne other than the meek one he had bargained for. The Bishop and an oracle seal the substitution: Decima will be Queen forever, and the other players will be exiled.

Though *The Player Queen* was meant to be a final illustration to *Per Amica Silentia Lunae*, a dramatic counterpart to its lyrical introduction *Ego Dominus Tuus*, it rather undermined Yeats's "old dream of symmetry", whereby every character would become an example of the search for the Antithetical Self. What is so clearly antithetical if the actress's most natural, real occupation is to play, to seem? As Septimus and Decima find out, life and letters are intricately linked. The idealistic set-up in a cosmos of symmetries and antinomies was dislodged in the figure of Decima, who does play a Noah-play, but one in which the Prime Minister's "circumstantial realism" has shifted into the realm of the most "unreal theatre" Yeats could have dreamt of. The distinction between life in reality and in the theatre is wiped out, as Decima mixes professional with non-professional actors. Another principle of the idealistic canon, the idea of mind over matter, is varied in a way which questions traditional value judgments, without simply reversing them. In so far as the people acknowledge Decima because she wears the prescribed golden coronation dress, the aspect of matter is decisive, but her mind is also important. Since both meet so effectively in Decima's expression, people admire her, instead of killing her. So, this Actress proves to her Poet that the slight dress of expression on her naked face proves to be a better mask than anything.

From the play's first line, where Old Men with "grotesque masks" simulate sleep, the townspeople are said to be actors. A professional actor and playwright, Septimus, mixes with them; he is drunk, and mixes reality with his fantasy. He has just written a play about Noah and his "bad wife" and her sister, one of whom was "drowned". So, when he talks about his real wife, he refers to the role he has given her, and "[she] has drowned herself". Thereupon, a woman pours water over him, and he complains that he is "drenched to the skin ... trampled upon ... Robbed, so to speak; naked, so to speak" (*CPl*:390-91). Thus the poet offers a prologue to the play, in which the main metaphors of drenching waves (which will turn out to symbolize signifiers that permeate intention), of people-trampling unicorns (that is, people made and unmade by stories about unicorns), and of the theft of texts and textile are presented. As the metaphors will turn out to be more decisive for the course of the story than for the individuals who pronounce them, it is only just that they are presented so early.

The second part of the play starts with the Prime Minister's trouble with "the leading lady [who] is lost". When Nona chances upon her and tries to make her fit into the Prime Minister's plan, they have an argument which brings out the major differences between hard-headed idealistic thinkers and more emotional ones, who take the playful aspect of life seriously. In that discussion, Decima moves from the first to the second position.

At the start, the leading lady wants to live according to the principle of absolute purity. Like a pathological hysteric, Decima wants to be a mere *uxor spiritualis*, ignoring the concrete needs of her husband. Sending him into exile from her bed is intended to kindle the desire which should inspire him to write great poetic texts, all in praise of his cruel Petrarchan *donna*. But the *Ego domina tua*-stance is unmasked as an illusion, when Decima discovers that the verses made about her were written on a woman colleague's shoulder. The fact that Septimus has sought consolation with Nona is the first incident in the play in which Decima's intention is thwarted. The second occurs when Septimus, following Nona, leaves his wife alone to die. The third occasion is when Decima is prevented from committing suicide; the fourth is when Decima, expecting to die at the hands of the people, is honoured by them instead. As a fifth and final demonstration of the futility of a man or a woman expecting to be able to satisfy their own intentions, the Player Queen's newly inspired deception is shown to have a basis other than that of her own ambition when it is sealed by the oracle (*CPl*: 426-29).

The stages in Decima's development are marked by the text metaphor, in which the material aspect is foregrounded. The initial breakdown of the *domina*'s cosmos is caused by the text betrayal: Septimus' verses, which Decima carried on her heart, prove to be the *hypomnèsis* Plato had warned against.[6] One should know a text by heart, because all that is not

---

6. In "La Pharmacie de Platon" Derrida focuses on Plato's insistence that writing is an ambiguous, dangerous instrument to the memory: a piece of written paper may help one to remember that which escapes one's memory, but it is also an exteriorization, hence liable to be misused, as a text can be stolen and misused in different contexts. "Ce *pharmakon* n'est-il pas criminel, n'est-ce pas un cadeau empoisonné?" (*La dissémination*, Paris, 1972, 87).

interiorized is subject to contamination. But Decima has always been marked with exteriorities: she knows nothing about her birth except the piece of text(ile), the "sheet that was stolen from a hedge" she was "wrapped in". Nona interprets this story in a simple, causal way. She draws a straight *Blut-, Boden- und Beruf*-line (in the "Naturalist" way Yeats hated): if she were born in a ditch, "Low comedy is what you are fit for". Decima sees her future in a different way. Her point of reference is a song Septimus wrote for her to perform as "the mad singing daughter of a harlot" who had a vision that her child would some day wear a golden dress and "carry/The golden top of care" (*CPl*:407-408). The outcome of the play does not confirm Nona in her identification of causality — logical simplicity — interiority — truth: as Decima is acknowledged by the people as Queen because the royal golden dress she has borrowed from the Queen fits her so well, it is the marginal remark in its unforeseeable influence, the illogical impact of metaphor on reality that proves how the complexity of images should not be discarded, and that people must be ready to accept that their interactions will always have something indeterminate about them. They must admit that an insistent exteriority is part of that reality, from which idealists and planners want to clean superfluous, distracting detail.

Men, women and metaphor
The idealists and planners are represented by the two main male antagonists: Septimus, the poet and playwright, and the Prime Minister, the man of action. Both are "authors": the first one wants to be the playwright of Decima's life, the other the creator of a *polis*, a state. Both are cheated out of their authority.

Septimus, Decima's first husband, loses control of her, as his authority starts to lead a life of its own in his metaphors. His song about the harlot's daughter who is destined to wear a golden dress becomes as real and as material as the Japanese horses had done:

> How therefore could she help but braid
> The gold upon my hair,
> And dream that I should carry
> The golden top of care?

> (*CPl*:407-408)

But the playwright's texts disown their author: since the Poet's Actress interprets his texts so well, she becomes the queen and marries the second author. The actors of the theatre group, who are the only ones who know Decima, are "pitched over the border". Thus, the poet is sent into exile by his own texts. Once more, metaphors show they cannot be controlled: the song with which Septimus gave Decima an origin, turns against him, as she acts as a bad daughter to the father of her desires.

This is also true for the man of action, the Prime Minister. Though he hates "dull, poetical plays", he ends up, wrapped in Septimus' esoteric writings, as the husband of an actress who indeed performs the song about the golden dress. Moreover, his own sayings turn against him: his repeated curse on "the sleep of Adam", the moment when woman came into being and man lacked control turns into reality:

> O Adam! why did you fall asleep in the garden? You might have known that, while you were lying helpless, *the Old Man in the Sky would play some prank upon you* (*CPl*:404; my italics).

When the Prime Minister is compelled to marry the Player Queen, he becomes what Septimus calls "the New Adam", the husband of a wild Eve, an actress who is herself led by an unfathomable force, a "circumstantial realism" which is very unreal to all actors, especially to the non-professional ones. The "player Queen" is a riddling figure to both the idealist Septimus and the realist Prime Minister — but also to herself.

The male world of the poet's and politician's power is not simply turned upside down by Decima's perfect acting. The women, like men, are not in control, but, paradoxically, Decima is more in command of the situation than the others, because she lets herself be dictated by circumstances. She is the perfect improviser, "empty" and versatile like the signifiers and metaphors themselves. The woman seems to give the law, but she can only do this because she knows she does not possess it. We will see this as we go through the different rituals which constitute this play.

As Yeats had asked in *The Trembling of the Veil*, "How could life be ritual if woman had not her symbolical place?" (*Au*:302), Decima indeed assumes her "symbolical place", and ritual abounds. We can distinguish three ritual actions, all variations on the theme stated earlier, that man's life is subject to his style — the expression that is beyond his own deliberate intention. As such, man and woman are ruled by metaphors, signs which are open to interpretation and misinterpretation by others.

First, there is the instauration rite with the animals. When Decima refuses to play Noah's wife, she calls upon her colleagues who are dressed as Noah's animals, to improvise an alternative play with her. She

starts dancing and all dance round her, so that she can pick a new
husband, as since his betrayal Septimus has been discarded. While she
dances, Decima sings:

> Shall I fancy beast or fowl?
> Queen Pasiphae chose a bull,
> While a passion for a swan
> Made Queen Leda stretch and yawn,
> Wherefore spin ye, whirl ye, dance ye,
> Till Queen Decima's found her fancy.

(CPl:416)

Here, the fact that politics are also a matter of sexual difference,
becomes more pronounced. We find the men invoking strong masters of
creation. The Prime Minister, who had cursed Adam for having been
cheated by a woman, invokes a strong Noah, who "beat his wife into the
ark" together with the other animals and women; Septimus recalls his
fame with Kubla Khan; another player remembers how successfully he
identified with Agamemnon when playing that role. However, the women
call up revolutionary, anarchic figures such as Eve, Noah's sister,
Pasiphae, and Helen's mother Leda. Whereas the patriarchs owe their
reputation to their privileged link with God, truth, and order, the women
are associated with the devil, lies, and anarchy. Noah's sister, according
to Septimus, "was drowned because she thought her brother was telling
lies"; and she herself has a "drowned, wicked mouth" (*CPl*:420).[7]

More than Adam's descendants, the Ledaean figures of mythological
women are aware of the barbarous influence of their dependence on
language, which Lacan calls "the symbolic order". In their acceptance
of the law of the signifiers (that is, by their admitting they possess only

---

7. Some Celtic myths account for the anarchic features of Irish history and
society, saying the island's population was started by a branch of Noah's family that
had been disobedient to the Master sailor. If this Noah play specifies that branch as
being the female members of it, this explains why it has always been the women
who have been such fierce, shape-changers and unsettlers of culture. Their
continually metamorphosing ways (*phusis kruptesthai philei*, nature likes to hide, as
Heidegger remarked) would then at once account for the "raving wombs" (Greek
hustera) which no country escapes, but particularly not Ireland, which is so full of
old stories about the secret life in the countryside — linked with the hysteria that has
plagued Eire for so long. That the drowning metaphor occurs here regularly, is also
not surprising, as the male researchers of women's vices from the fourteenth century
had already enumerated woman's quality as a *naufragii nutrix* (see P. Verhaeghe,
Tussen hysterie en vrouw: Een weg door honderd jaar psychoanalyse, Leuven, 1987,
71).

"forms", representations, a reality that is made, mixed, with language with its complexity of shifting connotations, rather than pure meaning or the thing itself), they irritate the man who believes in his ability to deal directly with meaning, truths, fact. Therefore the man needs a philosophy that argues in terms of entities, continuities, unbroken self-presence, on the basis of which he would be the giver of the law (of chronology, causality, and similar theories based on a linear logic of progression). With her existence, however, her necessary interaction with men, the woman protagonist in *The Player Queen* smuggles in a logic that does not agree with the ontological object-based thought and tries to forget its need of the dimension of language. (The Prime Minister explicitly states that he hates poetic language, probably because it is a more complex form of language; he also hates sleep, that is, images and words which occur in dreams or hallucinations, and other phenomena which unsettle reality.) The Player Queen accepts rupture in continuity, and parody that unsettles the symmetry of analogy.

In the second ritual, we find the Queen's act of dressing the Player Queen and the ensuing adoration by the bishop and the people, who are subject to powerful, persuasive images. Once more Decima contradicts Yeats's theory that nobility is a matter of personality, since it is her position in a configuration of signs — the Prime Minister's announcement to the people that the Queen intends to marry him, and the fact that Decima is sitting on the throne in the Queen's coronation dress — that makes her such a convincing sovereign. In the law of the signifiers, where the stress is on the dress, the Player Queen is "hollow", ready for death, but her ability to fit her outfit saves her. The golden gear and mules allow Decima to find herself as an actress, one who is always other. Thus, in saving herself, Decima is herself the first victim of that fictionalizing order, which calls for a conscientious interpretation of signs that are always more complex than one can know.

Yeats's Keatsian ideals of the identity of truth and beauty prove to be a fantastic scheme, and not the rule of reality. Instead of an organic unity, Decima illustrates the Lacanian experience, that there is nothing natural in the signifier.[8] First, she was wrapped in a sheet that was stolen from somewhere else; second, the poems closest to her heart could only be written in another's company; and third, she was invested with an authority she did not draw from any ancestral house. Once more, the

---

8. As Paul de Man observes, Wordsworth, in Michael Robartes-style, says "If words be not ... an incarnation of the thought but only a clothing for it, then surely they will prove an ill gift" (Paul de Man, "Autobiography as De-Facement", *The Rhetoric of Romanticism*, New York, 1984, 79).

straight genealogical line turns out to be insufficient as the sole principle of reality.

In the figure of the Player Queen, the distinction between form and content becomes blurred. In traditional ontological thought systems, content is given, while form is added. Decima finds her way into queendom by the form, which cannot be isolated from her function. She becomes a champion of the surface arts: "she refuses entrance, inserts distance".[9] She must embellish herself, "go into the maquis" of beauty, to conceal that she has no origin, is nobody, and later, that the subjects like her because she is a mistress of arts, of seeming. She is the living proof that it is style that makes the truth.[10]

When, in the third ritual, an oracle with a donkey's voice brays in trance, as he always does when the right sovereign has assumed the throne, even the sceptical Prime Minister is astonished: "God or the Fiend has spoken ... fate has brayed on that man's lips" (*CPl*:429) The decisive *coup d'état* is felt as a *coup de théâtre*, where a *hierosgamos* becomes a doubtful business in which a ludicrous and capricious incident (the old beggar's donkey-voice) assigns authority to an era in which both man and woman are imposters. Yet they are deceivers whose world view, whose certainty, is more subject to assault than the citizens, who simulate on a more innocent level: the Old Men only pretend to be asleep, the middle-aged men commit adultery in secret, and all relish the telling of fables. When the royal couple's deceit is sanctified by bishop and oracle, the Player Queen's theatricality becomes of the abyssal kind.

This is a line of thought that Yeats had started to develop at the time he was working on *The Player Queen*. In *A Vision*, an old Era becomes

---

9. Nietzsche was fascinated with women because they function according to the "feinere Gesetze": "sie halten zugleich ferne, sie schaffen Distanz ... sie verbieten 'den Eingang', das Verständnis" (*Die Fröhliche Wissenschaft*, in *Werke*, II, ed. Karl Schlechta, Frankfurt, 1984, aphorism 60). Derrida's views, given in his book *Epérons: Les styles de Nietzsche*, Paris, 1978, provides us with interpretations of the older philosopher which may not fit Yeats's theories, but they do shed light on the "difficult women" of his plays and poems.

10. In his division in types, Yeats had stressed the difference between the man of action who writes into his flesh and the poet who does so on parchment. This difference, however, can no longer be made in the case of the Player Queen, where her body, formed in a bodice lined with verses, was but a preplay for the woman who must "obey" her dress.

the pivot of a new dispensation at the moment of the kind described in "Long-legged Fly":[11]

> Our generation has ... stood at the climax, at what in *The Trembling of the Veil* I call *Hodos Chameliontos* .... there came ... organisation where there is no masterful director, books where the author has disappeared ... and I notice that when the limit is approached or past, when the moment of surrender is reached, when the new gyre begins to stir, I am filled with excitement (*AVb*:299-300).

However, in *The Player Queen* the fact that one's unconscious is not checked by an ultimate instance that would divide Good from Evil hits home in a more striking way.

At these turning points in the world's cultural history, Yeats sees a change occurring in human nature. As in Adam's sleep, something happens in which woman has a part man cannot reflect on, because he has not witnessed it; the part woman plays and plays with has even been taken out of him, as the creation story in Genesis confirms. Therefore, he exists with a lack, which makes him dependent on that other, who is his supplement, because Eve, woman, is not only an addition to him, but also one who can supplant him. She is derived from him, but she is also an extra, and hence, unlike the complement, does not fit into the old dreams of symmetry, which have inspired so many philosophical systems. Like Eve, invented by male authors, the Player Queen's role was conceived both by Septimus and by the Prime Minister. Only, they could not foresee that the roles they had prescribed would contaminate each other, from which mixture the Player Queen arises as the sovereign of all.

In this new era, the boundary between art and nature which Yeats often tried to draw ("Art is art because it is not nature"), puts the royal couple "in troubled ecstasy" over the truth of reality which lies in its seeming, since they experience that art as convincing art because it is second nature. Once more, the oppositional scheme proves to be

---

11. This poem describes a moment of thoughtlessness, as when Caesar is sitting with "the maps spread", but "His eyes fixed upon nothing", with a lack of focus that prepares for the conquest of Gaul; or when Helen of Troy, distractedly, is trying out "a tinker shuffle/Picked up on a street", giving her the elegance with which she will conquer the world; or when Michelangelo's hand is casually "mov[ing] to and fro" so "That girls at puberty may find/The first Adam in their thought" and create the ideal figures that will stir and mould the Western imagination for centuries.

inadequate.[12] *The Player Queen* shows that one should rather think in terms of first and second, more and less, original and derived; and that the fascinating sides of reality can best be seen if one looks at the "first, more, original" in sympathy with the "second, less, derived"; with extra attention to that which has always been discarded in traditional, male, ontologizing Western thought. This is a challenging way of reading, for it will question many old and deep-rooted and even in-grown certainties. Yet, one should, as reader and spectator, accompany Decima's former colleagues when they are exiled from the scene of the inconceivable deceit. They, the critics of the enigma of communication (of which one can never say with certainty whether the reality it constitutes is natural or artistic, real or fictional), will swarm out, always adding to the incommensurable story about man and his image which they will now disseminate in the world as the perpetually puzzling news.[13]

Yeats, Nietzsche and Lacan

Instead of dramatizing Yeats's mask theories, *The Player Queen* illustrates Nietzsche's and Lacan's theories in their endeavour to shed man's habit of ontologizing thought. In so far as Yeats fails to achieve clarity, he fares like the Prime Minister, who orders a play to present his intentions to the people, only to be presented by the people's interpretation of the substituted play, which reveals his ignorance of the relation between man and his words. Yet Yeats liked Nietzsche's theories, which Lacan, with a detour round Freud, develops. We will therefore follow their interpretation of the human subject as a speaking

---

12. Yeats's tendency to formulate his doctrine of the masks in terms of self and anti-self comes from his habit of thinking in antinomies, which Boehme and Blake saw as the two oars with which one could proceed through the water of human existence. Nietzsche is more nuanced: "Der Mensch selbst hat einen unbesiegbaren Hang, sich täuschen zu lassen ... wenn der Rhapsode ihm Märchen erzählt ... oder der Schauspieler im Schauspiel den König noch königlicher agiert, als ihn die Wirklichkeit zeigt" (Friedrich Nietzsche, "Über Wahrheit und Lüge im außermoralischen Sinn", *Werke*, III, ed. Schlechta, 1028).

13. Dissemination, as Derrida explains it, is to be distinguished from polysemy. The latter implies that a signifier has a certain meaning, but can have others also, whereas the disseminating process has no truth-form entity to start from: language makes sense in so far as it is a differential system. Whereas the older Yeats (in his last letter) wrote that "man can embody truth, but he cannot know it", the Player Queen has to teach the Prime Minister, that man can unknowingly embody something which is not necessarily truth, nor a lie, but an undecidable. In this situation, this "un-ethos", the Player Queen is not at home with her "self", and therein offers the reader a variation on Yeats's changeling motif.

being from the three classical points of view — that of author, text and context, and interpreter.

First, the author: both Septimus and the Prime Minister, are taught that it is not the character of the speaker but his language that confers the greatest power on a man's existence. He clearly lives under Adam's Curse, which is to say that his being depends on the effects of his speech. Yet this condition is usually successfully mastered by poets, who have to work harder than businessmen or paupers in a quarry. If poets set themselves to it, they can "articulate sweet sounds together" and command their public by persuasion.

In Lacan's theories, the *parlêtre* cannot ultimately steer his speech: signifiers are a "fonds incontrollable" and go their own way, independent of the speaker's intention.[14] This is clear when what one says about another person proves to be more revelatory of the speaker than of the theme. Or, as the Prime Minister discovers, the things said about, or even wholly apart from him, have greater determining power over him than his own plans. (For example, the gossip about the Queen and the unicorn, which he thinks is merely silly talk, will be sealed as reality by the oracle.) Every aspect of his plan is inverted: although, to show male supremacy over both animals and women, he had ordered "The Tragical History of Noah's Deluge" to be performed, this becomes a prank played on him, so that he too must be drowned in the *Hodos Chameliontos* of language, and set free by Septimus' best improviser, Decima. The planner and speaker who had identified with Noah is overcome by the "règnes flottants des signifiants" that always change their meaning, as they always move into other contexts. Thus, we find Lacan's view on the "speaking being", who is always "thrown", *jeté*, in signifiers (either as su*jet*, pro*jet*, ob*jet*), perfectly illustrated in the Prime Minister's case, as he is one of those who practise rhetoric, and will die through rhetoric.

In "the New Adam", as Septimus calls the Prime Minister, Adam's Curse is both a subjective and an objective genitive, but whether the first has caused the second or whether it is the other way round, remains undecidable. Unlike the Adam of Genesis who had all the creatures under his command, these animals turn out to be but images who command the New Man. With the New Woman, Decima, he will learn to unify with the movements of the signifiers, without identifying with them. If they

---

14. In *The Symbolist Movement in Literature*, which he dedicated to Yeats, Arthur Symons indicated this: "He knows that words are living things, which we have not created, and which go their way without demanding of us the right to live" (86).

do not play their roles as royals convincingly, if the people discover the deceit, they will be killed: so they assimilate themselves to their new function as best they can. At the same time, they are "thrown out" of understanding when the oracle sanctifies this very deception. The author remains powerful as long as he keeps up his or her paradoxical situation — like Decima: it is the champion improviser, the one who picks up the metaphors that befall her, who becomes the determiner of the new state's policy.[15]

The text and context: such improvisers who accept their being "done up" and undone by the signifiers of the moment, illustrate the fundamental hysteric's attitude. They differ clearly from the pathological hysteric, who merely manifests an exaggerated narcissism, practising her versatility merely to hide a deepest self, which she herself considers as something very special, although underestimated by normal people.

That the most influential speakers of this play are all given a name which is an ordinal instead of cardinal number, stresses the fact the players of the abyssal understanding of existence have no identity, except in their difference from each other: all are but signs in the differential system of language. Moreover, there is no "Number One": the Prime Minister, as we see at the end of the play, has become page to the Player Queen, being her first representative, executive, servant; while she herself is but a player queen, an Actress depending on a text.[16]

As language is a differential system, those signifiers are themselves subject to their context. In *The Player Queen*, four traditionally clear differences become problematic: between the marginal and the central; between the poetic and the real, or political; between entities and

---

15. In her ability to adapt readily to the changing expressions of the moment, Decima is a *Haec*-version of the *Hic*-figure of *Ego Dominus Tuus*. But she annuls the strict difference the poet wanted to maintain between *Hic* and *Ille*: the more she lives in the moment (the attitude *Hic* advocates), the more she is exiled from the possibility of experiencing the idea of reflecting, self-conceiving, continuous "identity" (and hence near to *Ille*'s condition).

16. That the name "Decima" is chosen for this woman who believes that her fate is written in the "stitch song" which the harlot sung at her work, is oddly appropriate, since a "decima" is also the name of a "'rhapsody' or '*stitch* song', which was sung, partly from memory, partly improvised, a song to accompany work" (J.A. Cuddon, *A Dictionary of Literary Terms*, London, 1979). The coincidence reinforces the link between the woman protagonist and the text metaphor. At different hinge points of the action she repeats the lines: "How could she help but braid/The gold upon my hair" (*CPl*:407); "She pulled the thread, and bit the thread/And made a golden gown" (*CPl*:428).

signifiers; and finally, between figural and literal understanding of words.

Let us start with the development, wherein the marginal plot grows to dominate the central plot. The first thing a reader (or a member of the audience) may observe in *The Player Queen* is how both content and form of the animal metaphors become contaminated. Animals from heterogeneous traditions — Kubla Khan's creatures mix with those of Adam and Noah; the masters of Xanadu and Troy face each other on fictional scenes — are brought together in this comedy and flow into each other.

On the level of form, more specifically that of genre, we find that elements of Noh drama mix with the "Noah play", so that an aristocratic Eastern Noh genre mixes with an aristocratic Western court play. The Noah tragedy, as ordered by the Prime Minister, had much of the mask play in it, that is it was a piece to be played on the occasion of a coronation; it had a noble main story, and some intervals played by fauns, or other animal players.[17] These actors playing satyrs, animals that should be driven together into the patriarch's saving ark, were originally meant to add a light touch to the tragedy, by way of interludes. But the marginal intrigue has overtaken the main purpose, and it is not entities which count but images. Whereas the Prime Minister and Decima as individuals had nothing in common, the metaphors that are ascribed to them fit perfectly, so that the "New Unicorn" marries the woman who has been "a badger and a weasel and a hedgehog and a polecat". When the Prime Minister's lesson to the nation is supplemented by the comedy, this is transformed into reality, turning the man's wishes upside down (the woman ordering the man) and inside out, as the figural signs become literal: the mulish obstinate woman becomes the true authority, when she, thanks to her "golden mules" and their sanctioning by the oracular "mule's voice", ass-sign the Prime Minister his place.

The interpreter: like the author and the signs, the interpreter is not a self-sufficient, ultimate authority, but he or she depends on shifting contexts. At times, Yeats acknowledged that the ways of the imagination were more like a labyrinth than a neatly laid out race-course. From the

---

17. Robert Graves indicates that centaurs, which later changed to satyr figures, were connected with "a royal wedding feast, divinely patronized" (*The Greek Myths*, Penguin, 1980, I, 362). In this version, the actors, who remind us of the Lacanian view of signifiers, do so more strongly: they are metaphors, themselves constituted of several signifiers, as the centaur is made of man and animal. Lacan's view that the signifier only makes sense in a context is also symbolized in the naming system with ordinal numbers.

Pre-Raphaelites and the Arts and Crafts Movement, he knew that the number and kinds of signs that form trivial tales, but which can set people dreaming and therein "change some childish day to tragedy", are unlimited. This play indeed shows him that "a fragment of gold braid" can be "an originating impulse to revolution or to philosophy" (*Au*:263). The philosophy we read in this comedy sends us once more in the direction of Nietzsche, whose "Geschichte eines Irrtums" we find exemplarily illustrated.

To conclude let me summarize the three main new elements that *The Player Queen* brings to Yeats's work. For a start, Septimus states that "Man is nothing till he is united to an image" (*CPl*:420).[18] Secondly, images are not absolutes either: "we merely play with images" (*CPl*:417), Septimus says slightly earlier. The art of being a noble human being consists in enduring the non-finality of meaning one has attained at a certain stage in one's life. Decima thus exemplifies what Yeats said in his typical obscure way in *Per Amica Silentia Lunae* that "the ringers in the tower have appointed for the hymen of the soul a passing bell" (*Myth*:332). Men and women must accustom themselves to the changing signifiers or conditions of life. Thirdly, the paradoxes of the *parlêtre*, the speaking being who is both united by and playing with images, will call up more paradoxes, as man must habituate himself to the question of "What is true, what is seeming?" In Nietzsche's work we find two answers. The first one declares that "Ich habe für mich entdeckt, daß die alte Mensch- und Tierheit ... und Vergangenheit alles empfindenden Seins *in mir fortdichtet, fortliebt, forthaßt*". Even in one's most intimate moments, for instance in giving oneself in love, one borrows "stolen sheets" and golden dresses, to express one's emotions, which in their turn are inspired by "beautiful old books" — the source of words to be used both by the lover in "Adam's Curse" (*CP*: 89) and by Septimus (reader of the beasteries), when he eulogizes Decima.

A second suggestion to be taken from Nietzsche is that to maintain a balance, to stay sane, life or history is not to be seen as progress, but as a continually recurring translation from dream to reality and back. The

---

18. Once more, he reminds us of Nietzsche, who says that man works and perceives, but only thanks to fictionalizations: notions of time and place that can be neatly categorized. Man cannot explain anything, he says, only play a game with images of things, not with things themselves: "Wir operieren mit lauter Dingen, die es nicht gibt ... teilbaren Zeiten, teilbaren Räumen ... wie soll eine Erklärung auch nur möglich sein, wenn wir alles zum Bilde machen, zu unserem Bilde!" (*Die Fröhliche Wissenschaft*, ed. Schlechta, aphorism 112).

cosmos of symmetries is wiped out, as "seeming is certainly not the antinomy of some essence":

> ... ich bin plötzlich mitten in diesem Traum erwacht, aber nur zum Bewußtsein, daß ich eben träume und daß ich weiterträumen muß, um nicht zugrunde zu gehn .... Was ist mir jetzt "Schein"! Wahrlich nicht der Gegensatz irgendeines Wesens — was weiß ich ... als eben die Prädikate seines Scheins!... Schein ist für mich das Lebende und Wirkende selber, das so weit in seiner Selbstverspottung geht, mich fühlen zu lassen, daß hier Schein und Irrlicht und Geistertanz und nichts mehr ist ....[19]

As for an alternative way of considering the relation between essences and accidental qualities, once more it will be women who will have to lead the author or philosopher or father of his writings to a "Selbstverspottung". As a Michael Robartes, or as any father figure, or any other male, he will confront women young and old, and both the inquisitive men and the dancing, singing, confessional women will be fascinated with each other and with their relationships, which will always remain difficult.

---

19. *Ibid.*, aphorism 54.

THE EROTICS OF THE BALLAD: "A MAN YOUNG AND OLD"

ELIZABETH BUTLER CULLINGFORD

Yeats's sequence of love poems, "A Man Young and Old", was written during 1926 and 1927, and first published as "More Songs from an Old Countryman" and "Four Songs from the Young Countryman".[1] In 1928 Yeats removed his attribution of the speaker's social origin, and placed the poems near the end of *The Tower*. The sequence manifests a complex intersection between contemporary Irish social history and Yeats's formal modernization of the love lyric. As often in Yeats, this modernization consisted in a turning backwards: a reversion past the renaissance iambic pentameter and the courtly sonnet to the popular ballad. Ballad metrics, folk simplicity, and peasant speakers combine to produce political as well as literary effects. "A Man Young and Old" begins that attempt to construct the erotic as a site of popular political resistance which was to culminate in Crazy Jane's defiance of the Irish Episcopate.

Marjorie Perloff has called these poems a "sequence of mythic ballads".[2] Their metrical pattern is consistent: alternating tetrameters and trimeters, rhyming on the even lines. Seven of the eleven poems use a six-line stanza rather than the Child quatrain:[3] Yeats's formal models included literary ballads, translations from the Gaelic, and Anglo-Irish

---

1. "More Songs from an Old Countryman" (numbers 6, 7, 8 and 10 of "A Man Young and Old") were first published in *The London Mercury* of April 1926, and "Four Songs from the Young Countryman" (numbers 1-4) in *The London Mercury* of May 1927. A different version of this paper is to be found in Elizabeth Butler Cullingford, *Gender and History in Yeats's Love Poetry*, Cambridge, 1993, 164-84 (Chapter 9, "The Erotics of the Ballad").

2. Marjorie Perloff, "'Heart Mysteries': The Later Love Lyrics of W.B. Yeats", *Contemporary Literature*, X/2 (Spring 1969), 266-83.

3. The five-volume *The English and Scottish Popular Ballads* (1882-98) by Professor Francis James Child "contains the definitive ballad canon" (Alan Bold, *The Ballad*, London, 1979, 1).

broadsides, which employ differing stanzaic forms.[4] He varies his structure without deviating from what he called "an old 'sing-song' that has yet a mathematical logic" (*UP2*:462) by combining his rhyme units into longer stanzas. The *Oedipus* translation that concludes the sequence is in "fourteeners", or seven stress lines; the fourteener may be the origin of the 4/3/4/3 ballad stanza.[5] Yeats encountered it among the Irish street ballads collected by his brother Jack.[6]

Numerous twentieth-century English poets wrote "folk" poetry: Thomas Hardy, A.E. Housman, Walter de la Mare, and W.H. Auden, for example. Introducing his *Oxford Book of Modern Verse* Yeats noted that folksong, "unknown to the Victorians as their attempts to imitate it show, must, because never declamatory or eloquent, fill the scene".[7] In Yeats's devotion to the ballad form, however, aesthetics cannot be separated from national loyalties and social critique. The Anglo-Irish ballad has, since the late eighteenth century, frequently been the vehicle of anti-Imperialism,[8] and in his youth Yeats celebrated the propagandistic advantages of the genre. Adopting the form which was to dominate his later love poetry, "A Man Young and Old" signals a return to early enthusiasms.

In "Popular Ballad Poetry of Ireland" (1887) Yeats had praised both the native Gaelic tradition, which died out under colonial rule, and nineteenth-century patriotic ballads written in English, the "pseudofolk tradition" that transformed the melancholy passivity of native poetry into stirring and "manly" verse.[9] Yeats admired popular ballads which

---

4. In "Tam Lin" the repeated stanzas about Janet and her green kirtle have six lines, a pattern which Coleridge borrowed in "The Ancient Mariner" where he employs six lines to distinguish the metaphoric stanzas from the narrative quatrains.

5. See *Princeton Encyclopedia of Poetry and Poetics*, ed. Alex Preminger, enl. edn, Princeton, 1974, 64. What is unusual about "From 'Oedipus at Colonus'" is that instead of seven stress couplets Yeats employs seven stress triplets: the lines can be analysed into sixains rather than quatrains. In this, however, Yeats is consistent with the six line norm of "A Man Young and Old".

6. See Hilary Pyle, *Jack B. Yeats: A Biography*, London, 1970, rpt. 1989, 67-68.

7. *The Oxford Book of Modern Verse, 1892-1935*, chosen by W.B. Yeats, Oxford, 1936, xiii (hereafter referred to as *OBMV*).

8. See M.H. Thuente, "Folklore of Irish Nationalism", in *Perspectives on Irish Nationalism*, eds Thomas E. Hachey and Lawrence J. McCaffery, Lexington, 1990, 42-60, *passim*.

9. Thuente, 46-47.

produced an image capable of arousing erotic desire and displacing it towards the nation, represented as a beautiful woman:[10] "Irish Jacobites ... have substituted some personification of Ireland, some Dark Rosaleen, for a mortal mistress" (*Ex*:283). Yeats's early project was the formation of the Irish subject into a nationalist subject through a poetics of desire for the free nation.[11] As a medium long associated in Ireland with both love and patriotism the ballad provided an inspiration for this poetics, although it was not until the nineteen-twenties that Yeats made his most effective use of the form.

Yeats included the Fenian Charles Kickham's "The Irish Peasant Girl" in his selections for *A Book of Irish Verse*. Less obviously militaristic than Mangan's "Dark Rosaleen", Kickham's poem nevertheless suggests the power of erotic sentimentality to form patriotic emotion. It is generically indebted to Wordsworth's "Lucy Grey": "She lived beside the Anner,/At the foot of Sliev-na-mon".[12] The poem is therefore an imitation of an imitation. As Yeats observed, "Coleridge and Wordsworth were influenced by the publication of Percy's *Reliques* to the making of a simplicity altogether unlike that of the old ballad-writers" (*Ex*:211). Yeats did not, however, dismiss literary ballads as inauthentic, and in this he was in tune with current, anti-hierarchical thinking about the genre.[13] He bore personal witness to the emotive capacity of mediocre popular verse:

> I began idly reading verses describing the shore of Ireland as seen by a returning, dying emigrant. My eyes filled with tears and yet I knew the verses were badly written (*Au*:102).

"The Irish Peasant Girl" also deploys the well-used trope of the dying emigrant, playing skilfully with the superior pathos to be elicited when the victim is a pretty young girl. The fate of the dead girl is linked to the fate of her country: she becomes a surrogate for Ireland. Her death alone can move the hardened speaker to sympathy:

---

10. I am indebted here to David Lloyd's unpublished lecture on *The Tower*, delivered at the Yeats International Summer School, Sligo, 1990.

11. Lloyd, unpublished lecture.

12. *A Book of Irish Verse: Selections from Modern Writers*, with an introduction and notes by W.B. Yeats, 2nd rev. edn, London, 1900, 180 (hereafter referred to as *ABOIV*).

13. See J.S. Bratton, *The Victorian Popular Ballad*, London, 1975, 4-7.

> Ah, cold and well-nigh callous,
> This weary heart has grown
> For thy helpless fate, dear Ireland,
> And for sorrows of my own;
> Yet a tear my eye will moisten
> When by Anner's side I stray,
> For the lily of the mountain foot
> That withered far away.
>
> <div align="right">(<i>ABOIV</i>:181)</div>

The tear which will moisten the speaker's otherwise dry eye represents the surplus emotion generated when the figure of Ireland's plight is also the focus of sexual desire. Yeats was determined to harness that surplus emotion while writing less hackneyed verse:

> When the Fenian poet says that his heart has grown cold and callous — "For thy hapless fate, dear Ireland, and sorrows of my own" — he but follows tradition, and if he does not move us deeply, it is because he has no sensuous musical vocabulary that comes at need (*Au*:151).

Yeats's ambivalence about the literary quality of Anglo-Irish nineteenth-century ballads never led him to discount their popular appeal or their propaganda value. At the end of his life he reiterated his appraisal of the ballad writers of *The Nation*: "they had one quality I admired and admire: they were not separated individual men; they spoke or tried to speak out of a people to a people; behind them stretched the generations" (*E&I*:510). He knew that at "the close of the eighteenth century Dublin street singers had some wealth and much influence; a political ballad had more effect than a speech". Arguing that "the political ballads have never ceased to be written and sung",[14] he forged a relation between genre, national pride, and social history:

> It is centuries since England has written ballads. Many beautiful poems in ballad verse have been written; but the true ballad — the poem of the populace — she has let die; commercialism and other matters have driven it away: she has no longer the conditions (*UP1*:147).

---

14. Foreword to *Broadsides: A Collection of Old and New Songs* (1935), in *Prefaces and Introductions: Uncollected Prefaces and Introductions by Yeats to Works by other Authors and to Anthologies Edited by Yeats*, ed. William H. O'Donnell, London, 1988, 177 (hereafter referred to as *P&I*).

Yeats's criticism is permeated by the materialist analysis of literature he learned from William Morris.[15] English "commercialism" accounts for the degeneracy of her artistic production, while Ireland's underdeveloped industries and rural economy allow access to the source of artistic health — the populace. As Matthew Hodgart points out, "the concept of an art belonging wholly to the folk is a fiction";[16] it is nevertheless a politically useful one. Yeats constructs a right-wing populist vision of the Irish ballad as the oral expression of a communal folk culture, contrasted negatively with the bourgeois, capitalist, and individualist print culture of England.[17] Unlike the purist devotees of Child, who established a rigid hierarchy of ballad genres, he does not scorn the hybrid form of the street or broadside ballad, which was particularly rich in Irish patriotic material. Since he does not distinguish between rural Gaelic, street, and political ballads, his definition of "the populace" perforce includes the urban community.

Many years after he had become "less of a socialist" (*Mem*:21) Yeats still saw the ballad as a crucial site of national and class antagonism. In 1906 he wrote:

> Ireland, her imagination at its noon before the birth of Chaucer, has created the most beautiful literature of a whole people that has been anywhere since Greece and Rome, while English literature, the greatest of all literatures but that of Greece, is yet the literature of a few. Nothing of it but a handful of ballads about Robin Hood has come from the folk or belongs to them rightly, for the good English writers, with a few exceptions that seem accidental, have written for a small cultivated class; and is not this the reason? Irish poetry and Irish stories were made to be spoken or sung, while English literature, alone of great literatures, because the newest of them all, has all but completely shaped itself in the printing-press. In Ireland to-day the old world that sang and listened is, it may be for the last time in Europe, face to face with the world that reads and writes, and their antagonism is always present under some name or other in Irish imagination and intellect (*Ex*:206).

---

15. For a full discussion of the influence of Morris on Yeats's politics, see Elizabeth Cullingford, *Yeats, Ireland and Fascism*, London, 1981, Chapter Two.

16. M.J.C. Hodgart, *The Ballads*, London, 1950, 159.

17. Colin Meir, *The Ballads and Songs of W.B. Yeats: The Anglo-Irish Heritage in Subject and Style*, London, 1974, 8-9, claims that Yeats's eliding of the difference between translations from the Gaelic and Anglo-Irish political ballads is misleading.

Yeats's political partiality is evident in his exclusion of all but the Robin Hood ballads from "English Literature". He polemically (and incorrectly) assigns to the Celtic North all the traditional ballads collected by Child in the 1890s,[18] and persists in describing the traditional ballad as "Scots" (*Au*:150).[19] Yeats is, however, accurate in his identification of early twentieth-century Irish culture as more orally based than English culture. Even in 1982 Walter Ong could still call Ireland "a country which in every region preserves massive residual orality".[20]

The hypothetical orality of poetry became one of Yeats's central aesthetic principles. "I naturally dislike print and paper" (*E&I*:13), he claimed, and insisted hyperbolically: "I have remembered nothing that I read, but only those things that I heard or saw" (*Au*:47). On revising the proofs of his collected edition in 1932 he observed that his lyric verse was "all speech rather than writing" (*L*:798).[21] The aesthetic of speech imposed on his verse standards of comprehensibility and dramatic immediacy which distinguish it from that of élitist modernists like Eliot. In the Foreword to his 1935 collection of Broadsides Yeats noted that street singers "had to shout, clatter-bones in had, to draw the attention of the passer-by" (*P&I*:176).

For Yeats the poetics of orality is also a politics, rejecting bourgeois individualism and the solitude of the study in the interests of public, communal experience. This utopian vision derives ultimately from the Tory mediaevalism of Carlyle and Ruskin, but Yeats first acquired it

---

18. Hodgart concludes that attitudes like Yeats's were nationalistic rather than accurate: "Because the best collections of the early nineteenth century were made in Scotland, and therefore so many of Child's versions are in a Scottish dialect, the basic identity of Scottish and English balladry has been obscured, and the facts have been distorted by nationalistic Scots and sentimental Englishmen" (19).

19. For a discussion of this hierarchy, see Bratton, 3-8.

20. Walter Ong, *Orality and Literacy*, London, 1982, 69.

21. Post-Derrida, Yeats's absolute distinction between speech and writing may appear naive. In his discussion of the feudal ballad in *Poetry as Discourse*, London, 1983, Antony Easthope argues that "the opposition cannot be maintained in the face of Derrida's demonstration that the graphematic is a feature of both writing *and* speech" (79). I am primarily concerned, however, with how Yeats used the concept of orality as a political marker for "Irishness", rather than with the accuracy of his linguistic analysis.

from the communist William Morris, even though Morris's literary ballads failed to be "popular":[22]

> I owe to [Morris] many truths, but I would add to those truths the certainty that all the old writers, the masculine writers of the world, wrote to be spoken or to be sung, and in a later age to be read aloud for hearers who had to understand swiftly or not at all and who gave up nothing of life to listen, but sat, the day's work over, friend by friend, lover by lover (*Ex*:221).

Ong discusses what he calls the "psychodynamics of orality" in terms which resemble those of Yeats's ideal: "Oral communication unites people in groups. Writing and reading are solitary activities that throw the psyche back on itself."[23]

Yeats celebrates the dialogue between literacy and orality. He was delighted by evidence that the popular voice could be anonymously augmented by the literate poet: "One day thirty years ago, walking with Douglas Hyde I heard haymakers sing what he recognised as his own words and I begged him to give up all coarse oratory that he might sing such words" (*Ex*:337). For Yeats a necessary corollary of the communal ideal was the abdication of authorial privilege. He describes the anonymity conferred by absorption in the popular memory in terms that anticipate the currently accepted theory of "communal re-creation", which explains the ballads as individual compositions taken up, altered, and orally transmitted by illiterate people:[24]

> In Ireland, where still lives almost undisturbed the last folk tradition of western Europe, the songs of Campbell and Colum

---

22. In Bratton's opinion, Yeats's comments were perspicacious. She argues that Morris's "Chants for Socialists", for example, "are outstanding as literary rather than as popular ballads, their diction and tone inextricably entwined in literary and ideological medievalism .... this kind of success, connected with the whole Victorian movement to improve popular taste by education in the fine arts, is in no way connected with the tradition of popular poetry, and indeed is seeking to supplant and suppress it" (152-53).

23. Ong, 69.

24. See the *Princeton Encyclopedia of Poetry and Poetics*: "Current opinion concedes that the traits of 'balladness' may be explained by the communal theory, but holds that all extant ballads are the work of individuals originally. As the individualists failed to understand, however, the work of an individual poet does not become a ballad until it is accepted by the folk and remodeled by the ballad conventions in the course of its tour in tradition" (63).

draw from that tradition their themes, return to it, and are sung to Irish airs by boys and girls who have never heard the names of the authors (*OBMV*:xiii).

The modern lyric appears between the covers of a printed book on which the author's name stands as a claim to individual intellectual property. Yeats began writing drama to break away from the commodification of the word and the notion of literary proprietorship:[25]

> I disliked the isolation of the work of art. I wished through the drama, through a commingling of verse and dance, through singing that was also speech, through what I called the applied arts of literature, to plunge it back into social life (*Ex*:300).

Writing drama prompted a new appraisal of Shakespeare, whom he could never completely forgive for being English. Shakespeare belonged to the Renaissance, which Yeats, following Ruskin and Morris, identified as the originating moment of capitalism: "The capture of a Spanish treasure ship in the time of Elizabeth made England a capitalist nation" (*Ex*:334). Capitalism spelt the end of orality, for in the time of Elizabeth "English ballad literature began to die" (*UP1*:147), while in subjugated but still pre-capitalist Ireland the Gaelic ballad thrived. The poetic language of the English folk was superseded by alien neo-classical models:

> The metaphors and language of Euphuism, compounded of the natural history and mythology of the classics ... injured the simplicity and unity of the speech! Shakespeare wrote at the time when solitary great men were gathering to themselves the fire that had once flowed hither and thither among all men, when individualism in work and thought and emotion was breaking up the old rhythms of life, when the common people, sustained no longer by the myths of Christianity and of still older faiths, were sinking into the earth (*E&I*:110).

Yeats's suspicion of English Renaissance individualism is inseparable from his suspicion of the blank verse line as its prosodic expression. This expression is one wholly inappropriate to Irish culture:

---

25. For a discussion of print as furthering "the private ownership of words", see Ong, 131: "Typography had made the word into a commodity. The old communal oral world had split up into privately claimed freeholdings. The drift in human consciousness toward greater individualism had been served well by print."

When I wrote in blank verse I was dissatisfied … our Heroic Age went better, or so I fancied, in the ballad metre of *The Green Helmet*. There was something in what I felt about Deirdre, about Cuchulain, that rejected the Renaissance and its characteristic metres …. When I speak blank verse and analyse my feelings, I stand at a moment of history when instinct, its traditional songs and dances, its general agreement, is of the past (*E&I*:523-24).

Yeats's prosodic choices, therefore, are consciously oppositional. The "lectures and pamphlets" of Morris which turned him briefly into a socialist also enabled him to anticipate the speculations of contemporary aestheticians like Antony Easthope, who claims that the pentameter is a hegemonic form:

There is a solid institutional continuity of the pentameter in England from the Renaissance to at least 1900. Like linear perspective in graphic art and Western harmony in music, the pentameter may be an epochal form, one co-terminous with bourgeois culture from the Renaissance till now.[26]

Easthope sees the accentual-syllabic pentameter as relegating the older accentual or pure stress metre (four stresses to the line, with an indeterminate number of unstressed syllables) to a subordinate or oppositional position as "the appropriate metre for nursery rhymes, the lore of schoolchildren, ballad, industrial folk song".[27]

Modernists like Ezra Pound, determined to break the tyranny of the "goddam iamb", elude the pentameter by moving into free verse. Yeats goes back to popular tradition for his metrics. Parkinson asserts that there is no reason to suppose that Yeats ever composed in accentual-syllabic feet: "The main modes of his prosody are either the stress line or the syllabic line."[28] He identifies even those lines that appear to be pentameter as decasyllabics.[29] According to Easthope, one of the crucial distinctions between pure stress metre and pentameter is that

in accentual metre the stress of the intonation and the abstract pattern coincide and reinforce each other; in pentameter they are

---

26. Easthope, 53.

27. *Ibid.*, 65.

28. Thomas Parkinson, *W.B. Yeats: The Later Poetry*, Berkeley and Los Angeles, 1971, ix.

29. *Ibid.*, 187.

counterpointed. The coincidence in accentual metre calls for an emphatic, heavily stressed performance, one typically recited or chanted, often in association with rhythmic gestures, clapping, dancing. In chanting, rhythmic repetitions take complete priority over natural intonation, subsuming it, and this is the metrical "space" for a collective voice.[30]

From his early experiments with chanting to the psaltery to the late radio broadcasts where he incorporated clapping into the recitation of his political ballad "Come Gather Round Me, Parnellites", Yeats was obsessed by the relation of poetry to song. Because he was tone deaf his command of pitch was non-existent, and appreciation of counterpoint impossible, but rhythm was paramount. He disliked "art" music intensely, probably because he was unable to recognize its melodic and harmonic forms, and had numerous battles with composers who attempted to set his verse.[31] He never ceased, however, to search for the perfect marriage between words and music, in which verse

> must be set for the speaking voice, like the songs that sailors make up or remember, and a man at the far end of the room must be able to take it down on a first hearing .... I have but one art, that of speech, and my feeling for music dissociated from speech is very slight .... I hear with older ears than the musician, and the songs of countrypeople and of sailors delight me (*Ex*:217-18).

Yeats's nautical poetics reinforced his folk aesthetics since sea shanties are work songs, organically connected to the labour of those who sing them.[32] If as a child his absorption in traditional ballads stimulated a lonely longing "for some such end as True Thomas found" (*Au*:78), he also socialized happily with the sailors on his grandfather Pollexfen's vessels, and the fishermen and pilots of Rosses Point.

After 1926 the ballad came to compete with Yeats's more complex stanzaic forms as the dominant prosodic structure of his verse. Once the vehicle of nationalist politics, it now became the vehicle of sexual politics instead. In public life Yeats opposed the clerical vision of the State, arguing for divorce and contraception and against all forms of censorship, suggesting that it would exclude from Ireland "all great love

30. Easthope, 73.

31. For a full discussion of Yeats and Music, see Ann Mann, unpublished lecture delivered at the Yeats International Summer School, Sligo, 1989.

32. See Hodgart, 160.

poetry".[33] In an erotophobic culture that tried to define indecency as "calculated to arouse sexual passion", he deployed the love lyric as a strategy of poetic resistance.[34] In a culture rapidly becoming bourgeois he marshalled the popular resonances of the ballad form. He adopted not only its metrical structure, but also its emotional atmosphere and attitude towards the body. The Child ballads are characterized by their matter-of-fact acceptance of sexuality. Love is often passionate and enduring but seldom sentimentalized, and nearly always physically expressed. Most ballad heroines who are in love turn out to be pregnant, often with bloody consequences.[35] This stark aesthetic is softened neither by chivalry nor by religion.[36] "The ballads take a simple view of sex, uncomplicated by Christian ethics or by mediaeval Courtly Love".[37]

Just before he wrote "A Man Young and Old" Yeats was forcibly reminded of the power of ballad sexuality to disturb bourgeois clerical sensibilities. The Christian Brothers made a public bonfire of *Pear's Annual* (1925), because it contained "The Cherry Tree Carol", a folk ballad unusual in having a religious theme and treating it naturalistically. In the ballad the pregnant Virgin feels a craving for cherries that the sexually jealous St Joseph is disinclined to satisfy:

> Then up spake Joseph
> With his words so unkind
> Let them gather cherries
> That brought thee with child.

Yeats's brother Jack, a ballad enthusiast and collector, had published "The Cherry Tree Carol" in the Broadside series issued by Cuala Press

---

33. *The Senate Speeches of W.B. Yeats*, ed. Donald R. Pearce, London, 1961, 177.

34. For Yeats's objection to this definition see "The Censorship and St. Thomas Aquinas", in *UP2*:477.

35. See, for example, "Jellon Grame", "Child Waters", "Fair Annie", "Leesome Brand".

36. Hodgart notes that "Christianity does not appear to have modified the background of the Scottish ballad versions" (129). There are also a few ballads, like "The Cherry Tree Carol", on religious subjects. Elsewhere, the Church has left little trace (130). Hence it was a socially appropriate form for Yeats to have used in the context.

37. *Ibid.*, 135.

from 1908 to 1915.[38] In "The Need for Audacity of Thought" (refused publication in *The Irish Statesman* by the prudent AE) Yeats defended the orthodoxy of the Carol, which expresses the mystery of the Incarnation by showing "God, in the indignity of human birth ... I can see no reason for the anger of the Christian Brothers, except that they do not believe in the Incarnation". He concluded combatively that "The intellect of Ireland is irreligious" (*UP2*:464). Calling the Carol a "masterpiece" he invoked the popular mind in its defence: "It has been sung to our own day by English and Irish countrymen, but it shocks the Christian Brothers" (*UP2*:462). In attacking a popular ballad, the priests attack the wisdom of the people, the countrymen.

Apart from Peter, "a pushing man", Yeats's "countrymen" are not the strong farmers, but the "peasantry" whom he instructed Irish poets to "sing" in "Under Ben Bulben". The cultural values of the new state after 1922 were not only Catholic, they were rural petty-bourgeois. "Familism", which ensured the continuity of inheritance and prevented the splitting up of farms,[39] encouraged sexual conservatism: independent sexual behaviour was likely to lead to economic disaster.[40] Against post-Famine sexual restrictiveness and consolidation of Church control, Yeats posited an image of the class below the farmers, the landless peasantry and the migrant labourers or "journeymen", a class that rapidly declined in numbers after the Famine, as preoccupied with desire and sexuality. Studying the conservative small farmers of Clare in the 1930s Arensburg and Kimball noted that landholders identified sexual behaviour that flouted the familistic pattern with "the debased conduct of the lower ranks of the landless and disreputable of the countryside" (204). At issue in Yeats's aristocratic "dream of the noble and the beggarman" was a construction of the role of the landless peasantry as desiring subjects in the new Free State, and of the Free State itself as a political body open to desire. Hence the original attribution of "A Man Young and Old" to the young and old *Countryman*, and the formal claim, registered through the ballad metre and rhyme scheme, to participate in the popular consciousness.

---

38. Broadside no.7, Dublin: Cuala Press, 1909 (for Jack Yeats's ballad enthusiasms, see Pyle, 67-68).

39. See David Cairns and Shaun Richards, *Writing Ireland: Colonialism, Nationalism and Culture*, Manchester, 1988, 115.

40. See Conrad M. Arensberg and Solon T. Kimball, *Family and Community in Ireland*, Cambridge: Mass., 1968, 94 ff.

It was not sufficient to posit the countryman as the locus of desire: at stake for a love poet was the question of what kind of desire, and for what kind of woman. The group of poems to Maud Gonne in *The Wild Swans at Coole* remains within the courtly framework of the abject lover and the cruel mistress, despite his acknowledgement that the lady, like her poet, is past the age when this devotion might seem appropriate. In 1915 Yeats was still "the poet stubborn with his passion ... /When age might well have chilled his blood." Ten years later, the short lyrics of "A Man Young and Old" use the ballad form to criticize the assumptions and the diction of the Petrarchan lover.[41]

The young countryman is a peasant afflicted by the courtly ethos. In "First Love" Yeats returns to the relation between the doomed lover and the murderous, moon-identified beauty that had provided the staple of his own early verse:

> Though nurtured like the sailing moon
> In beauty's murderous brood,
> She walked awhile and blushed awhile
> And on my pathway stood
> Until I thought her body bore
> A heart of flesh and blood.
>
> *(CP:*249; *PNE:*227)

The aristocratic origins of the convention are undercut by the linguistic awkwardness of the peasant speaker, a parody of the "palely loitering" knight from the greatest of Romantic ballads, "La Belle Dame Sans Merci":

> She smiled and that transfigured me
> And left me but a lout,
> Maundering here, and maundering there ....

The anti-poetic line "maundering here and maundering there", with its awkward repetition of a semi-colloquial and unmusical word, de-romanticizes the speaker. His lady is less a Keatsian "faery's child" than an unsympathetic version of Kathleen ni Houlihan. If the speaker is a country-man, she is his country. The quasi-oxymoronic expression "beauty's murderous brood" suggests the more famous oxymoron from

---

41. Hazard Adams, *The Book of Yeats's Poems*, Tallahassee; 1990, 175, sees them as "a complicated manipulation of voice" in which the poet attempts to "sum up in a fiction the life of male human desire".

"Easter 1916", the "terrible beauty" born of patriotic sacrifice. The moon-woman has a "heart of stone", which reflects Yeats's previous fear that excess of nationalist desire "May make a stone of the heart"; and the image of the countryman "transfigured" into a lout bathetically undercuts the heroic transformation of the patriots of "Easter 1916", who are "changed utterly". The flirtatious appeal of the lady who deliberately blocks the speaker's way, blushing and smiling, but who never delivers on her apparent sexual promise, figures the seductions of Kathleen ni Houlihan, who demands that her male devotees give her all but who has "never laid out the bed for any". "First Love" can be read as a rejection of the nationalist poetics of desire for the woman-nation. Such rejection was facilitated by the fact that after the Treaty, according to Sean O'Casey, "the terrible beauty was beginning to lose her good looks".[42]

"Human Dignity" (*CP*:250; *PNE*:228) extends the imagery of moon and stone and continues the intertextual reference to "Easter 1916".[43] The iconic moon, like the ideal of the patriot, repays no-one on the personal level; in its universal "kindness" it is indifferent to particular sorrows or private desires. The lover invokes the verbal code of the Renaissance lyric in which the "kindness" of a mistress ought to signal her sexual willingness. The mistress refuses to recognize this code. Her "heart of stone" turns human sorrow into lapidary myth, "a scene/Upon a painted wall", and the dumbstruck lover himself into a "bit of stone".

In "The Mermaid" the lyrical "I" yields to a condensed third person ballad narrative:

> A mermaid found a swimming lad,
> Picked him for her own,
> Pressed her body to his body,
> Laughed; and plunging down
> Forgot in cruel happiness
> That even lovers drown.

(*CP*:250; *PNE*:229)

Yeats here alludes to Burne Jones's "The Depths of the Sea" where an enigmatically smiling mermaid clasps a young man whose posture suggests that of a moribund captive. Yeats, however, is not merely

---

42. Sean O'Casey, *Inishfallen, Fare Thee Well*, in *Autobiographies*, London, 1980, II, 72.

43. The whole sequence is organized around a remarkably coherent set of verbal patterns: moon, stone, tree, heart, body, pleasure; old, broken, wild, murderous; shriek.

reproducing the *fin-de-siècle* cliché of the vampire woman: the poem's context within this sequence suggests that he is criticizing male representations of the woman-nation, including his own, as insisting on the displacement of desire into death. Unlike the first two poems, which draw on his unrequited love for Maud Gonne, "The Mermaid" figures a sexually aggressive woman who has "picked" the man, and taken the physical initiative.[44] She appears absent-minded about his oxygen deficit, guilty not of murder but of criminal negligence, yet her oxymoronic "cruel happiness" marks her as another "terrible beauty".

Reversing gender roles but retaining the tragic outcome, Yeats in "The Death of the Hare" reflects on woman as prey rather than woman as predator. His juxtaposition of radically opposed definitions of the female role in love exhibits both representations as ideological. Acknowledging the coercive force of apparently dead metaphors, Yeats deliberately deconstructs the traditional trope of love as a hunt. If the male is a hunter, the only possible end for the prey is death. The game of compliment is the social equivalent of loosing the "yelling pack" on the hare, and implies the curtailment of the woman's freedom, the loss of her "wildness":

> Then suddenly my heart is wrung
> By her distracted air
> And I remember wildness lost
> And after, swept from there,
> Am set down standing in the wood
> At the death of the hare.

> (*CP*:251; *PNE*:230)

Yeats, who valued wildness, understood that for women patriarchal marriage represents capture. In his youth he had worshipped heroines like Shelley's proto-feminist Cythna, "lawless women without homes and without children" (*Au*:64). On one of the rare occasions when his courtship of Maud Gonne was going well, he wrote, "I had even as I watched her a sense of cruelty, as though I were a hunter taking captive some beautiful wild creature" (*Mem*:49). Of "The Death of the Hare" he

---

44. Perloff sees the mermaid as Maud Gonne (270), but John Harwood, *Olivia Shakespear and W.B. Yeats*, London, 1989, argues that "The Mermaid" and "The Empty Cup" offer "precisely contrasted evocations of his affair with Olivia, departing in opposite directions from parallel opening lines by way of the opposed images of drowning and thirst. Yeats did, in a sense, "drown" in a love that was only half-tasted, and it was precisely this paradox which had coloured much of his reflection upon the affair" (183).

said, "the poem means that the lover may, while loving, feel sympathy with his beloved's dread of captivity" (*L*:840-41). The young countryman poems thus provide meta-commentary on the traditional rhetoric of poetic love: its tropes point inexorably towards death for both male and female protagonists. The references to "Easter 1916" also allow us to read them as encoding a critique of the nationalist tradition of self-sacrificial love for Ireland, which also leads towards death.

The poems attributed to the old countryman abandon this worn-out rhetoric to challenge the discourse of purity that controlled official Free State policy. Anticipating his later declaration that lust and rage were just as appropriate for the pensioner as for the man in his prime, Yeats sets out to destroy the conventional image of the old as the peaceful repositories of wisdom and good counsel. The central trope in this poetics is that of desire out of season — the sexual desire of the old. In "A Man Young and Old" this desire is rendered doubly anomalous and improper in being attributed to what Daniel O'Connell had called "the finest peasantry upon earth" (quoted by Yeats in *Au*:204.)

A poem that Yeats places immediately after "A Man Young and Old" provides the political context for the old countryman poems:

> They hold their public meetings where
> Our most renowned patriots stand,
> One among the birds of the air,
> A stumpier on either hand;
> And all the popular statesmen say
> That purity built up the State
> And after kept it from decay;
> Admonish us to cling to that
> And let all base ambition be,
> For intellect would make us proud
> And pride bring in impurity:
> The three old rascals laugh aloud.
>
> (*CP*:255-56; *PNE*:238)

"The Three Monuments" is usually glossed from Yeats's divorce speech in the Senate, in which he evidenced the sexual immorality of O'Connell, Nelson, and Parnell in order to oppose indissoluble marriage and affirm the sacredness of individual desire. In a crude sexual pun the three "stand" in public to remind the Irish of the erotic energies they seek to suppress. Superior to contemporary "popular statesmen", they look down on their squeamish successors with Nietzschean gaiety: "The three old rascals laugh aloud." (Although Parnell died young Yeats makes him an honorary "old rascal": only in age can one cast aside prudery.)

Ambition, intellect, and pride are boldly and approvingly associated with decay, baseness, impurity, and age. Yeats defends this paradoxical association with increasing energy in the last phase of his political and poetic career.

Yeats's association of ribaldry with the countryman is not merely fanciful: writing of the late 1920s Arensberg and Kimball record that even the prudish small farmers indulge in

> taunts about prowess and mild ridicule for the possession of a greater relish than is meet, or fanciful recitation of past magnificent misdeeds .... Details of amorous desire and accomplishment are given with considerable gusto, and greeted and reiterated again and again amid hearty laughter.

They caution, however, that the country tradition of verbal ribaldry is no indicator of sexual activity, and reinforces through the sanction of laughter the strict moral code of the farmers.[45] Yeats wishes to disrupt that code. The old countryman, instead of reflecting wisely at the fireside, is driven "crazy" by the thought of lost sexual opportunities. "The Empty Cup" (*CP*:251; *PNE*:231) laments Yeats's inability to appreciate the sexual generosity of Olivia Shakespear.[46] Yeats later wrote to her: "I shall be a sinful man to the end and think upon my deathbed of the nights I wasted in my youth" (*L*:790). "Moon-accursed" by the *femme fatale* of "First Love", the young man "hardly dared to wet his mouth" with the sexual fluid contained in the symbolically feminine cup, for fear that he would be overwhelmed by the experience. Now the cup is "dry as bone". The lover exchanges the lyric form of Petrarchan sublimation for the ballad form of active and practical desire only to discover that although the spirit is willing the flesh is weak.

The decay of the body, however, increases the vehemence of desire. In "His Memories" (*CP*:251-52; *PNE*:232) the broken tree under which the young countryman lay in dumb endurance becomes a metaphor for the grotesque body of the old countryman, whose arms are "like the twisted thorn". The rural images which pervade the whole sequence become crudely colloquial as the old man describes himself as a "holy show" and asserts that women would "sooner leave their cosseting/To hear a jackass bray" (the jackass is a traditional image of sexual potency). Yeats's persona is autobiographical, but the "old sing-song" of the simple form permits him to take extravagant attitudes towards his

---

45. Arensberg and Kimball, 199-200.

46. See Harwood, ch. 3, for an account of their sad affair in 1896.

experience. In a move that anticipates his later construction of female desire as obsessed with "desecration and the lover's night", the old man reflects on his "magnificent misdeeds", recounting with relish his physical conquest of the *femme fatale*, who once enjoyed his lovemaking to the point of sado-masochistic ecstasy:

> The first of all the tribe lay there
> And did such pleasure take —
> She who had brought great Hector down
> And put all Troy to wreck —
> That she cried into this ear,
> "Strike me if I shriek."
>
> (*CP*:252; *PNE*:232)

The inaccessible woman of the courtly poetic tradition, the Helen of "No Second Troy", is represented as eager for her own debasement, begging to be beaten. "His Memories" raises the same problems as "Leda and the Swan": in his eagerness to deconstruct the courtly form and to exalt the pleasures of the body in the teeth of religious repression, Yeats swings from deathly asexual adoration to outright sexual violence. The liberationary power of an insistence on female *jouissance* in a culture dominated by the Virgin Mary is undercut by his presentation of that pleasure as another form of female victimage. In this he may have been influenced by his formal model, the ballad, in which numerous heroines gladly endure physical abuse from the men they love.[47]

Ballad cruelty, and the unsentimental tone of ballad narrative in the face of tragedy, colour Yeats's depiction of "The Friends of his Youth", Old Madge and Peter. In a new development of the "stone" image Madge carries "a stone upon her breast" and sings it a lullaby:

> She that has been wild
> And barren as a breaking wave
> Thinks that the stone's a child.
>
> (*CP*:252; *PNE*:233)

The word "wild" carries stronger sexual connotations in Irish speech than in English, so we infer that Madge has had an interesting but

---

47. Burd Ellen in "Child Waters", pregnant and close to term, follows willingly at the heels of her lover's horse, is forced by him to swim the Clyde, dress as a page and perform the duties of a servant, until she finally gives birth unassisted in a stable. See also "Fair Annie", "Jellon Grame", "Lord Thomas and Fair Annet".

infertile past; now in age her motherhood is a crazy masquerade. Through the image of the moon she is connected with the equally barren woman of "First Love", but in keeping with the coarseness of the old man's diction the moon is presented as "pot-bellied", pregnant, rather than as a virginally romantic ideal. The image of the barren mother nursing a stone can be unpacked politically: Yeats thought Maud Gonne's work to free the treason felony prisoners "brought out the woman in her" and identified her with "Mother Ireland". Later disillusionment with what he saw as her political inflexibility led him to formulate the idea that "women give all to an opinion as if it were some terrible stone doll". "Easter 1916" took up the image of the stone as obsessive political commitment and contrasted it with the living mother who murmurs tenderly over her sleeping child. In the Twenties Maud Gonne was famous as one of the founders of the Women's Prisoners' Defence League, popularly known as "the Mothers". Every week, dressed in flowing black clothes, she led a march to O'Connell Street and made a speech demanding the release of Republican prisoners.[48] Yeats described with a mixture of awe and disapproval

> those dwindling meetings assembled in O'Connell Street or at some prison gate by almost the sole surviving friend of my early manhood, protesting in sibylline old age, as once in youth and beauty, against what seems to her a tyranny (*UP2*:487-88).

One of "The Friends of his Youth", then, is certainly Maud Gonne: not Maud Gonne the mother of two but Maud Gonne in her guise as Mother Ireland, the mother of prisoners. After the experience of Civil War Yeats charges that Mother Ireland is barren, and has nursed not a living child but a nation with a heart of stone. Mrs Boyle in O'Casey's *Juno and the Paycock* (1924) uses the same metaphor:

> Mother o' God, Mother o' God, have pity on us all! Blessed Virgin, where were you when me darlin' son was riddled with bullets, when me darlin' son was riddled with bullets? Sacred Heart o' Jesus, take away our hearts o' stone, and give us hearts o' flesh![49]

---

48. See Margaret Ward, *Maud Gonne*, London, 1990, 134-36, and 153-55.

49. Sean O'Casey, *Juno and the Paycock*, in *Collected Plays*, London, rpt. 1967, I, 87.

Disillusionment with Mother Ireland was common in the 1920s: in *Ulysses* Joyce satirized her as "old Gummy Granny", and after *The Plough and the Stars* riot O'Casey grumbled in *Inishfallen, Fare Thee Well* that "the one who had the walk of a queen could be a bitch at times".[50] In male authors this attitude is problematic. Hatred of a stereotype created by men slides easily into a hatred of women men see as conforming to that stereotype. Yeats, on the other hand, refuses to dissociate himself from Old Madge. He had attacked the "shrieking" of political women in "Michael Robartes and the Dancer", but here he admits with tears that "her shriek was love". The politics of the oxymoron are the politics of admitted contradiction, opposites not reconciled but yoked by violence together. The paradox of the "terrible beauty" is that terror can still be beautiful, that excess of love is still love, and that the speaker's memories of Madge are partly tender.

These memories are passionately evoked in "Summer and Spring", a parody of "Among School Children" (1926), in which Aristophanes' tale of lovers as separated halves of an original sphere symbolizes a moment of ecstatic union. In "Summer and Spring" the lecherous old countryman debunks the Aristophanic myth. He and Madge once sat under that ubiquitous old thorn-tree

> And when we talked of growing up
> Knew that we'd halved a soul
> And fell the one in t'other's arms
> That we might make it whole;

Their symbolic mathematics, however, are confounded by the revelation that Madge has also halved a soul with Peter, and also healed the split, "under that very tree". The sphere was divided into three. Instead of developing the tragic potential of Peter's "murdering look" into a traditional ballad tale of violence occasioned by sexual jealousy, Yeats ends his poem with a jaunty and (in the Irish context) shocking affirmation of the wild woman with two lovers:

> O what a bursting out there was,
> And what a blossoming,
> When we had all the summer-time
> And she had all the spring!

(CP:253; PNE:234)

---

50. *Autobiographies*, II, 150.

The word "blossoming" evokes the last stanza of "Among School Children", in which "The body is not bruised to pleasure soul". Here the reference is not ironic: the stately decasyllabics and the brisk ballad metre carry the same impassioned protest against the mutilation of the whole person perpetrated by those who devalue physical experience.

The traditional ballads were predominantly transmitted by women,[51] and "The Secrets of the Old" are female secrets, including the fact that women fantasize about sex more in age than they did when they were young and lusty. The speaker's ignorance about what women really want is belatedly corrected by Madge, who "tells me what I dared not think/When my blood was strong". She and dumb-struck Marjorie are just as sex-obsessed as he is, sharing with him their memories of satisfied female desire: "How such a man pleased women most/Of all that are gone." The "stories of the bed of straw/Or of the bed of down" with which they regale each other clearly do not conform to what Denis Johnston satirized as official cultural policy: "Clean and pure Art for clean and pure people."[52]

The "wildness" which in Yeats's poetic vocabulary is almost always attributed to women, is transferred in "His Wildness" to the male speaker. He must "mount and sail up there", appropriate the woman's role as moon, because the female imaginative space is unoccupied:

> For Peg and Meg and Paris' love
> That had so straight a back
> Are gone away ....

Once up "there" with the sailing moon he will combine Peter's peacock cry of male pride with Madge's thwarted maternal impulse: "Being all alone I'd nurse a stone/And sing it lullaby" (*CP*:254; *PNE*:236).

Like the equally mysterious poem "What Magic Drum", which also features a nursing male, "His Wildness" disturbs the categories of masculine and feminine by hybridization rather than inversion. Together with the "peacock cry" of male memory, the speaker takes on the lunar image of the traditional beloved, the maternal pose of Mother Ireland, and the barrenness of crazy Madge. His willingness to nurse a stone suggests an assumption of responsibility for the cultural and political conditions he intellectually deplores, and a desire to break down the

---

51. See Allan Bold's *The Ballad* (n. 3 above), and the same author's *The Sexual Dimension in Literature*, London, 1982.

52. Denis Johnston, *Selected Plays*, Gerrards Cross, 1983, 55.

intolerable separation imposed by gender between the male lover and the inaccessible woman with the "heart of stone".

Irish cultural critics link Yeats with de Valera as responsible for imposing a constricting stereotype of Irish rural life upon the new State. "The pastoral Ireland of Yeats and de Valera has now become a downright oppression", writes Declan Kiberd. "The 'revival' which they led was in no sense a national revival, but a sentimentalisation of backwardness in Ireland, a surrender to what Marx once called 'the idiocy of rural life'".[53] If we think only of the rural romanticism of Yeats's early writings we may be tempted to agree. A comparison between his ballads of the young and old countryman and de Valera's famous St Patrick's day radio broadcast, however, invalidates the comparison. De Valera notoriously envisaged Ireland as

> a land whose countryside would be bright with cosy homesteads, whose fields and villages would be joyous with the sounds of industry, with the romping of sturdy children, the contests of athletic youths and the laughter of comely maidens, whose firesides would be forums for the wisdom of serene old age.[54]

Yeats's ballad poetics of old age eschew wisdom for sexuality, exchange cosy homesteads for the open road and the broken thorn, replace athletic youths by twisted "holy shows", and comely maidens by demented old women whose memories are well stocked with illicit episodes. The romping of sturdy children (the only justification for desire in the Catholic sexual ethic) is notably absent as wild and barren Madge sings her lullaby to a stone. Neither Yeats's vision or de Valera's has any claim to so-called objective truth: both are consciously ideological, and offer competing constructions of "the folk". Although de Valera's speech was made after Yeats's death, its contents epitomize the type of discourse against which he posed his defiant celebration of geriatric desire. As a popular form the ballad provided an appropriate vehicle for Yeats's oppositional sexual poetics.

---

53. Declan Kiberd, "Inventing Irelands", *The Crane Bag*, VIII/1 (Spring 1985), 15.

54. *Speeches and Statements by Eamon de Valera 1917-73*, ed. Maurice Moynihan, Dublin, 1980, 466.

THE BANG THAT WAS GREECE, THE WHIMPER THAT WAS ROME: A GRAND TOUR THROUGH YEATSIAN POLITICS

PETER LIEBREGTS

Anyone who has ever taught in primary or secondary school has had to deal at one time or another with the far-reaching attempts of some parents to adapt the curriculum to the unrecognized genius of the apple of their eye. Yet it is doubtful if one ever received such a letter of meddling advice as the one we may find in William Butler Yeats's *Pages from a Diary in 1930*. In that letter, entitled "A Letter to Michael's Schoolmaster", the poet ordered the teacher of his son Michael, age ten, to immediately start teaching his pupil classical Greek by the Berlitz method so "that he may read as soon as possible that most exciting of all stories, the *Odyssey*, from that landing in Ithaca to the end. Grammar should come when the need comes." Yeats himself would tell his son about Plato. The schoolmaster was strictly forbidden to teach Michael any Latin, because the "Roman people were the classic decadence, their literature form without matter". Greece, however, "could we but approach it with eyes as young as its own, might renew our youth". Besides further detailed instructions about the curriculum, the letter stated that if Michael wanted "to learn Irish after he is well founded in Greek, let him — it will clear his eyes of the Latin miasma". The letter ended on a note which marked its author as a concerned and passionate parent: "If you will not do what I say, whether the curriculum or your own will restrain, and my son comes from school a snotterer like his father, may your soul lie chained on the Red Sea bottom" (*Ex*:320-21).

Remarkable in all of Yeats's writings, as we witness here and may see many times in the whole of his *oeuvre*, is his admiration for anything Greek and his strong antipathy to the Latin language, culture and literature. This polarity has various reasons, as I have shown in my book

on Yeats and the Classical tradition.[1] For the purpose of this article, I
will focus on the general background of his use of the Classics, and his
analysis of Greek and Roman culture in the nineteenth century as a
rhetorical means of distinguishing the young and budding national Irish
literature from what he considered to be the old dying English tradition.

Introduction: the Victorians and ancient Greece

William Butler Yeats came of age in an era of paradox and polarity.
Torn between the soothing certainty of traditional values and the alluring
but uncertain prospects of progress, Victorian England was in constant
flux between conflicting opposites. We may see this exemplified in
Matthew Arnold's distinction between Hellenism and Hebraism, and in
the tendency of critics to oppose two kinds of poetry, one of which dealt
with contemporary affairs and one which did not.[2] This thinking in
polarities often derived its examples and analogies *pro* and *contra* from
the Greek and Roman Classics, since the Victorian era had a general
admiration for the perfection of antiquity.

As Richard Jenkyns and Frank Turner have shown, the classical
world stood at the very heart of Victorian criticism, historical thought
and formal education.[3] The Victorians regarded the "ancients" as
"distant contemporaries who had confronted and often mastered the
difficulties presenting themselves anew to the nineteenth century".[4] Yet
even in this identification, Victorian polarity was not absent. Though
there was a strong sense of kinship with Greek society, the Victorians
also felt that perhaps they were more like the Romans. For like the
Roman poets, who in looking back with envy and admiration to the
Greeks, felt like dwarfs upon the shoulders of giants, the Victorians also
sensed they were living in a secondary age. Thus Walter Pater situates
his *Marius the Epicurean* (1885) in the Italy of the second century AD
and stresses the parallels between that age and the nineteenth century. In
later Rome, the earliest freshness of "*Hellas* ... looked as distant ... as

1. Peter Th.M.G. Liebregts, *Centaurs in the Twilight: W.B. Yeats's Use of the Classical Tradition*, Amsterdam and Atlanta: GA, 1993, *passim*. The research for this present article was made possible through the financial support of the Netherlands Organization for Scientific Research (NWO).

2. See Isobel Armstrong, *Victorian Scrutinies: Reviews of Poetry 1830-1870*, London, 1972, 13.

3. Richard Jenkyns, *The Victorians and Ancient Greece*, Oxford, 1980; Frank M. Turner, *The Greek Heritage in Victorian Britain*, New Haven and London, 1981.

4. Turner, xii.

it does from ourselves".[5] And Oscar Wilde made Dorian Gray admire such very late Greek authors as Philostratus and Procopius. Ultimately, the Victorian generally identified themselves more with Greece than with Rome because it was the very feeling of living beyond the *akmè* of a glorious past and of being more akin to the Romans that made the Victorians look back with admiration to that distant Greek achievement.

In this regard the Victorian age turned out to be the culmination of the Romantic *Hellenismos* and its exaltation of the Greek ideals of democracy, literature and philosophy as a reaction to the severe *Latinitas* of the late seventeenth and early eighteenth centuries. The Romantics sought inspiration in classical Greece instead of in ancient Rome as the Augustans had done. Keats was inspired by Chapman's translation of Homer and Lemprière's classical dictionary, while Byron demonstrated his philhellenism by giving his life for Greece in its war against the Turks. Shelley even claimed that all men were Greeks and turned Aeschylus' Prometheus into a champion of the free will and of the creative spirit of mankind.

In the first quarter of the nineteenth century this Hellenism remained limited as "education made practically no allowance for Greek and was still concentrated on the study and imitation of the Latin poets".[6] However, it gradually became clear that Roman-Christian culture was no longer a sufficient format for the literary expression of the revolutionary changes in every part of society at large. The intellectual evolution of the self-reflective study of man, and the demands for political changes and social reforms also led to an enormous Greek revival in the arts between 1820 and 1860, causing a gradual reorientation at the schools and universities from Latin authors to Greek writers. Consequently, "by 1860 every Oxford Greats man would be reading Plato and Thucydides and nearly everyone at Oxford was reading Greats".[7]

Many intellectuals in the second half of the nineteenth century began to see classical Greece as a mirroring image of Victorian Britain. In "On the Modern Element in Literature" (1857), Matthew Arnold stressed the common characteristics between classical Greece and Victorian England, and by putting contemporary problems into this historical perspective, he implied that Greek literature contained the answers to many a Victorian predicament. Similarly, in his *Plato and Platonism* (1893) and *Greek*

---

5. Walter Pater, *Marius the Epicurean*, ed. Michael Levey, Penguin, 1985, 91.

6. R.M. Ogilvie, *Latin and Greek: A History of the Influence of the Classics on English Life from 1600 to 1918*, London, 1964, 82.

7. *Ibid.*, 102.

Studies (1895), a collection of essays written in the 1870s and 1880s, Walter Pater regarded Greek society as struggling, like Victorian England, to maintain the balance between material and spiritual improvement while preserving its moral values and social order. The Hellenism as described in *Social Life in Greece from Homer to Menander* (1874) by the eminent Irish classical scholar Sir John Mahaffy flourished in this Victorian matrix in which every sensible man felt Greek blood flow through his veins:

> Every thinking man who becomes acquainted with the masterpieces of Greek writing, must see plainly that they stand to us in a far closer relation than the other remains of antiquity .... They are the writings of men of like culture with ourselves, who argue with the same logic, who reflect with kindred feelings. They have worked out social and moral problems like ourselves, they have expressed them in such language as we should desire to use. In a word, they are thoroughly modern, more modern than the epochs quite proximate to our own.[8]

Particularly Homer, who "voiced contemporary aspirations and ideals",[9] was seen as the champion of Hellenic values. Between 1850 and 1870 there appeared twelve translations of his epics.[10] And on the frieze of the Albert Memorial, unveiled in 1876, Homer takes the place of honour before Shakespeare, Dante, Virgil and Milton. The adoration of the heroic values of Homeric society also led to an emphasis on athletics and games as means of building character, especially in England's Public Schools where more than ever *mens sana in corpore sano* was emphasized as an ideal. A sound classical education combined with severe physical training would transform Englishmen into superior individuals who would resemble the Homeric heroes in their courage, their swiftness of thought and mutual respect. They would make sure that the sun would never go down on the British Empire.[11]

Yet already in this still seemingly stable "Homeric" nineteenth century, one of the pillars of the temple of the *Pax Britannica* threatened

---

8. J.P. Mahaffy, *Social Life in Greece from Homer to Menander*, London, 1874, 1.

9. Ogilvie, 138.

10. *Ibid.*, 160.

11. For several parallels believed to exist between Victorian England and the Athenian *polis* of the 5th century BC, and between the growth of the British Empire and the expansion of Athenian power, see Ogilvie, 106-108.

to crack. On the western side of the Irish Sea, the cries for Home Rule were becoming louder and louder. The Prime Minister, William Gladstone, one of the most prolific Homeric scholars of his time, almost casually expressed this situation when he wrote in his diary in 1887, a year after his third Liberal government had introduced the first Home Rule Bill for Ireland: "Worked on Homer, Apollo, etc. Then turned to Irish business and revolved much." Irish politics and Homer seemed to be interchangeable interests to him, as we may infer from his statement in 1888: "There are still two things for me to do! One is to carry Home Rule — the other is to prove the intimate connection between the Hebrew and Olympian revelations!"[12]

Like Gladstone, William Butler Yeats was equally preoccupied with Home Rule and Homer, but it was part of his literary and nationalist strategy that he connected the two quite differently. He used the Greek poet and all he stood for as weapons in his efforts to secure independence for Ireland from a country which saw itself as the cradle of Homeric men. As we will see, Yeats made Ireland into the true heir of ancient Greece, and referred England back to the second division, to that of ancient Rome.

Ireland and ancient Greece

Yeats was not alone in his equation of ancient Greece with Ireland, although most of the nineteenth-century Irish writers do not seem to share his general dislike of classical Rome. In the first half of the century the Gaelic tradition was rapidly becoming the most powerful ideological force in Irish nationalism, yet the Classics, so much admired in England, also continued to exert their influence in Ireland.[13] We may see this, for example in the patriotic poetry of Thomas Davis. The poem "A Nation Once Again" opens as follows:

> When boyhood's fire was in my blood
> I read of Ancient freemen,
> For Greece and Rome who bravely stood,
> Three hundred men and three men ....[14]

---

12. Quoted in Jenkyns, 200.

13. For the examples given of nineteenth-century Irish writing, I am much indebted to W.B. Stanford, *Ireland and the Classical Tradition*, Blackrock, 1984, 217-20.

14. For this and the following two quotations see W.H. Grattan Flood, *The Spirit of the Nation*, Dublin, 1911, 237, 161, 262.

Another poet in *The Nation*, R.D. Williams, recalls the Greek fighting spirit at Salamis in "The Patriot Brave" and prays:

> Great spirits who battled in old time
> for the freedom of Athens, descend!

Using the image of the same historical event William Mulchinoeck in "A Patriot's Haunts" has a vision of an army of the sons of Ireland

> With banners flaunting, fair, and free,
> Fit for a new Thermopylae;
> And in the dark and narrow pass
> I place a new Leonidas ....

And in the ballad "The Bunch of Loughero", it is not Cathleen ni Houlihan, but Penelope who takes her son Telemachus-Ireland in her arms:

> She took him in her arms,
> Between joy and hope did smile
> Saying, O my lovely child
> Abandon all such slavery and toil.

Yet these classical allusions and equations gave way to Gaelic ones when the Celtic revival came into its full strength towards the end of the nineteenth century. The Greek and Gaelic heritage were now sometimes opposed to each other, and in his two-volume *History of Ireland* (1878-80) Standish O'Grady even declared the old Gaelic epics superior to the Homeric and tragic poetry of Greece:

> I cannot help regarding this age and the great personages moving therein as incomparably higher in intrinsic worth than the corresponding ages of Greece. In Homer, Hesiod, and the Attic poets, there is polish and artistic form, absent in the existing monuments of Irish heroic thought, but the gold, the ore itself, is here massier and more pure, the sentiment deeper and more tender, the audacity and freedom more exhilarating, the reach of imagination more sublime, the depth and power of the human soul more fully exhibit themselves .... Out of the ground start forth the armies of her demigods and champions — an age bright with heroic forms, loud with the trampling of armies and war-steeds, with the roar of chariot-wheels, and the shouting of warriors.[15]

15. Standish O'Grady, *History of Ireland*, London, 1881, 201.

Yet whether Ireland and Greece were linked by resemblance or by contrast, the relationship kept cropping up, not only in literature but also in scholarly works of this period. We may see an analysis of the connection in *Le Cycle mythologique irlandais et la mythologie celtique* (1884) by Henri D'Arbois de Jubainville, Professor of Celtic Languages and Literature in Paris, and in Alfred Nutt's and Kuno Meyer's *The Voyage of Bran* (1895-97). Yeats himself stated in 1898 that he regarded these books as those "without which there is no understanding of Celtic legends" (*UP2*:119).

It is very likely that John Synge had directed Yeats's attention to De Jubainville. While still a student of classics at Trinity College Synge had attended the latter's lectures in Paris. These stressed the affinities between the Celtic heroic tales and the Homeric epics, and compared the Irish and Greek languages, as De Jubainville believed that the Celtic and the Greek races originally had been one. The notes that Synge attached to *Le Cycle mythologique irlandais* especially focus upon this idea.[16] When Yeats was a Senator of the Irish Free State between 1922 and 1928, he gave a speech in which he referred to D'Arbois de Jubainville's belief that through the study of the old Irish literature, one could shed light

> on the most important secular event in human history. Going back 1,000 or 1,200 before Christ we find Dorian tribes descending on the Mediterranean civilization. They destroyed much and wandered much, and it has been held that we owe to their destruction, the story of the Fall of Troy, and to their wandering, the Story of Odysseus.

Through Irish literature one could rediscover the civilization of these tribes before they entered the Mediterranean: "That does not mean that our people were the Greeks or that our literature is as old as 1,200 years before Christ, but our legends and our books have preserved and gathered together the old literature and much of the history of a similar period."[17]

Alfred Nutt traced the association of gods with certain places back to the time when natural locations such as rivers, trees and mounds were still worshipped. He also suggested a common origin for certain features of Greek and Irish mythology, particularly the doctrine of re-birth, and

---

16. See Declan Kiberd, *Synge and the Irish Language*, London, 1979, 32-35.

17. *The Senate Speeches of W.B. Yeats*, ed. Donald R. Pearce, London, 1961, 76.

pointed out the many similarities between Greek and Irish beliefs. Of course, this not only appealed to Yeats's feeling of nationalism, but it also addressed his passionate interest in the occult. In two essays on primitive folklore and religion which he appended to *The Voyage of Bran*, Nutt had stressed the afterlife and the soul. In his review of Nutt's work in *The Bookman* in September 1898 Yeats wrote that Celtic legends formed "our principal way to an understanding of the beliefs out of which the beliefs of the Greeks and other European races arose", since the scholar had shown the resemblances between "the Celtic and Greek doctrine of the rebirth of the soul" and "the Greek cult of Dionysius [*sic*] and the Irish cult of the fairies". Yeats, quoting Nutt, noticed that "'Greek and Irish alone have preserved the early stages of the happy other world conception with any fulness', and that Ireland had preserved them 'with greater fulness and precision' than the Greeks" (*UP2*:119-20). The Irish folk in this respect had carried on the Greek tradition, since "the Galway peasant, like the Greek peasant, has named the gods" "'the Others'" (*UP2*:59).[18]

These books confirmed Yeats's idea that the Greek tradition was still very much alive in the West of Ireland. In his 1889 edition of William Carleton (1794-1869), Yeats had selected two tales, "The Poor Scholar" and "The Hedge School", from *Traits and Stories of the Irish Peasantry* (1830-1833) about the value of learning among the peasants. The protagonist from "The Hedge School" feels confident enough to rebuke an Englishman when the latter scoffs at Irish education: "What was Plato himself but a hedge schoolmaster? and, with humble submission, it casts no slur on an Irish teacher, to be compared to him, I think."[19] To the Irish of the West, the Greeks were like distant relatives about whom they were well informed. Lady Gregory was told by an informant that Aristotle had been a Greek Druid who wandered in Ireland, while Douglas Hyde recorded how a man familiarly referred to Aristotle as "Harry".[20] Stanford cites a report in 1843 from a German traveller to Kerry in which he describes how he had met a Kerry fisherman who spoke of Aristotle as "a wise and mighty king of Greece".[21]

---

18. Cf. *UP2*:76, where Yeats in 1898 described how the Irish peasants call the gods "'the others', as the Greek peasant calls his Nereids".

19. William Carleton, *Traits and Stories of the Irish Peasantry*, first and second series, London and New York, 1877, I, 238-39.

20. See M.H. Thuente, *Yeats and Irish Folklore*, Dublin, 1980, 249.

21. Stanford, 14.

Yeats's writings on ancient Greece and Rome, then, form a reaction against the Victorian view of England as the true heir of Greek culture, and are partly a product of the recurring literary and scholarly equation of Ireland with Greece. But Yeats in an idiosyncratic way expands and adapts this matrix to his own purposes as he tries to connect these views on the classics with his own attempts to create a national Irish literature.

Yeats, Greece and Irish nationalism

In the latter part of the 1880s Yeats became involved in Ireland's growing nationalism through the influence of the Fenian John O'Leary. In his enthusiasm for O'Leary's adage that "there is no nationality without literature, no literature without nationality", Yeats began to see himself as an Irish artist who could use his art as a means to give Ireland an identity of its own. For his *The Wanderings of Oisin*, written between 1886 and 1888, and published in January 1889, the poet used a variety of Irish sources to create a poem as a contribution to the Irish cause. However, one may also detect some parallels between *Oisin* and Homer's *Odyssey*.[22] The first Island of Yeats's poem bears some resemblance to Scheria, the home of the Phaeacians, while Oisin's encounter with the demon in Book II shows a similarity to the *Odyssey* 4. 351-582, where Menelaus wrestles with Proteus. And Book III of *Oisin* is reminiscent of *Odyssey* 9. 82-104, the passage dealing with the island of the Lotus-eaters. These parallels are hardly accidental, but spring from Yeats's belief in the close connection between Irish and Greek mythology.

Given Yeats's deep love for Homer and the similarities between the *Odyssey* and *Oisin*, the poet was of course pleased that Oscar Wilde in conversation favourably compared his story-telling to Homer's (*Au*:135). Wilde's praise encouraged Yeats in his belief that would revive Greek art in an Irish setting and thus foster a national spirit. In Greece, Homer and the great dramatists had given literary form and expression to Greek mythology, but in the nineteenth century the Celtic sagas were still relatively untouched by literature. A whole range of specific Irish images from a heroic past was still unadulterated enough to be employed for the expression of the Irish national identity. Therefore, Irish writers should study their heritage and national character, as Yeats stated with a reference to the Greek γνῶθι σέαυτον on the temple of Apollo at Delphi: "'Know thyself' is a true advice for nations as well as for individuals" (*UP1*:250). Yet for the expression of this national character, Irish writers should make discriminate use of foreign literatures and study

---

22. See my *Centaurs in the Twilight*, 42-46.

internationally acclaimed authors to discover "the secret of their greatness", that is their style, which is "the only thing in literature which is immortal" (*UP1*:273). In this respect Yeats often refers in his numerous early critical articles to classical Greece, and appeals to Irish artists to study, alongside Celtic mythology, Homer and the Greek poets. By studying and adapting the methods of Greek literature, Irish authors could not only contribute to the great tradition of world literature, but also represent the Irish national character in a truly Irish manner and turn their land into a "Holy Land ... as the Greeks made the lands about the Ionian Sea" (*UP2*:56). Yeats thus wanted a national literature which used the Homeric expression of the essence of the Greek race in an Irish context so that Irish authors could represent the Irish national character in an inalienable Irish way.

His whole life Yeats would hold on to this idea as we may conclude from an interview given in 1931 in which he refers to Aeschylus' *Oresteia*:

> I hate international literature. The core of a thing must be national or local. But at the same time it ought to be a fundamental piece of human life, which is the same everywhere .... I'd like to make Agamemnon a publican who comes home from America to Patrick Street, Dublin, and finds his wife has been carrying on with the bartender, and I'd like to turn Cassandra into an old char prophesying in a tea-cup. Any great play can be put into any other nation or age, but at the same time it is essentially local. A great piece of literature is entirely of its own locality and yet infinitely translatable.[23]

We see how Yeats, despite his insistence on the study of the Irish heritage, kept his eyes fixed on ancient Greece. One advantage was that through the resemblances between Celtic and Greek mythology, the use of Irish folklore in literature would strike a modern Irish audience as at the same time new and familiar. In this respect Frayne has made the following astute observation:

> The name Cuchulain was unknown to most English readers, yet his personality and deeds were close enough to those of Achilles and Siegfried to mitigate the novelty. Deirdre could be treated by Yeats as a composite of the queenly heroines of Greek tragedy, a mixture of Elektra, Ariadne, and Antigone (*UP1*:48).

---

23. *W.B. Yeats: Interviews and Recollections*, ed. H. Mikhail, 2 vols, London, 1977, II, 202.

Indeed, there are many similarities between the epic heroic world of Homer and that of the Irish cycles as described in *History of Ireland: Heroic Period* (1878) by Standish O'Grady, and later by Lady Gregory in her *Cuchulain of Muirthemne* (1902) and *Gods and Fighting Men* (1904). Alfred Nutt even called one of his books *Cuchulainn, the Irish Achilles* (1900), a copy of which can still be found in Yeats's library. Lady Gregory's translations from the Gaelic heroic tales deeply impressed Yeats, who called her *Cuchulain of Muirthemne* "the best book that has come out of Ireland in my time" (*Ex*:3). In the "Scylla and Charybdis"-episode of Joyce's *Ulysses*, Buck Mulligan adds to this a remark which undoubtedly had been in Yeats's mind too:

> - Couldn't you do the Yeats touch?
> He went on and down, mopping, chanting with waving graceful arms:
> - The most beautiful book that has come out of our country in my time. *One thinks of Homer.*[24]

In Lady Gregory's books Yeats saw a reflection of the epic and high imaginative quality of the Irish spirit, and in *Gods and Fighting Men*, he discovered descriptions of Ireland's heroic past that closely resembled Homeric Greece. The Irish warriors lived life to the full, and like the Homeric heroes they all hoped to be "great gentlemen and be worthy of the songs of poets". In these Irish-Greek heroes Yeats saw the "four essential virtues": "to be generous among the weak, and truthful among one's friends, and brave among one's enemies, and courteous at all times" (*Ex*:21).

This insistence on the connection between Greece and Ireland can be seen over and over again in Yeats's work. He stated, for example, in 1893 that "Homer, Aeschylus, Sophocles ... were little more than folk-lorists with musical tongues. The root-stories of the Greek poets are told to-day at the cabin fires of Donegal" (*UP1*:284). In his description of his childhood days, Yeats later recalled that his mother "and the fisherman's wife would tell each other stories that Homer might have told" (*Au*:61). This idea is also put forward by the would-be writer Michael Hearne in *The Speckled Bird*, when he describes some Irish fishermen:

> They talk of the same things the shepherds talked of before there was a town in all Europe. I want to share their thoughts and emotions — only I want to think with more subtlety and feel with

---

24. James Joyce, *Ulysses*, ed. H.W. Gabler, New York, 1986, 178 (my italics).

more delicacy than they do. To do that is to have the wisdom of Odysseus as distinguished from modern wisdom.[25]

Therefore Yeats in many of his critical articles of the period 1885-1900 urged Irish artists to focus upon Irish folklore, while emphasizing the connection between Greece and Ireland: "The literature of Greece and India had just such a foundation, and as we, like the Greeks and the Indians, are an idealistic people, this foundation is fixed in legend rather than in history" (*UP1*:273-74). Therefore one should use folklore as the basis of art, as it was in folklore that the "soul" of the Irish race resided.

Throughout Yeats's early work we see how he continually stresses that folklore must be used consciously by artists to express the "soul" of a race into art:

> Might I not ... create some new *Prometheus unbound*; Patrick or Columcille, Oisin or Finn, in Prometheus' stead; and, instead of Caucasus, Cro-Patrick or Ben-Bulben? Have not all races had their first unity from a mythology that marries them to rock and hill? (*Au*:193)

Poets are essential in this respect, because "they create national character; Goethe, Shakespeare, Dante, Homer have so created, and many others in less degree" (*Mem*:248). This ideal of giving a personal expression to the imagination of the race as Homer had done, is a reflection of Victorian thought and is connected with the Victorian admiration for the Greek epic poet. We may read, for example, in Wilde's "The Artist as Critic" how Ernest, one of the two characters of the dialogue, asks Gilbert whether "the great poems of the early world, the primitive, anonymous collective poems" are the result of "the imagination of races, rather than the imagination of individuals". Gilbert replies:

> Not when they became poetry. Not when they received a beautiful form. For there is no art where there is no style, and no style where there is no unity, and unity is of the individual. No doubt Homer had old ballads and stories to deal with ... but they were merely his rough material. He took them, and shaped them into song. They become his, because he made them lovely .... The longer one studies life and literature, the more strongly one feels that behind everything that is wonderful stands the individual, and

---

25. W.B. Yeats, *The Speckled Bird*, ed. William H. O'Donnell, 2 vols, Dublin, 1973, I, 69.

that it is not the moment that makes the man, but the man who creates the age. Indeed, I am inclined to think that each myth and legend that seems to us sprung out of the wonder, or terror, or fancy of tribe and nation, was in its origin the invention of one single mind.[26]

This idea may be fruitfully compared to Walter Pater's concept of the evolution of literary myth. The original story is not the product of a single poet, but of "the whole consciousness of an age", while there may eventually appear a man eminent "above a merely receptive majority", who attaches "the errant fancies of the people around him to definite names and images".[27] That this idea was also accepted among Homeric scholars may be seen in, for example, the introduction to Butcher's and Lang's 1879 translation of the *Odyssey*. In their speculations about the poem's possible origin, they postulated that the many legends, myths and stories about the Trojan War had to be shaped "into a definite body of tradition" by "minstrels, priests, and poets, as the national spirit grew conscious of itself". Butcher and Lang claimed that at the time of the composition of the *Odyssey*, "it is certain that a poet had before him a well-arranged mass of legends and traditions from which he might select his materials". They therefore call the *Odyssey* "a tissue of old *märchen*".[28]

In all this Yeats found confirmation for his claim that Homer could serve as an example for a modern artist and his ambition to shape folklore into literature: "we may have to go where Homer went if we are to sing a new song" (*Ex:*25). As Yeats states in his Preface to Lady Gregory's *Gods and Fighting Men*, this was exactly what the Greeks had done when they produced their admirable body of national literature: "Was it not Aeschylus who said he but served up dishes from the banquet of Homer?" (*Ex:*25). This is a reference to a statement in the *Deipnosophistai* VIII.347e ("Wise Men at Dinner") by the Greek philologist Athenaeus (3rd century AD):

---

26. Oscar Wilde, *The Artist as Critic: Critical Writings of Oscar Wilde*, ed. Richard Ellmann, New York, 1968, 356.

27. Walter Pater, *Greek Studies*, London, 1895, 100.

28. S.H. Butcher and A. Lang, *The Odyssey of Homer (Done into English Prose)*, London, 1928 (1879), xi-xii.

τὸ τοῦ καλοῦ καὶ λαμπροῦ Αἰσχύλου, ὅς τὰς αὑτοῦ
τραγῳδίας
τεμάχη εἶναι ἔλεγεν τῶν Ὁμήρου μεγάλων δείπνων.[29]

The saying of the noble and illustrious Aeschylus, who said that
his own tragedies were slices from the great meals of Homer.

Yeats comments on these lines that Homer had found the great banquet
"on an earthen floor and under a broken roof" (*Ex*:25) — in other words,
in folklore. The Irish poet also used Athenaeus' image in his description
of Thomas Davis and of the other poets associated with *The Nation*, who
"spoke or tried to speak out of a people to a people; behind them
stretched the generations". Though Yeats disliked the political rhetoric
of their poetry, their use of Irish material inspired him to "get back to
Homer, to those that fed at his table" (*E&I*:510-11).

But Yeats as an Irish nationalist went even a step further by claiming
that there existed a far greater kinship between Ireland and Greece than
between England and Greece. He also used Athenaeus' image in his
attempts to disengage the course of the young Irish literature from the
dying English tradition. He wrote in "The Rhymers' Club", published in
April 1892 in the *Boston Pilot*:

> the literature of Ireland is still very young, and on all sides ... is
> Celtic tradition and Celtic passion crying for singers to give them
> voice. England is old and her poets must scrape up the crumbs of
> an almost finished banquet, but Ireland has still full tables
> (*LNI*:60).

In the same year he wrote that he sometimes heard men in England
"complain that the old themes of verse and prose are used up", but he
asserts, with the sculptural imagery he would later often use, that in
Ireland "the marble block is waiting for us almost untouched, and the
statues will come as soon as we have learned to use the chisel" (*LNI*:66-
67).

This belief culminated in 1893 in "Nationality and Literature", the
most important exposition of Yeats's early beliefs in the future of Irish
literature and of his efforts to separate the Irish and English literary
traditions. In this lecture given in May 1893, Yeats wanted to examine
the stages of "the general course of literary development" and attempt to

---

29. Greek text is taken from Athenaeus, *The Deipnosophists*, London, 1930, IV,
74.

"point out what stage the literature of England is, and in what stage the literature of Ireland is" (*UP1*:268). To analyse the different directions art can take in various cultures, Yeats in his essay proposes to take as his examples the evolution of the literatures of Greece and England, in which there are three "clearly-marked periods" (*UP1*:269), namely the epic, the dramatic and the lyric.

This method of comparison and systematization through the application of the idea of rise and fall was a common one in the nineteenth century, in which the confrontation with the monumental status of classical poetry had led to a sense of defeat and despair. Thomas Love Peacock's essay "The Four Ages of Poetry" (1820), for example, divides history into the four ages of Iron, Gold, Silver and Brass, an idea derived from classical poets like Hesiod and Ovid who in this way had analysed history to explain the decay of mankind. In his scheme Peacock describes how after the Iron period of the uncivilized bards, the Golden Age had included Homer, lyricists like Pindar and tragic poets like Aeschylus and Sophocles, when poetry was as yet unrivalled by science and prose. But in the Silver Age poetry lost its unchallenged position through the rise of Greek prose and of Roman poets like Virgil who, in the imitative spirit of Latin poetry, tried to restore the naturalness of the Golden Age. Finally the Brass Age has to admit the failure of its attempts to return to the Golden Age. Peacock thus turns Latin literature into a lesser successor of Greek culture. He also attempts to show that post-classical literature has known these four stages, from medieval romance, via the golden age of Shakespeare, to the Silver Augustans, to end in our contemporary brass period. In other words, every illusion of emulating Homer's universal epic poetry should be abolished.

In his 1893 lecture, Yeats seems to agree with this pessimism by presenting a picture of Greek literature as a process of decline, from Homer's description of the character of the entire Greek race to the minute depictions of subjective experiences in the Greek Anthology:

> In Greece the first period is represented by Homer, who describes great racial or national movements and events, and sings of the Greek race rather than of any particular member of it. After him come Aeschulus [*sic*] and Sophocles, who subdivide these great movements and events into characters who lived and wrought in them. The Siege of Troy is now no longer the theme, for Agamemnon and Clytemnestra [*sic*] and Oedipus dominate the stage. After the dramatists come the lyric poets, who are known to us through the Greek anthology. And now not only have the racial events disappeared but the great personages themselves, for

literature has begun to centre itself about this or that emotion or mood, about the Love and Hatred, the Hope or Fear which were to Aeschulus and Sophocles merely parts of Oedipus or Agamemnon or Clytemnestra, or of some other great tragic man or woman. The poets had at the beginning for their material the national character, and the national history, and the national circumstances, and having found an expression of the first in the second, they divided and sub-divided the national imagination, for there was nought else for them to do .... When they could subdivide no more, or when the barbarian had defeated them into silence there came a long blank until the next great creative period, when the literature of England arose and went through the same stages, and set to music its very different national character, national history, and national circumstance of climate and of scenery (*UP1*:269-70).

We see here Yeats's characteristic sweeping mode of generalization which he also used in the "Dove or Swan" chapter in *A Vision* to describe the evolution of Unity of Culture and its disruption. He attempts to show how the disintegration of the Homeric-epic age, which had been concerned with the national destiny, had led to the creation of literature intent on the description of isolated examples of great characters, and had ended in the total self-centredness of lyricism, the expression of the *minutiae* of the subjective moods of the individual poet. This logical way of reasoning clearly had no need of the lyrical stage between Homer and the Attic dramatists of the fifth century BC. Yeats could not account for the subjectiveness and self-expression in early Greek literature, and thus for convenience's sake, he ignores the whole period of the archaic lyricists ranging from Archilochus (*c.* 650) to Pindar (518-450), and sees Greek lyric poetry as being that of the Greek Anthology, written after the age of Aeschylus, Sophocles and Euripides.

   We may also detect in the passage quoted above the influence of Shelley with regard to the presentation of Rome as the "barbarian" who defeated the Greeks "into silence". Shelley tended to play down Rome's role in history — and in view of Yeats's admiration for his Romantic precursor, Shelley may be said to be partly responsible for Yeats's disapproving views on ancient Rome. In *A Defence of Poetry* Shelley made Rome into the symbol of "the extinction or suspension of the creative faculty of Greece".[30] But Shelley also knew Horace's tag that captive Greece had in turn made the conqueror captive, and he claimed

---

   30. Quotation taken from *A Study of Shelley's A Defence of Poetry: A Textual and Critical Evaluation*, ed. Fanny DeLisle, 2 vols, Salzburg, 1974, I, 92-93.

in the preface to *Hellas* that but for Greece, "Rome, the instructor, the conqueror, or the metropolis of our ancestors, would have spread no illumination with her arms".[31] In *A Defence of Poetry*, Shelley declared that the "great writers of the Virgilian age, saw man and nature in the mirror of Greece", but that they were less poetical "as the shadow is less vivid than the substance".[32]

After classical literature, English art is put on the Yeatsian bed of Procrustes. Chaucer and Mallory are compared to Homer, but England's epic stage is not carried to the same perfection as in Greece, "for her genius inclined her rather to dramatic and lyric expression". The rise of the theatre is therefore typical of England with its "isolated colossal characters"; yet English writers went further with their self-analysis, "expressing more and more minutely and subtly [their] own profound activity". Byron, Shelley and Keats, "the most characteristic writers", took for their themes "the passions and moods that were once but parts of those great characters, and again the part drove out the whole" (*UP1*:270). The extreme subjectivity of these poets and their devotion to great emotions such as "Hatred, Fear, Hope and Love" made art unnational.

Arthur Hallam, in his essay on Tennyson so much admired by Yeats, had also made the distinction between contemporary writers and the "eminent spirits" of Homer, Dante and Shakespeare, who had spoken to the entire nation, because they were "assigned by destiny to the most propitious eras of a nation's literary development"; these "youthful periods" were characterized by an "expansive and communicative tendency".[33] Hallam, anticipating T.S. Eliot's "dissociation of sensibility", regarded his own age as divided: no longer did sensation, thought and feeling form a harmonious whole; art had lost contact with society and had become increasingly subjective. Likewise, modern lyrical poetry in Yeats's eyes is characterized by a growing complexity and obscurity of language and thought. In "Dr. Todhunter's Latest Volume of Poems" (1889), for example, Yeats gives "complexity of phrase" and

---

31. Percy Bysshe Shelley, *Longer Poems, Plays and Translations*, London, 1970, 315.

32. DeLisle, 100-101. We may compare Shelley's attitude with that of the Victorian Hellenist Wilde who in *Salomé* referred to the Romans as "brutal and coarse, with their uncouth jargon. Ah! how I loathe the Romans! They are rough and common, and they give themselves the air of noble lords" (Oscar Wilde, *The Complete Works*, ed. John Gilbert, London, 1985, 185).

33. Quotation is taken from Armstrong, 90.

of "ever-increasing subdivision of thought" as the signs of an old
literature (*LNI*:89). Yeats seems to imply, in tune with the tenor of the
Victorian age, that modern English art lacked universal validity, that it
was as inferior to Greek poetry as Roman art had been, and that epic
poetry was no longer possible.

The Victorians had inherited the Romantic feeling of having failed to
supply the reader with a modern epic that could equal Homer or even
Virgil. Since the Victorians regarded epic as the loftiests of poetic forms
and the supreme literary genre, it was natural that the absence of a
rivalling contemporary heroic and universal poetic resulted in the
conviction that modern times lost on points to antiquity. William Morris's
Life and Death of Jason, and his *Earthly Paradise*, and Tennyson's *Idylls
of the King* were brave attempts to restore Homeric qualities to English
art, but in "On the Modern Element in Literature" (1857), Matthew
Arnold dismissed epic poetry as a definite thing of the past. Though he
claimed that Victorian poets should imitate the Greeks, he made an
exception for Homer as the one poet who could never be rivalled, since
epic poetry was the perfect expression of a primitive age. It is this idea
that Yeats has in mind when, after his description of the dying English
art, he argues that Irish culture still stands at the beginning of its
evolution, as Homer had stood at the beginning of Greek literature:

> Look at our literature and you will see that we are still in our epic
> or ballad period. All that is greatest in that literature is based upon
> legend — upon those tales which are made by no one man, but by
> the nation itself through a slow process of modification and
> adaption, to express its loves and hates, its likes and dislikes
> (*UP1*:273).

Unlike the situation in English literature, the Irish character is still
unexpressed though there is abundant unexhausted material ready at hand
to build the nation. In this respect Yeats regards Ireland as unique in
Europe: "Alone, perhaps, among the nations of Europe we are in our
ballad or epic age" (*UP1*:273). All that Ireland needs now are artists who
can shape into form "a wild anarchy of legends", an "epic needing only
deliberate craft to be scarce less than Homer" (*UP1*:166;1890).

Given Yeats's belief in Homer as a literary model, in the "freshness"
of the Irish literary tradition and in the connections between Greece and
Ireland, it will cause no surprise that in the poet's early criticism we may
find on many occasions the epithet "Homeric" tagged to any book or
poem that made Irish mythology and history part of the literary revival.
In the 1880s, Yeats called Sir Samuel Ferguson (1810-86) the greatest

Irish poet, "the one Homeric poet of our time", because he had restored to Ireland's "hills and rivers their epic interest" (*UP1*:90), while his poems "embody more completely than in any other man's writings, the Irish character" (*UP1*:87). Yeats praised the "epic measures" of Ferguson's *Lays of the Western Gael* and *Conary*, which he called "the best of all Irish poems" (*CL1*:444;457-58), and credited Ferguson's *Deirdre* with every possible laudatory epithet, as in this work the poet did not only restore "to us a fragment of the buried Odyssey of Ireland", but as every line was beautiful and could not be taken out of its context, Ferguson "was like the ancients" (*UP1*:92). In later years Yeats would mitigate some of his initial admiration for Ferguson, but his primitive quality and simplicity was always hailed as Homeric: "At his worst he is monotonous in cadence and clumsy in language; at his best a little like Homer in his delight of savage strength, in tumultuous action, in overshadowing doom" (*UP1*:363; 1895). Ferguson, "a singer of heroic things unrivalled in our days, the ballad Homer" (*LNI*:80), was thus an Irish Homer and his poetry demonstrated the way for Irish art to develop along its own lines, instead of slavishly following the traditions of English literature.

Similarly, Yeats praised Standish O'Grady's two-volume *History of Ireland* (1878-80) as a "bardic" attempt to re-vitalize and immortalize Ireland's heroic age by "condensing and arranging" the old Irish sagas "as he thought Homer would have arranged and condensed" (*Au*:220-21). He regarded the retelling of the Cuchulain-myth by O'Grady, "his mind full of Homer", as an attempt to "bring back an heroic ideal" (*VPl*:567). Ferguson and O'Grady were two of the men used by Yeats to show the path Irish literature should take for a national art to arise through the practice of the Homeric manner in an Irish context.

Another reason why Yeats linked Greece with Ireland, and associated England with Rome, was his belief that the first two nations shared a common heritage through folklore. In his review of Alfred Nutt's work in *The Bookman*, Yeats wrote that Celtic legends formed

> our principal way to an understanding of the beliefs out of which the beliefs of the Greeks and other European races arose .... The main argument of Mr. Nutt's book is the argument of Mr. Frazer's *Golden Bough* applied to Celtic legends and belief, and being itself a deduction from peasant custom and belief, and not, like the solar myth theory, from the mythology of cultivated races, it must look always for the bulk of its proofs and illustrations to peasant custom and belief (*UP2*:119-21).

As we have seen, Yeats was confirmed in his belief that the Irish peasant in this respect had carried on the Greek tradition, because "'Greek and Irish alone have preserved the early stages of the happy other world conception with any fulness', and that Ireland has preserved them 'with greater fulness and precision' than the Greeks" (*UP2*:119). This folklore was still very much alive in the West of Ireland:

> The Country of the Young, as the poets call their country, is indeed the country of bodiless beauty that was among the Celtic races, and of which (if D'Arbois de Jubainville has written correctly) the Greek mythology and all that came of it were but the beautiful embodiment; and it still lives, forgotten by proud and learned people, among simple and poor people (*UP2*:58).

Yeats was convinced that due to the rise of material civilization man had lost the ability to see the world as symbolical of the spiritual existence: the material world had become an object as such. In ancient times, however, when "a man beheld a natural object the spiritual thing it expressed came at once into his mind".[34] In ancient Greece, matter and spirit, form and essence had still been one before they were severed by science, materialism and empiricism. Yeats therefore disliked Roman literature because in his view its works were written when man had already turned away from nature and had started to question the relation between essence and its material embodiment: "No passing beggar or fiddler or benighted countryman has ever trembled or been awe-struck by nymph-haunted or Fury-haunted woods described in Roman poetry. Roman poetry is founded upon documents, not upon belief" (*Ex*:438-39). In "The Celtic Element in Literature" (1897), Yeats, deriving his arguments from Matthew Arnold's *On the Study of Celtic Literature* (1867), argues that the ancient descriptions of nature made "in what Matthew Arnold calls ... 'the Greek way'" would not be less if a fountain or a rose had been an actual object, but Yeats denounces Virgil for being a real Roman by looking

> at nature without ecstasy ... with the affection a man feels for the garden where he has walked daily and thought pleasant thoughts. [He] looked at nature in the modern way, the way of people ... who have forgotten the ancient religion (*E&I*:177-78).

---

34. *The Works of William Blake: Poetic, Symbolic, and Critical*, eds Edwin J. Ellis and W.B. Yeats, 3 vols, London, 1893, I, 291.

Contrary to the Roman poet Virgil, the ancient Greeks "had imaginative passions, because they did not live within our own strait limits, and were nearer to ancient chaos, every man's desire, and had immortal models about them" (*E&I*:178). Yeats viewed Ireland as a nation of the imagination in which people still lived a Homeric life. In this respect the Celts were still like the ancient Greeks who, in Blake's words, had "animated all sensible objects with Gods or Geniuses, calling them by the names and adorning them with the properties of woods, rivers, mountains, lakes, cities, nations, and whatever their enlarged & numerous senses could percieve".[35]

In the context of the Victorian admiration for Greece, Yeats turns the tables by claiming that there exists a far greater kinship between Ireland and Greece than between Greece and England. Yeats generally associates England with Rome, thus implying that English art, like the Roman, can no longer produce such divine poetry as the Greeks had done. Ireland, however, still possesses a living tradition resembling that of Greece:

> There is still in truth upon these great level plains a people, a community bound together by imaginative possessions, by stories and poems which have grown out of its life, and by a past of great passions which can still awaken the heart to imaginative action. One could still, if one had the genius ... write for these people plays and poems like those of Greece (*E&I*:213).

In "The Celtic Element in Literature" Yeats describes the Celts as passionate visionaries, believing in an animated, supernatural nature and in dreams as reality. In "Dr. Todhunter's Latest Volume of Poems" (1889), Yeats states that as "a literature ages it divides nature from man", as in English-Roman art, but Todhunter's poems are Celtic, "Greek-like and young", full of the "sentiment that fills morning twilight". In his poems "man and nature are one, and everywhere is a wild and pungent Celtic flavor" (*LNI*:89).

Besides this perceived difference between Greece-Ireland and Rome-England with regard to their beliefs, Yeats also distinguished between the oral and the written tradition to make different claims for Irish and English literature. Throughout his work, he repeatedly emphasized how "Greek literature was founded on a folk belief differing but little from that of Ireland" and "that Roman, like English literature, was founded upon the written word" (*VPl*:574). The poet believed that the Irish folk,

---

35. William Blake, *The Complete Poetry and Prose*, ed. David V. Erdman, New York, 1982, 38.

like the ancient Greeks, had preserved their perceptions of the world in their stories which they had passed on to many later generations through an oral tradition. In a 1902 lecture, Yeats wrote that this tradition was broken some "three hundred or four hundred years ago", when "the power went into the hands of the masters of the written book and went away from the unwritten book of the folk, and the written book is still, perhaps will always be, fully possessed only by those that have leisure". Yet for the common man it is still a more natural thing to listen than to read: "It is natural for him to sit among his friends and listen to a tale told or a song sung, but not natural for him to mope in a corner with a book."[36]

In that same lecture Yeats referred to his story "'Dust Hath Closed Helen's Eye'" (*Myth*:22-30), in which he compares the Irish girl Mary Hynes and the blind Irish poet Anthony Raftery to Helen and Homer.[37] Yeats states that Mary Hynes, who had died sixty years before in the village of Ballylee, had been "a beautiful woman whose name is still a wonder by turf fires". Yeats connects Gaelic folklore with Greek mythology or, more specifically, Mary Hynes with Helen, in his claim that the "spirit of Helen moves indeed among the legends that are told about turf-fires, and among the legends of the poor and simple everywhere" (*UP2*:190). He continually emphasizes the Homeric parallels of his story. He describes, for example, how the "hard" peasants, when they talk about Mary Hynes, "grow gentle as the old men of Troy grew gentle when Helen passed by on the walls" (*Myth*:28). This is a direct allusion to the *Iliad* III. 153-58:

> Thus sat the Trojan elders upon the tower. When they saw Helen coming to the tower, they said softly to one another winged words: "Small blame that Trojans and well-greaved Greeks should suffer pains for a long time because of such a woman: very much like the immortal goddesses is she to behold." (my own translation)

Several men and women in Ballylee had told Yeats about Mary Hynes' beauty, the blindness of Raftery, and the poem in which the latter had celebrated her. In "The Literary Movement in Ireland" (1899) Yeats quotes from Raftery's poem and comments that it came out of

---

36. "Four Lectures by W.B. Yeats, 1902-4", ed. Richard Londraville, in *Yeats Annual No. 8*, ed. W. Gould, London, 1991, 84.

37. On this story and Yeats's use of Mary Hynes and Raftery, see my *Centaurs in the Twilight*, 84-88.

the same dreams as the songs and legends, as vague, it may be, as the clouds of evening and of dawn, that became in Homer's mind the memory and the prophecy of all the sorrows that have beset and shall beset the journey of beauty in the world (*UP2*:190).

In "'Dust Hath Closed Helen's Eye'", everyone in Ballylee praises Mary Hynes in unison as the "most beautiful thing ever made" (*Myth*:25), just as Helen was the paragon of Greek beauty. Mary died young "because the gods loved her ... and it may be that the old saying, which we forget to understand literally, meant her manner of death in old times" (*ibid.*:28). This is an allusion to a statement by Menander (342/1-c. 290 BC), the Greek poet of the New Comedy, that

῎Ον οἱ θεοὶ φιλοῦσιν ἀποθνῄσκει νέος [38]

He whom the gods love dies young.

Yeats comments upon this sentiment in "'Dust Hath Closed Helen's Eye'" with a display of his anti-academic attitude: "These poor countrymen and countrywomen in their beliefs, and in their emotions, are many years nearer to that old Greek world, that set beauty beside the fountain of things, than are our men of learning" (*Myth*:28). Yeats claims that these Irish folk were like the ancient races before the written word came to determine their way of life and thought. He believes that those telling him about Raftery "think and feel as probably the farming people thought and felt when Homer wrote". Yeats sees then in Ireland how the opposition of the oral and the written traditions is a distinction between Irish and English literature, or, in larger terms, between Greek/Irish and Roman/English civilization. Anyone who attempts to keep alive the first and to drive out the latter is "really striving to keep alive the old poetry of the world".[39] For an Irish artist writing in English, there arises the problem of the absence of a tradition if it is to be defined through the medium of letters. But if one resorts to folklore instead of the written book, one may "recover again something of the old art of the troubadour", and write poems which can be spoken or sung, "that ancient art".[40]

---

38. Greek text is taken from *The Penguin Book of Greek Verse*, ed. Constantine A. Trypanis, Penguin, 1979, 281.

39. "Four Lectures by W.B. Yeats, 1902-4", 86.

40. *Ibid.*, 88.

We find the same sentiment in the short account Yeats wrote in 1904 of his pilgrimage to Raftery's grave the previous year. In this essay, "Literature and the Living Voice" (*Ex*:202-21), he claimed that Ireland has created "the most beautiful literature of a whole people that has been anywhere since Greece and Rome", while English literature is "yet the literature of a few". The reason is that "Irish stories were made to be spoken or sung", while English literature "has all but completely shaped itself in the printing-press" (*Ex*:206). He regarded the written tradition as "the poetry of the coteries", whereas "true poetry" presupposed "the unwritten tradition" (*E&I*:8). Therefore, the Gaelic Movement must keep "this old culture" or "exaltation of life itself" alive (*Ex*:207). This idea would eventually lead him to re-make his "written" style to come closer to the oral tradition, since "literature is but recorded speech" (*Ex*:95). That Yeats held on to this idea for the rest of his life is clear from a letter to Dorothy Wellesley, written in May 1936, in which he explained to her why he had changed some of her poems; he called them "'literary' & the writers of ballads must resemble Homer not Vergil. His metaphors must be such things as come to mind in the midst of speech (the pen confounds us with its sluggish deliberation)." And in December of that same year he wrote that he felt that "one's verse must be as direct & natural as spoken words."[41]

This idea can be traced back to Wilde when he states that the Greeks regarded "writing simply as a method of chronicling", and that Homer's blindness may have been a myth to remind later generations "not merely that the great poet is always a seer, seeing less with the eyes of the body than he does with the eyes of the soul, but that he is a true singer also, building his song out of music", because the Greeks admired most of all "the spoken word in its musical and metrical relations".[42]

Though space prevents us from pursuing Yeats's identification of Ireland with Greece and his denunciation of Roman culture further throughout his entire *oeuvre*,[43] it may be said here that Yeats's ideas on this theme were never to wane, especially after he sanctioned them in a "scientific" way through his theory of the gyre and historical periods in *A Vision*. A few examples must suffice: in the Adelphi-text of *The Resurrection* (1927), in which Yeats referrs to "the dull Roman brain"

---

41. *Letters on Poetry from William Butler Yeats to Dorothy Wellesley*, ed. Kathleen Raine, London, rpt. 1964, 61 and 109.

42. *The Artist as Critic*, 351.

43. For this wider survey the reader will have to turn to my *Centaurs in the Twilight*.

(*VPl*:916), one of the players states that the Roman "eats too much and for that reason he cannot think, and so he lets the Greeks, who are a lean race, do it for him" (*VPl*:910); while in his draft for *Autobiographies*, Yeats refers to "something declamatory" about the style of Irish political leaders, "Latin in a bad sense" (*Mem*:41).

I would like to conclude this article by turning back to its beginning. It may now have become clear why Yeats in "A Letter to Michael's Schoolmaster" expressed such views on the values of a classical education. We see this belief recur again and again from the 1920s onwards, when the poet had been working on the idea of cyclical history in *A Vision* and had been a member of the Senate with the assignment to take care of educational affairs. When in the 1930s education became a recurrent theme in his critical writings because of his notion that the modern world in almost every respect was declining, his attitude towards Greek and Latin continued the earlier stance which he had derived from the Victorian and Gaelic matrices. In his introduction to *Fighting the Waves* in the *Dublin University Review* of April-June 1932, he refers to Lionel Johnson's adage that "A gentleman is a man who knows Greek", and states that the

> pressure of other subjects has decided that one of the classical languages must go, and every man not a pedant or a man stupefied by the memory that Latin was once the Volapuk or Esperanto of Europe, knows that it should be Latin. Latin literature had great style and an air of authority but it lacked always fundamental thought.

Among his many suggestions for school reform he urged that one should

> compel a boy to begin Greek with his school life, when well grounded to learn Irish by the "direct method", school and university to teach him the two languages, the two literatures, in association. Let him translate Greek into Irish and learn that our chariot fighting Red Branch resembled the chariot-fighting Greeks and Trojans; that D'Arbois de Joubainville spent his life in the study of Irish for no other reason; that the sacred grove where Oedipus was carried off by the gods differed in nothing from the groves where, according to Connaught tales, men, women and children are carried off ... (*VPl*:572-74).

Even in as late an essay as "Ireland after the Revolution" (1939), Yeats still vehemently rejected Latin as a "language of the Graeco-Roman decadence, all imitation and manner and other feminine tricks"; only a priest, a doctor or a lawyer had need of a "little Latin" (*Ex*:438). He again expounded that one should teach, besides mathematics, nothing but Greek, Gaelic and one modern language, and that the children "should speak [Irish and Greek] as fluently as they now speak English" (*Ex*:440). One must "teach Irish and Greek together, make the pupil translate Greek into Irish, Irish into Greek" (*Ex*:439). Though, as we have seen, Yeats's use of the classical tradition is partly determined by Victorian and "Gaelic" influences, it is this particular idealization of Ireland and Greece that has made the poet's view of the classics so idiosyncratic. Anyone familiar with Yeats's work will know that oppositions formed the substructure of the whole of his life and thought. His ideas about Ireland/ Greece *versus* England/Rome are no exception to the rule.

WHOSE REVIVAL? YEATS AND THE SOUTHWARK IRISH LITERARY CLUB

PETER VAN DE KAMP

On 21 March 1888 W.B. Yeats paid his first visit to an Irish Club in London which had been described by one of its members as "a centre of vigorous Irish life" with "a deal of the zest and comradeship that afterwards marked the greater days of the London Gaelic League".[1] To this view of the club Yeats's was diametrically opposed:

> There was a little Irish society of young people, clerks, shop-boys, and shop-girls, called "The Southwark Irish Literary Society", and it had ceased to meet because the girls got the giggles when any member of the Committee got up to speak. Every member of it had said all he had to say many times over. I had given them a lecture about the falling asunder of the human mind, as an opening flower falls asunder, and all had professed admiration because I had made such a long speech without quotation or narrative (*Au*:199).[2]

Yeats's impressions are not incorrect. By 1889, the society which he had joined the previous year had lost much of its zest; *United Ireland*, William O'Brien's Home Rule weekly, ceased to publish the reports of

---

1. W.P. Ryan, as quoted in Martin J. Waters, *W.P. Ryan and the Irish Ireland Movement*, Ph.D. thesis, University of Connecticut, 1970, 12. This present article has been made possible by the financial support of the Ireland Fund in the form of a UCD Newman Scholarship.

2. In his private memoirs, Yeats further diminishes the import of the club: "I had occasionally lectured to a little patriotic society of young Irish men and women at Southwark, clerks for the most part, and their sisters and sweethearts. I made an appointment with the most energetic of them to explain my new plan. He was ready for it, for his society had ceased to meet. The women had taken to laughing at the lectures — they were always the same and they had heard them so often — and nobody would give another lecture" (*Mem*:51-52). Yeats is here referring to Frank Fahy, whose brother and sister were committee members of the club.

its meetings, many of the prominent members had left London, and the club had been adversely affected by its move from Bath Street to Clapham.[3] Yet the club had been very active in the years before Yeats joined it, and his impressionistic view of its proceedings has biased commentators' assessments of its merits,[4] despite W.P. Ryan's cautious and yet controversial annals, *The Irish Literary Revival.*[5]

The title of my essay is derived from an article by Declan Kiberd, "The Perils of Nostalgia", which disavows any *engagé* dimension to the revival:

> The real question must surely be: whose revival? There was certainly no great change in the conditions of the Dublin poor in the early decades of the century, which began with the announcement that the death-rate in Dublin 'has reached the awful proportion of 46 per 1000, while in English cities it is 18.0 or 19.0.' By 1913, the Government Housing Commission revealed that 1/3 of the population of the city lived in tenements. The average wage for men was 14 shillings for a 7-day week.[6]

Some people might feel that Kiberd's figures are irrelevant; a literary Revival, they might argue, does not encompass a social one — cultural and social prosperity being unrelated. This, we may assume, would have been the view of Yeats and Co. at the height of the Revival. But this view would not have been shared by the original Revival orchestrators,

---

3. W.P. Ryan, *The Irish Literary Revival*, London, 1894, 33.

4. See Richard Fallis, *The Irish Renaissance: An Introduction to Anglo-Irish Literature*, Dublin, 1978, 10-11, and Wayne E. Hall, *Shadowy Heroes: Irish Literature of the 1890s*, Syracuse: NY, 1980, 41 ff. These, and other commentaries do not provide a detailed analysis of the club. John Wilson Foster, in *Fictions of the Irish Literary Revival: A Changeling Art*, Dublin, 1987, pays due homage to one of the foremen of the Southwark workers, William O'Brien, judging his *When We Were Boys* on its true merits, but his literary vantage point prevents him from paying attention to the first stage in the revival.

5. The book was considered controversial, mainly because of its covert disclosure of the rows that surrounded Duffy's New Irish Library project.

6. In *Literature and the Changing Ireland*, ed. Peter Connolly, Gerrards Cross, 1980, 3. In his article Kiberd focuses on the interchange of literature and society in the first decade of the twentieth century. By that time, the revival had lost much of its revival impetus. And while it had become a marketable commodity, the first generation of revivalists, including Moran and Fahy, had taken up their roles as Nestors of Irish society.

journalists, civil servants, clerks, fathers of the band of men that people *Dubliners*, a professional class which had emerged all over Europe in the latter half of the nineteenth century as the nationalist intelligentsia.

These Irish Revivalists modelled themselves on continental nationalist movements which had been successful, never forgetting the economic viability of the country that had emerged. Belgium was often quoted as an example, what with its successful fight for freedom in the nineteenth century against the French and Dutch despite a language — and hence culture — rift. In Switzerland, a three-language state, peasant liberation had been effected, and Hungary, which was to become Arthur Griffith's obsessional model, had managed to manifest itself as every nineteenth-century's nationalist's ideal. Denmark was the economic ideal of the emerging co-operative movement, and The Netherlands had managed to maintain its own independence with an embarrassment of riches.

With the success of these European counterparts in mind, these Irish Revivalists raised a spirit of cultural nationalism which Yeats and his friends of the higher echelons of society — O'Leary, Sigerson, Rolleston, Todhunter — tried to transform into cultural internationalism, refining the spirit of Young Ireland out of the heated air of the popular platform into the luminous ether of the literary salon.

The Southwark literary renaissance: 1881-1889

As a movement, the Irish Literary Revival had its roots, not in Dublin, nor in the work of any of the renowned Renaissance writers, but in the poor and overcrowded industrial district of Southwark, which in the 1870s and 1880s became a prime London centre for Irish political, intellectual and social activity. Here in 1873 Isaac Butt's Irish Home Rule Confederation of Great Britain had established its first Irish political club. And here, in February 1883, in the early years of the Land League, the force of Irish Land Agitation led to the formation of the Southwark Irish Literary Club at 132 Blackfriars Road, by a civil servant of the Board of Works, called Francis A. Fahy, who had settled in London in 1873, and who had become involved in the Southwark Branch of the Land and Labour League. Fahy, who had a tendency to lecture to people rather than talk to them, outlined the importance of the club:

> I did not suggest ... that the Southwark Club was the great and sole creator of the revival. Manifestly this would be claiming far too much .... The Southwark strain in one way or another ran through the whole revival. Southwark had some share in the inspiration of the Pan-Celtic Society, it led directly to the formation of the Irish Literary Society, London, it had even

something to do with the Dublin National Literary Society ....
Southwark did good work and wielded much influence in the Land
League days. Of course we know that there were much bigger
Irish litterateurs outside it, that far finer Irish work than it ever
saw was done in quiet ways apart from it in the eighties; but for
many years it was the one ardent centre of Young Ireland
propagandism that we had, the one clear index of anything like a
literary movement.

It was Fahy who pointed out the role of the League in its formation:

When all is said and done you must go back to the Land League
for its origin. The Land League agitated and thrilled Ireland at the
outset. Generous and educated young men who left down their
"Speeches from the Dock", and "Spirit of the Nation" to take out
their Land League cards, had dreams of a new and picturesque
National struggle somewhat on Young Ireland lines.[7]

The shortcomings of the Land League's policies have been well-
documented and do not concern us here. What must be pointed out is that
the League brought about a bundling of intellectual optimism among the
Irish middle classes in Ireland and England. This is apparent even in
Anna Parnell's *Tale of a Great Sham*, when she points out that

When O'Connell saw a famine approaching, he ran to the English
government for help .... The Young Irelanders wrote poetry. The
Land League went neither to the English government nor to the
muses, but ... became ... a government *de facto*.[8]

A motley proliferation of societies sprouted under the rays of the Land
League, such as the Shepherd's Association, the Workmen's Club, the
Irish National Forester's Benefit Society, the West Clare National
Teacher's Association, the Duployan Shorthand Club, the Young Men's
Irish Historical Society, the Gentlemen's Bootmaker Society and the Irish
National Nailmakers' Union. Despite their obvious diversities these clubs
shared the League's belief that nationality — an awareness of one's Irish
identity — would benefit the Irish at home and abroad, not only
culturally but also socio-economically.

The Southwark Club belies Anna Parnell's observation: it offered
several of its Land Leaguers and Ladies Land Leaguers the opportunity

---

7. A letter to *United Ireland*, 28 April 1894.

8. Edited with an introduction by Dana Hearne, Dublin, 1986, 57.

to go to the Muses without deserting their pragmatic aspirations. The cultural dimension to the Southwark Club is apparent from its origin. It grew out of the Southwark Junior Irish Literary Club, which had been founded on 22 October 1881 to counteract the "sad but well-known fact that the children of Irish fathers and mothers in London are growing up with no knowledge of the land of their fathers, or knowing it only by the music-hall ditty, or the sneer of the daily paper where prejudice holds it up to scorn".[9] Meetings of this club were held every Sunday, and children were admitted for one penny, for which they were given an Irish book from John Denvir's Irish Penny Library — which, together with Edmund Downey's Irish Library was probably the most successful Irish popularist publishing venture in the late nineteenth century.

The political potential of the club was recognized by several members of the Irish Home Rule Party. On 27 January 1883 a meeting of its representatives at the office of the Irish Parliamentary Party decided to urge "the secretaries of the different branches of the Land League of Great Britain" to attend a "general meeting of all interested in the success of the Junior Irish Literary Club ... at the office of the Irish Parliamentary Party".[10] By this time, the success of the venture was paramount: a central committee had been established in London to administer the several branches that had sprung up throughout England — the Southwark branch then counted 140 members. It actively participated in Irish relief work, raising money through concerts for "the destitute poor of Loughrea".[11] And it gave financial and educational support to the Gaelic Union, the precursor of the Gaelic League.

Against the background of the success of the Junior Irish Clubs, the Southwark Irish literary society was established, with a similar mixture of social involvement and propagandism based on ethnocentricity. Literature for the sake of literature was as unthinkable to the founding members of the club as it had been to the leaders of the Young Ireland movement, upon which the club was grafted. More than being just a gathering of "ladies and gentlemen" with an active or passive interest in Irish letters, the club offered the opportunity for "active propagandism", of "becoming acquainted with the true facts of the history" of Ireland, and of counteracting the English "charges made against the Irish

---

9. Address by M.D.J. Sweeney, *United Ireland*, 2 September 1882.

10. *United Ireland*, 28 January 1883.

11. *United Ireland*, 10 March and 9 June 1883.

people".[12] Thus among its literary papers and lectures, which championed Mangan, Kickham and the poets of 1848, can be found such titles as "The Cost of Provincialism", "The Everyday Life of an Irish Labourer", "Labour Representation in Ireland".[13]

Combining an interest in Irish literature and history on the one hand and nationalist propaganda on the other was characteristic of the London-based Irish middle-class intelligentsia who became prime movers in the literary revival, exemplified in the writings of Francis A. Fahy himself. On the literary side, his lyrics, mostly published under the pen-name "Dreolin", attained considerable popular appeal — a Theresa Boylan could write in 1888 from Kilbrook to D.J. O'Donoghue: "Mr. Fahy's *Irish Songs and Poems* [1887] is a wonderful favourite with the peasantry here. 'Flower of the Flock' being I believe sung at every festive gathering of theirs."[14] And the young W.B. Yeats acknowledged Fahy's popularity in a letter to Katharine Tynan, dated 14th March [1888]:

Fahy I saw one day in the British Museum Reading Room, Sparling introduced us. A very brisk cordial neat little man — Asked me down to his Irish Literary Club. Seems a king among his own people and what more does any man want. I hear they — that is the members of the club — sing his songs and have quite a Fahy cult. Wish we had him in our ballad book ....[15]

---

12. *Freeman's Journal*, 6 February 1892; *United Ireland*, 11 November 1882 and 2 September 1882.

13. At the same time, the Southwark Irish Debating Society, an offshoot of the Southwark Irish Literary Society and the Southwark Branch of the Labour and Land League, established in September 1883, discussed such topics as "The Demand of the Highland Crofters", "Fenianism and its Consequences", and "Christian Socialism. What It Is". As for literature, Mangan was established as the major poet of the nineteenth century. Richard Dowling was the first to revive interest in Mangan, with an article in *Tinsley's Magazine*, entitled "A Forgotten Poet".

14. UCD D.J. O'Donoghue archives.

15. *The Collected Letters of W.B. Yeats, Vol. 1: 1865-1895*, eds John Kelly and Eric Domville, Oxford, 1986, 55-56. In a letter to D.J. O'Donoghue, 27 February 1888, Fahy gives his side of this first meeting, which took place on the 23rd of that month: "I saw Sparling at the British Museum on Thursday where he introduced me to Yeats. Both looked different to what my fancy painted them. I had my notes re 'Irish Minstrelsy' ready for Sparling, and we had a chat — not long — over them" (UCD D.J. O'Donoghue archives, LA15/1665).

Some of Fahy's songs and poems bear out his social concern. For instance, in "A Laughing Matter", published in *United Ireland*, 26 August 1882, he intones:

> "Society," whose revel song
> Drowned aye the poor man's curse and groan,
> That ground the weak, caressed the strong,
> To-day lies shattered, overthrown.
> While those it once could ostracise —
> The "rabble low," the "mere riff-raff" —
> In triumph o'er its ruins rise,
> And build a nation new, and laugh.
> Ha, ha, ha, ha! Ho, ho, ho, ho!
> A goodly pile, broad-set below.
>
> Oh, laugh, oppressed on every shore,
> When *Might* must strike its flag to *Right!*
> Laugh, nations call the world o'er,
> A sister leaps to life and light!
> Come ye who toil, and toiling weep,
> And read oppression's epitaph,
> By labour's hands cut broad and deep:
> "He laugheth best who last can laugh."
> Ha, ha, ha, ha! Ho, ho, ho, ho!
> A goodly pile, broad-set below.

Fahy's social conscience also shines through the guide to — but also for — the Irish in London, which he and D.J. O'Donoghue saw published in 1889; approximately one Londoner in forty-seven, he observes, was Irish-born, living "not in very affluent circumstances", "obliged to settle in the low rented neighbourhoods, where the scum and dregs of London generally live", and being "only thinly scattered through the higher class trades".[16] In *Ireland in London*, the message Fahy gives to his fellow Irish emigrants is one of social hope, based on national idealism:

> Irishmen need have no fear of being over-ambitious. They will doubtless continue to win their way to the chief positions in the empire they have helped so materially to build up. Strictly speaking, Englishmen are only its nominal rulers ....

---

16. F.A. Fahy and D.J. O'Donoghue, *Ireland in London*, Dublin, 1889, 8, 11, 9-10 (see also Waters, 9).

In 1886 Fahy gained the support of W.P. Ryan, an able administrator, and as ardent a nationalist as Fahy.[17] Some of the ambitious ideals of the Club are represented in Ryan's novel, *The Heart of Tipperary* (1893). Set in the 1880s, it depicts the attempts by supporters of the literary revival, and by leaders of the Land League, to free the Irish lower classes from the shackles of violently repressive forces such as the secret societies.

At this stage, the club had gained rapid support from Home Rule politicians like Justin McCarthy and Richard Barry O'Brien, who lectured in November 1883 on "Political Evolution in Ireland", and from littérateurs like D.J. O'Donoghue, who devoted his maiden speech on 30 October 1886 to convicting English critics of the densest ignorance, unfairness and prejudice with regard to Irish writers. Its number of active members had more than doubled, from thirty to eighty, and included Irish Irelander D.P. Moran, who would later describe Yeats's involvement in the Renaissance as "one of the most glaring frauds that the credulous Irish people have ever swallowed".[18] Its President was none other than the formidable T.D. Sullivan, Lord Mayor and M.P, editor of *The Nation*, leader of the Plan of Campaign, and, as "T.D.S.", author of propaganda verse, "one of the greatest poets who ever moved the heart of man", of whom T.F.R. wrote that "no latter-day Irish poet

---

17. Ryan, the child of evicted Tipperary peasants, settled in London in November 1886 as a clerk in the Pearl Assurance Company. Waters, in his excellent Ph.D. thesis describes him as follows: "Ryan belonged to a class of young Irishmen which had been created by the national schools. Literate, intelligent, and nationalist, but poor and unsophisticated, they followed the models laid down by the articulate nationalists of the late 1840s" (Waters, 42). At thirty Ryan had worked himself up to the position of literary editor for *The Sunday Special*. In 1905 he took up the editorship of *The Irish Peasant*, and became notorious for his criticism of the atavism of the Catholic Church. After the suppression of the paper by Cardinal Logue, he briefly edited *The Peasant* before returning to London, where he became a frequent contributor to socialist newspapers.

18. *The New Ireland Review*, X (September 1898-February 1899), 352: "A certain number of Irish literary men have 'made a market' — just as stock-jobbers do in another commodity — in a certain vague thing, which is indistinctly known as 'the Celtic note' in English literature, and they earn their fame and livelihood by supplying the demand which they have honourably and with much advertising created .... an intelligent people are asked to believe that the manufacture of the ... 'Celtic note' is a grand symbol of an Irish national intellectual awakening. This, it appears to me, is one of the most glaring frauds that the credulous Irish people ever swallowed ..." (quoted in *The Shaping of Modern Ireland*, ed. C.C. O'Brien, London, 1960, 111).

has been so popular with the large mass of the people".[19] His deliberative ballads are a more direct call to action than the work of such precursors in the genre as Thomas Davis and Lady Wilde. His "God Save Ireland" (1867), a poem in commemoration of the Manchester Martyrs, which has erroneously been attributed to his brother, A.M., was set to the tune of the American Civil War Song "Tramp, tramp, tramp, the boys are marching", and became a kind of nationalist Irish anthem — which up to recently was still taught in Irish primary schools and is still intuned at many a market fare or small-town festival:

> High upon the gallow-tree
> Swung the noble-hearted Three,
> By the vengeful tyrant stricken in their bloom;
> But they met him face to face,
> With the courage of their race,
> And they went their souls undaunted to their doom.
> "God save Ireland!" said the heroes;
> "God save Ireland!" said they all:
> "Whether on the scaffold high
> Or the battle-field we die,
> Oh, what matter, when for Erin dear we fall!"

Yeats's Renaissance: 1891-1900

Yeats's disparaging comments about the Southwark Club are understandable considering the extra-literary dimensions of the literary society. It seems that for Yeats the club espoused all the values that, under O'Leary's guidance, he had learned to renounce. As journalists, men like Fahy, Moran and Ryan did not shun rhetoric to spread the word and to establish a popularist movement with an appeal similar to that held by the Young Irelanders.

Yeats's disparagement might further be attributed to personal motives. We know that Yeats was the odd-man-out in the Southwark Club; Ryan describes him as "a little weird" and "eerie", speaking "as one who took his information firsthand" from the fairies, and Ryan records, not without glee, how the *bon-vivant* Fleet Street journalist John Augustus O'Shea teased Yeats by pointing out, after the latter's lecture on Sligo folklore, on 13 June 1888, that "there were more fairies on a square foot of Knockshegowa than in all the county Sligo".[20]

---

19. *Irish Monthly*, XLIV (1914), 390.

20. Ryan, 30.

When in 1891 Yeats, with the help of T.W. Rolleston, set out to transform the Club into the Irish Literary Society, he received assistance from men like Fahy and Ryan because he worked under the guise of being counted one with Davis, Mangan, Ferguson, and with the view that "the work might be attempted upon a more ambitious scale". At the age of 21 he had expressed a wish for revival literature to reach "the great concourse of the people".[21] But once the Irish Literary Society and its Dublin counterpart were established, he began to challenge their social and political aspirations in his contributions to the society's meetings. He points out that rather than aiming to reach the masses, he was "anxious to ... make the upper classes read".[22] He lays "to the door of rhetoric that fault of the Irish character, which made it possible for a certain type of Irishman to be perfectly sincere on the other side tomorrow".[23] He argues against the Gaelicization of Ireland.[24] He prefers mythical histories to the chronologies of Ireland's colonized plight, which were deemed essential reading by most original revivalists.[25] And, after a

---

21. Review of Katharine Tynan's *Shamrocks* in *The Gael*, 11 June 1887.

22. *Irish Literary Society Gazette*, I/4 (June 1899), 5.

23. *Irish Literary Society Gazette*, I/6 (January 1900), 5.

24. The opposition which Yeats received on this account can be illustrated by a letter by William Boyle to D.J. O'Donoghue, dated 4 June 1896: "We had the last lecture of the season in connexion with the I.L.S. last night with E. Gosse in the chair. In a sly way he threw a good deal of cold water on the Irish revival. 'If you write English what is the use of trying to be other than English' was the burden of his somewhat sneering observations. Yates attempted a reply, but it was rather weak and ineffective. Ashe King, Greene, Graves & B. O'Brien also spoke but let the thing go by without reply ..." (UCD D.J. O'Donoghue Archives, LA15/73).

25. W.P. R[yan], *The New Ireland Review*, IV (December 1895), 224-26: "Mr. Yeats does not believe that Irish history has ever yet been satisfactorily written (though, by the way, in a recent English article he included Dr. Joyce's history in an unconvincing list of the best Irish books [in the *Bookman*, October 1895]). He speaks of Nationalist history as a mystery play of angel and devil; but he never mentions the books or authors that suggest the conclusion, and in truth he leaves strong doubt in the hearer's mind that he has fully read the Irish historians, or that he has given thought and attentions to the materials of Irish history which are essential to the realisation of the variety, vividness, and far-reaching interests of its drama .... Mr. Yeats' theory that Irish history was never understood till the nineties is gentle comedy, all the more so in view of the recent work of Dr. Todhunter and Mr. Standish O'Grady. Mr. Yeats told the Irish Literary Society that his preference for Mr. O'Grady's history arises from the fact that the historian in [*sic*] so 'strange'. We thank him for the word. In his philosophy, beauty and strangeness are everything, truth a mere consideration. We now know how the land lies, and there shall

lecture by Fahy on Jacobite songs, he clings to his conviction that Davis's "Battle of Fontenoy" was "a clever imitation of Macaulay, and was very useful in its way; but after all it was mere journalistic and rhetorical poetry" — remarks which were received with "laughter and cries of 'No'". (Davis's poetic account of the Irish Brigade's heroics in the field of Fontenoy had reached the status of an Irish battle song).[26] The Yeats of "He Reproves the Curlew" dissociated himself from the Yeats of "How Ferencz Renyi Kept Silent".

The Irish Literary Society had not made that step towards 'pure' aesthetics. Yeats's poetic genius was recognized, but his ideology was taken less seriously by the members of the Literary Society. He never gained the large popular following in the Irish Literary Society that, for instance, Francis Fahy commanded; year after year the latter was elected on to its Committee with most votes — even when Yeats's sisters and father were among the voters. Yeats's speeches induced the bemused tolerance to which Katharine Tynan had treated him in the latter part of the 1880s. On April 23 1899 he unfolded his plans for a National Irish Theatre in what he must have considered a stirring address to the Society. The reactions were less enthusiastic than Yeats might have expected. Clement Shorter pointed out in the ensuing discussion that "mere attempts to appeal to a limited audience was the way in which Mr.

---

be no more misunderstanding .... The baffling fact is that Dr. Todhunter, Mr. Rolleston, and our new order of critic-historians have been as far from the whole truth as the most perverted of nationalists engaged in weaving that 'mythology of angel and devil,' which I am sorry to see, has given much pain to Mr. Yeats and the *Bookman.*"

26. *Irish Literary Society Gazette*, I/3 (March 1899), 7. The report of the proceedings continues to supply A.P. Graves's admonition of Yeats's point of view, and shows to what extent Yeats's ideas were at variance with the Society's view at large: "Mr. Yeats, interposing, said he had a great admiration for a certain amount of Davis's poetry, but not all.The Chairman said it was not the first time that Mr. Yeats had expressed these opinions at the lectures of the society. It was, no doubt, true that Davis hastily wrote many of his ballads for the Dublin journals. He had not had, perhaps, the leisure which Mr. Yeats enjoyed to polish his golden numbers. (Hear, hear.) But few could read these ballads without being deeply stirred — (hear, hear.) and he was perfectly certain that if 'The Battle of Fontenoy,' had been recited it would have evoked as much enthusiasm as any of the songs that were sung that night. (Applause.) Mr. Yeats was extremely eclectic in his views about Irish poetry; — (laughter) — and perhaps they ought to be thankful of having a man of so fine a discrimination and so delicate a taste as to be able to see, and the great courage to proclaim it to an Irish audience, that Davis's splendid ballad 'The Battle of Fontenoy,' was a piece of mere journalism. (Laughter and applause)."

Yeats could render the largest and most thorough service to the country he loved so well".[27] William Boyle, the playwright, represented popular opinion:

> The lecture by Yeats on Saturday on "The Ideal Theatre" wasn't up to much. He rambled, stuck & began sentences he never finished. Norrys Connell made a few happy remarks and the Chairman, E. Gosse, was capital. "We did not so much hear a lecture" he said "as overhear a poet preparing a lecture." That sums it up neatly.[28]

Yet Yeats had succeeded in taking the sting out of the Society by including among its statutes that "no religious or political discussion is allowed at the meetings of the Society".

Polarization between the Yeatsian literary ideas and the political and social intentions of Ryan, Moran and Fahy was inevitable. When Gavan Duffy's New Irish Library Scheme got under way, Ryan set up the colportage, and despite the economic depression in England, was very successful, selling 3,000 copies of Davis's *The Patriot Parliament* within less than four weeks. Yet he had grown increasingly dissatisfied with the society. In December 1893, he wrote to D.J. O'Donoghue:

> I had a long letter from MacDonagh & was surprised to find how much his ideas resemble my own, on the subject of the late programme, the movement, & certain guiding spirits of the Society .... He says, & I think justly, that the Society is being run in the interest of a few people — & every meeting we have shows the ring that speaks & rules. He says that he intends to withdraw from the whole business quietly and gradually. I think that if a feeling like this is allowed to develop that the Society in the end will collapse ignominiously. Other members I know to be very dissatisfied too with the progress of the Society, and the course things are taking. As one who has been in the Society since the beginning I am firmly determined to make a stand against the red-tapists, the snobs, the rule of B.A.'s. M.A.'s, & B.L.'s, and against what Dr. Downey calls "Old fogeyism." I want to see fair play, fair scope, fair credit all round .... The work of the Society is being cramped and narrowed by men whose place is on a Burial Board, or a Parish Council. By all means let us have them, but let

---

27. *The Irish Literary Society Gazette*, I/4 (June 1899), 7.

28. UCD O'Donoghue Archives, LA15/92, LS W.Boyle to O'Donoghue, 25/4/98.

them not be absolute monarchs. Rolleston in his letter of resignation said that the I.L.S. cannot afford to stand still — it must go on till all the Irish literary forces in Britain are brought into an intellectual union. In the provinces the people are working towards that end. We are doing nothing to help them, we do not even recognise them.[29]

In 1894, although privately disillusioned with the Society, Ryan publicly still extolled its potential — seeing as its salvation the aims which the society had lately shed. He wrote in *The Irish Literary Revival*:

Perhaps with the expansion and success of this revival — always remembering the educational and social, as well as the purely literary aims of it — the destinies of things Irish are more closely identified than many political students imagine.[30]

Eventually, disgruntled with Duffy's dictatorial management of the New Irish Library, despondent about the élitism of the Irish Society, disappointed with its non-committal stance, Ryan, together with D.P. Moran, became one of the society's most forthright critics, specifically in Father Thomas Finlay's *New Ireland Review*, which in the 1890s never ceased to offer the Irish Irelanders' enlightened alternative to the Celtic Twilight.

During that second decade of Revivalism, Fahy remained a Committee member of the Society, organizing its "Original Nights", but in the main concentrating his contributions on the furtherance of MacNeill's and Hyde's Gaelic League, of which he became the London President under the auspices of the Society. Ryan joined ranks with him, and against the ideas of "the Superior Person", who contends that "we ought ... in Ireland, instead of confining ourselves within such a narrow range as Gaelic offers, to take our share in the culture of the world".[31] The League's deliberative intention to de-anglicize Ireland gave people like Ryan and Fahy the clear-cut, albeit idealistic, aim which was germane to their commitment.

As the League slowly but gradually increased its middle class membership, counting 600 branches by 1908, the Irish Literary Society withdrew further into its élitist shell. The contemporary press time and

---

29. UCD D.J. O'Donoghue Archives, LA15. The letter is dated 12/12/93.

30. Ryan, 3.

31. Thomas Crosbie, "From the Study Chair", *The New Ireland Review*, VI (September 1896-February 1897), 109.

again criticized its alienated position. Of Rolleston, one of its original
foremen, it was pointed out that "suavity and sympathy carried him a
long way", but that "a sensitive shrinking from anything extreme or
revolutionary, an inability now and then to note an honest heart under
anything rude and crude in form, a half belief in Carlylean dogmatism,
a dash of stoicism, all kept him too remote from the people, and out of
accord with them". O'Leary is seen as a harmless old fuddy-duddy:

> one could hardly grow angry with Mr. O'Leary, or cease to
> regard him with indulgent respect and forgiving interest. For the
> sake of the past, one learned to pardon much, and in the course of
> time we came to look on his perennial opposition to everything,
> his hypercritical condemnation of the muddle of the Hibernian
> world, as a feature and a voice that somehow we should be lonely
> without.[32]

Todhunter and O'Grady are considered to be strangers of their time and
to "Irish ideals.[33] The nature of the coterie is summed up by an early
portrait of Yeats in the *Evening Telegraph* of 14 January 1888:

> Augustus Fitzgibbon, considered by himself and his friends to be
> a poet of Titanic power, who may accomplish great things, and
> who may not, but whose boyish head is in the meantime being
> turned in the most delightful and deplorable fashion by the circle
> which is fortunate enough to revolve round this elsewhere
> unappreciated star. His friends will gravely tell you that Ireland
> has not produced such a poet hitherto; that some of his
> unpublished songs are equal to Shakespeare, that in music he ranks
> with Shelley, in colouring with Keats; and that Coleridge himself
> was not more saturated with deep and transcendental philosophy.
> They will tell you that he is too exquisite and ethereal to be
> understood or appreciated by the common British reviewer, and
> hence his obscurity. All this, of course, Fitzgibbon fondly
> believes, and invites you to believe by the ingratiating sweetness
> with which he takes his spoiling. In his circle all are equally
> sincere in giving and returning flattery.

Yeats had turned the tide of organized Irish cultural life from well-
meaning and committed dilettantism to a specialized interest in literature,

---

32. "O.Z." [W.P. Ryan], *New Ireland Review*, I (March-August 1894), 254.

33. "O.Z.", "From a Modern Irish Portrait Gallery, VII. — Dr. John
Todhunter", *New Ireland Review*, III (March-August 1895), 228.

a Cheshire Cheese Revisited. However aesthetically right his orchestrations may have been, they tore the heart — made up of popular support — out of the movement. This is exemplified by a telling eye-witness account of the Inaugural Meeting of Yeats's most personal public venture, the National Irish Literary Society, by Richard J. O'Mulrenin, agricultural editor of the *Weekly Freeman*. The account is endemic of the contemporary popular view:

> As for the Irish Literary Society I joined it and was appointed a member of the Council with the intention of doing my part to assist any national movement. I have subscribed to everything of the kind for many years past. But I soon discovered that here in Dublin the society was run by a small exclusive clique whose only object was to make use of it for their own notoriety. The [*sic*] sheltered themselves under one or two distinguished names, viz. Dr Sigerson and Dr Douglas Hyde and made use of these two gentlemen to serve their own purpose. This clique exists of Messrs George Coffee [*sic*], Dr. Coffee [*sic*], W.B. Yeats, and three or four very young and inexperienced men but who have a great deal of vanity and little or no real Irish national feeling. In fact the feeling of nationality is conspicuously absent .... I was a member of the Pan-Celtic Society which was really a good little society .... They did not go on their knees to get outsiders [who] had made a name for themselves among English readers, but sturdily depended on themselves. Dr. Downy who was the life and soul of the society was thoroughly national of the Thomas Davis type .... There is nothing Irish or national about W.B. Yeats. He is permeated with Swinburnism, Tennysonianism, Browningism and so forth mixed up with the fanaticism of William Blake but he has nothing Irish in his composition and is personally a thorough crank. The others are nonentities and the whole is a sham as far as nationality is concerned. You can show this letter to whomsoever you like for I make no secret of my opinions .... The air of "respectable" Dublin seems to be poisonous to anything really national at present.[34]

---

34. UCD D.J. O'Donoghue Archives, LA15/1311, Richard J O'Mulrenin to O'Donoghue, March 3rd 1893. The letter is an important document, piercing various shibboleths of the Irish Renaissance, *vide*: "But as far as that goes I do not believe that Sir. C.G. Duffy has much national feeling. Dr. Sigerson is a man of genius and national but he is a crank and full of fads, the most conspicuous of which is his obtrusive admiration and praise, of those barbarians the Norse pirates and his belief of his descent from them. He drags this into every discussion .... Hyde is thoroughly national, modest, and has more common sense than most of them but he is rather weak and through politeness does not exercize [*sic*] his power as president. The

A Society of paradoxes

Although Yeats's Irish Literary Societies were heavily criticized by popularists, it would be wrong to dismiss them as altogether unsuccessful. Under the old Young Irelander, Sir Charles Gavan Duffy,

---

committee meetings are consumed in interminable talk about details without anything being finally settled .... The clique are mostly very great toadies to any one who has made any sort of a name. Thus instead of asking a member of their society to deliver a lecture they went out of their way to ask Standish O'Grady, a writer on the *Daily Express* and who had produced a rhapsodical book called the *Bardic History of Ireland*. It was not a history but a mere collection of imaginary events evolved from the author's inner consciousness to suit certain theories of his about myth. It was nicely written and evinced a firm imagination but as a contribution to Irish history it was a *reductio ad absurdum* of anything of the kind. It however made a name for the author among those who knew nothing of Irish history and did not want to know. On this account he was asked to give a lecture. The man is busy and did not want to do so but did not think it politic to refuse. Moreover he is a pronounced Tory, anti-Catholic, anti-Irish, anti-national, and in the employ of the Government having been appointed to something by Mr Balfour. The lecture consisted of scrappy notes about the Battle of the Curlew mountains connected by bits of conversational remarks not very well delivered. He apologised for this with the plea of hurry but in a manner rather contemptuous of his audience. Then by prearrangement John O'Leary got up to propose a vote of thanks and began a halting and exceedingly badly delivered speech by confessing that he had not the remotest knowledge of the subject matter of the lecture. O'Leary is I think, as far as delivery goes and also as far as matter, the worst speaker I ever heard, yet he's always put up on such occasions. I have seen him pause for five minutes to collect his few ideas keeping the audiences waiting the whole time .... He seems to know nothing whatever of Irish history. His sense of the fitness of things maybe gauged by the advice he gave some years ago to the citizens of Dublin viz. to read the works of Spinoza and Kant! You can judge from this what a crank he must be. But he has a name and so is made use of. Richard Ashe King rose by appointment to second the vote of thanks. But if O'Leary was bad he was worse for he began by confessing that not only did he know nothing about the battle of the Curlew Mountains but that he had not even endeavoured to obtain any information about it. This must have been very gratifying to the audience. But he proceeded further to flatter them by the statement that as he was ignorant on the subject everybody else then must also be so .... Then another appointed speaker rose, Mr Kelly, the proprietor of the *Tuam Herald* and he added to the mass of ignorance by similar declarations. Moreover he said that he did not think that the Curlew Mountains were so called from a bird but he confessed his ignorance .... Dr Hyde who was in the chair and who delivered a short and sensible speech [explained]. Such a disgusting exhibition of an Irish literary Society I never saw. Of course when the appointed speakers have wasted a lot of time in tiresome and irrelevant talk the audience become impatient and begin to leave and there is neither time nor opportunity for anyone else to speak. Such has been the course at every lecture of the Irish Literary Society that I have attended ...."

the London Irish Literary Society did make concerted efforts to appeal to the great concourse of the Irish. For Duffy, the aims of the society were to instil a pride in identifying with the ethnocentric as expounded in books. This nationalism was not without its practical aims; Gavan Duffy observes in two famous addresses to the Society,

> I have sometimes marvelled that no one has made it his special task to teach the "tenants at will," who have become proprietors under the Land Purchase Act, what wonders they may accomplish for themselves and the country.
>
> ... the discipline of education is not for ornament merely, but for practical use. Without it men and nations miss open roads to national prosperity ....[35]

Where in rural Ireland the Revival served the social purpose of retaining the infrastructure through instilling awareness of its cultural identity, in England and the industrialized parts of Ireland, it served as anodyne for the destitute masses. Ryan gives us an account of the practical work undertaken:

> Curious stories might be told of the movement for popularising these books amongst the masses, for carrying them and others to ground where Irish books had never been before. The mission was in reality the most important as well as the most difficult of all. In the face of poverty at home, and in Britain one of the most serious industrial crises of the century, the work of winning readers in the Irish Highlands, by the furnaces of the Black Country, the slums of Lancashire cities, or the mining stations of Northumbria, was sometimes a heart-wearing task ....[36]

The breadth of these concerted efforts is exemplified by the number of Irish literary societies that sprung up in English working class districts in the 1880s, and proliferated in the early 1890s. There was the Liverpool Irish Literary Society, established in 1884, by John Denvir, the first Secretary of the Home Rule Confederation of Great Britain. There was the East End Literary Society of Newcastle, under the National Leaguer, W.J. Ryan; the Dundee Catholic Literary Society, the

---

35. "Books for the Irish People", and "What Irishmen May Do for Irish Literature", in *The Revival of Irish Literature and Other Addresses*, London, 1894, 47 and 18.

36. Ryan, 71.

Manchester Irish Literary Society, with the ardent socialist, James Sexton, the Glasgow and West of Scotland Catholic Literary Association, the Sunderland Literary Society, the Irish Society of East Anglia, which had as its aims, "keeping fresh in the hearts of Irishmen ... the memory of the old country, and the relief as far as possible of the poorer classes of their fellow-countrymen", the Southampton Irish Literary and Social Club, the North London Irish Literary Society, the Birmingham Irish National Club and Literary Institute, founded by J.F. Cassidy, member of the Birmingham Branch of the Irish National League, the Edinburgh Literary Society, and the Coatbridge Irish Literary Society. In addition, Irish journalists and writers had grouped themselves in several charitable organizations, such as the Guild of Irish Journalists (est. 1895), which had as one of its aims the education of "young orphans of deceased writers", and counted among its members M.E. Francis, Katharine Tynan, T.D. Sullivan, W.P. Ryan and J.M. Tuohy.

Yet despite these concerted efforts to channel Irish literary activity through social work, the Revival could only be salvaged by élitism and purely literary activity, by the class of Revivalists that Kiberd singled out in "The Perils of Nostalgia". Thus in 1908 Katharine Tynan observed:

> There has been a literary revival ... of late years, much greater and more general than people imagined who talked of the little and poetical Irish revival, which meant mainly the poetry of W.B. Yeats and George Russell, and the scholarly genius of Douglas Hyde. But, alas! it is a one-sided revival, for although the writers have come there are no readers — among Irish people or elsewhere.[37]

This change of its fortune has been attributed to the fall of Parnell and the subsequent death of the Home Rule Movement. But what has not been acknowledged is that at the core of the Revival lay an irresoluble paradox that distinguished it from any other Renaissance — namely its self-consciousness. Terms like "Revival" and "Renaissance" are normally applied after the Rebirth, but with this Irish Revival, the child was born before it was conceived. A rondel of dubious literary merit, by T.P Stuart, which appeared in the *New Ireland Review* in 1894 sums up the spirit:

> The Newer Ireland looms along the marge
> And all the ways of song are glorified

---

37. "The Neglect of Irish Writers", *Catholic World*, April 1908, 92.

....
Erin renascent be our sacred charge;
Our aims the highest, our ambitions wide
For not in vain, has our dear country cried.
Since man, and maid, take up the spear and targe.[38]

That some critics have attributed this feeling of an impending Irish transfiguration to post-millenialism is not surprising, considering that this Newer Ireland remained on the brink of being born. For years, "Erin renascent be our sacred charge" lay at the basis of the Literary Societies, and for years it manifested itself in the intentions of individual writers. Between 1887 and 1899 it made its presence felt in Yeats's prose; for a considerably longer period it infused the work of AE, and it culminated in their combined effort to prepare Ireland through Orphic rituals for an impending rebirth.

But the idea also shone through the more practically deliberative lectures delivered to Irish Literary Societies by formidable figures like Gavan Duffy, Hyde, Sigerson, Todhunter and by many of — what now are considered to be — minor figures. For this generation, the appellation "Revivalist", then, is paradoxical, because their desire to effect a Revival is based on their observation of the want of one, not among the intellectuals that performed their literary or scholarly part in the societies but among the general population whom they were trying to target. As late as 1899, a correspondent to the *New Ireland Review* sums this up facetiously with reference to Art:

> Irish Art has entered on a new phase. *As yet no examples of the newer school have appeared* .... What is Irish is distinguished by its idealisation of the commonplace, its appeal to and stimulation of the higher imagination .... This new art-product, whose sacred cult they pursue in Grafton Street, Dublin, is none other than blackthorn bludgeon! ... We wonder how long it will take for a growth of public feeling which will make these things impossible. Or is there ever to be a public feeling amongst us which will discourage caricatures of ourselves by ourselves?[39]

Speaking to Irish Societies, lecturers constantly note the unwanted internationalization of the Celt, with the preponderance of foreign rags

---

38. *The New Ireland Review*, I (March-August 1894), 221.

39. *The New Ireland Review*, VII (March-August 1897), 242 (my italics).

in Irish households. Hyde, who calls the Irish of his time "the Japanese of Western Europe", notes:

> What have we now left ...? Scarcely a trace. Many ... read newspapers indeed, but who reads, much less recites, an epic poem, or chants an elegiac or even a hymn? ... We must set our face sternly against penny dreadfuls, shilling shockers, and still more, the garbage of vulgar English weeklies like *Bow Bells* and the *Police Intelligence*.[40]

In a similar vein, Gavan Duffy quotes a Father Hogan,

> "None like the working clergy ... can realise the baneful effects that are produced by pernicious books, and how fatal to the innocence of youth, and to the strength of national as well as of personal character, they so often prove." And Sigerson, capping the paradox, points out that "... our people, generally, drink no more at the high-head fountains of their island-thought. This is one of the greatest losses which can befall a nation, for it loses thus its *birthright* ...."[41]

That the Revival was considered to *have* a birthright was based on inherently conservative characteristics of the Celt, constantly harped on in reviews, like that of Nora Hopper: "It is Celtic to the core, as simple as it is sweet, possesses no trace of anything 'modern' or decadent."[42] Its ingredients were Celtic love of learning, contact with the soil, loyal comradeship, chivalric courtesy, great-minded heroism — in short, all those traits, as has been noted by Wilson Foster, Roy Foster and others, which set the Irish apart from the English, and which contrasted most distinctively with all that was West-Briton — a Celtic spirit which was essentially rural and conservative, exuding ceremony and innocence, an excellent prototype for an island of "athletic youths and happy maidens", "not needing or desiring great wealth, but enjoying free simple lives, ennobled by the perfect liberty which the poet declares is a child of the mountains".[43] In essence, then, the Revival was dependent on

---

40. "The Necessity for De-Anglicising Ireland", in *The Revival of Irish Literature and Other Addresses*, 159; original address delivered before the Irish National Literary Society in Dublin, 25 November 1892.

41. "Books for the Irish People", 50-51.

42. "With the Irish in Great Britain", *New Ireland Review*, III (1895), 59.

43. "What Irishmen May Do for Irish Literature", 19.

maintaining the social status quo; the ever-observant D.P. Moran pointed this out in "Is the Irish Nation Dying?":

> Improve the conditions of the peasant and you wipe out the traditions and the language; advance the more intelligent of the working men, as a consequence of material prosperity, into a higher class, and you weaken the prop even of "nationality", and add to the already large contingent of the vulgar-genteel.[44]

The social aims of the Revival, as propounded by Gavan Duffy, were exposed for what they were worth when the Societies actually did try to reach the common public. Ryan discovered that the people

> had not the heart for industrial or statesmanlike problems. Something which brought back a little of the joys of old times, the dew of Irish hills, the light of Irish hearths, the bonfire's night, the merry Christmas, some wand which waving showed them Rory's raids, or "Sarsfield's Ride," which opened the gates of the faery world, or whose touch brought the ghosts of the night-lands: these appealed to them, as did anything fresh and glowing with the new life and the new hopes of the old land, whose songs, dreams and traditions had followed them like guardian angels round the world.[45]

Bearing in mind the significance of the Irish Literary Societies in shaping the Renaissance, we can hardly be surprised that what emerged as dominant themes in Revival literature were suitably escapist and suitably removed from realism. In a sense, the second phase of the Revival, with its élitism and escapism, is not just the ingenuous product of Yeats & Co, but rather a direct consequence of the movement's limited appeal. The market for books in Ireland was extremely limited. Robert Blake noted in 1897:

> Publishing in Ireland ought to be a vast industry, administering enormous revenues, giving employment to large number of printers and workmen of all kinds, and bringing floods of money into the country. It is, unfortunately, nothing of the kind; Ireland is an importer, rather than an exporter of books. Scotland has her Blackwood and Blackie; Ireland has only her booksellers .... The fact that publishing cannot be said to exist, as a business, in Ireland, and that in consequence literature distinctively Irish has

---

44. *The New Ireland Review*, X (September 1898-February 1899), 214.

45. Ryan, 71-72.

ceased to be produced, not only implies the financial loss of all
that might be gained in the successful pursuit of publishing, but the
loss of all the influence Ireland might wield if she were properly
represented in the world of letters.[46]

This view is supported by several publishers, booksellers and writers.
Edmund Downey, the Revivalist's erstwhile publisher, wrote in 1896:

> I am now convinced all the talk ... about the "Irish Literary
> Revival" simply prevented any such literary revival. People got
> disgusted with the lies written & spoken. It was much easier to sell
> Irish books before any of the books began to be talked, &
> everything pointed to a real revival in the literature concerning
> Ireland — but the Book-Mongers spoiled it all. Christ save us from
> any more of them! The Scotch don't talk of literary revivals. Bad
> as their present literature is, at any rate they support it literally
> without screaming over it & lying about it.[47]

The renaissance reviewed

It would be wrong to conclude that the revivalists wholly escaped into a
world of romance. Take Katharine Tynan, whom George Russell called
the earliest singer in that literary awakening, and who is basically
remembered for such innocuous, homely verse as "Sheep and Lambs".
Tynan actually devoted numerous articles to the social ills in Ireland. A
member of the Ladies Land League, she gave eye-witness accounts of
evictions in Tipperary. Nor was she blind to the destitution in Dublin; in
1891, in "Christmas in the Coombe Hospital", she describes the extreme
deterioration of the former Dublin centre of linen trade into slums,
characterized by tenement houses where illness was rampant.

Tynan is just a case in point; in an essay on "Irish Novels" one critic
has noted that "there is not an Irish novelist ... whose work can be
judged by an exclusively literary or artistic standard" in that it was
inextricably linked with social and political movements. A plethora of
women writers like Jane Barlow, Katherine Purdon, Julia Crottie,
Charlotte O'Connor Eccles, M.A. Rathkyle, M. Hamilton, and M.E.
Francis gave vivid pictures of nineteenth-century Irish society, and, as
we have seen, several leading politicians such as T.D. Sullivan and

---

46. "From the Study Chair", *New Ireland Review*, VIII (September 1897-
February 1898), 112.

47. E. Downey to D.J. O'Donoghue, 14 Oct. 1896, UCD Archives LA15/488.

William O'Brien expressed their literary views of the stratification of the New Ireland.[48]

That these have become the forgotten writers of the Irish Revival is partly due to the tyranny of the canon — the literary merit of their work was rightly eclipsed by that of the great Renaissance authors. It led, at hindsight, to a misrepresentation of the Revival, which first comes across in Boyd's seminal study of the Renaissance (1916), which has been instrumental to all later studies.

Everything fits snugly in Boyd's history. He notes that Mangan and Ferguson

> lifted national poetry out of the noisy clamour of politics, and thereby effected that dissociation of ideas which was most essential to the existence of national literature, and which remains the best work of the modern Irish poets. The substitution of a sense of nationality for aggressive nationalism is the factor in the poetry of Mangan and Ferguson which distinguishes them from all their predecessors ....

On the next page we read, "The publication in 1878 of O'Grady's *History of Ireland: Heroic Period* marked the advent of a new spirit". Further on Boyd remarks:

> With his proud affirmations of belief in the ancient deities, and his wonderful evocation of the past, Standish O'Grady revealed to his countrymen the splendour of their own idealism, and restored to them their truly national tradition. All eyes were now turned towards the shining land of heroic story and legend, the footsteps of all were directed upon the path which led back to the sources of Irish nationality.[49]

The work of the translators and folklorists who collected, transcribed and translated these folk tales and songs, in which the old Celtic traditions still lived, was an important element in the forces that went to the formation of modern Anglo-Irish literature. Allingham had "worked apart from the popular literary movements of [his] day ... avoiding ... political

---

48. See Janet Madden, *This Dark Country: Irish Novels by Irish Women. 1875-1925. An Aspect of Irish Literature*, Ph.D thesis, UCD, June 1983.

49. Ernest A. Boyd, *Ireland's Literary Renaissance*, Dublin and London, 1916, 26-27, and 52-53.

nationalism".[50] "The National Literary Society in Dublin and the Irish Literary Society in London had come into being, and it was as President of the former that Sigerson was able to dedicate [his *Bards of the Getral and Gall* to Gavan Duffy, the President of the sister Society [in London], and to Douglas Hyde, the President of the Gaelic League".[51] And hey presto, we have a Revival, carefully avoiding nationalism and exuding an air of nationality — meaning what Yeats wanted it to mean.

I will not dwell on the obvious chronological pitfalls of Boyd's history. Nor will I expose his essentially post-romantic view of literature, essentially removed from anything that reeks of politics — a view as Platonic as it dismisses Plato's *paideia*. Instead, I should like to conclude with a contemporary reaction to Boyd and to Boyd's Renaissance champions. Katharine Tynan reviewed Boyd for *Studies* in 1917. After noting that Boyd disregards Herbert Trench and Somerville and Ross, she goes on to say:

> Unfortunately, the big book gives one a sense of partiality, as though the writer had been shown a corner of his subject and told to write from that. For instance, it used to be said by a little group of writers in the 'nineties, and an important group, that Standish O'Grady was their beginning. [Yeats made the remark, "whatever the future may bring forth will find its morning in these volumes"]. I doubt that many Irish writers could subscribe to that now .... The saying was a shibboleth — we were full of shibboleths in those days, and ever ready to acquire a new one; and we were quite conscious that they were shibboleths although we subscribed to them so cheerfully .... The movement became a Movement because the Irish were writing plays and poetry while England was losing her soul in money-getting.

Katharine Tynan concludes:

> The defect in Mr. Boyd's book is that he does not look beyond the Dublin group. He is, in fact, overweighted. And his Irish Protestantism gets in his way.... The critic, almost equally with the historian, needs the calm, unbiased mind, which Mr. Boyd does not possess.[52]

---

50. *Ibid.*, 81.

51. *Ibid.*, 57.

52. *Studies*, VI/21 (March 1917), 164-65.

Thankfully, no critic or historian of the Irish Renaissance has yet fully met those requirements.

IRISH PATRIOT ALIENS:
THE IRISH CAUSE AND THE EARLY RECEPTION
OF YEATS'S WORK IN THE NETHERLANDS

ROSELINDE SUPHEERT

In the 1880s and 1890s, when W.B. Yeats began publishing his work, and later, at the beginning of the twentieth century, the Netherlands could boast a considerable number of literary journals and influential writers and critics, but no journal or critic paid attention to the publications of the young Irish poet. This is not to say that Dutch critics were not interested in literature in English. Journals like *De Gids*, *De Nieuwe Gids*, *Den Gulden Winckel*, *Tweemaandelijksch Tijdschrift*, *Onze Eeuw*, and *De Beweging* regularly carried articles — or even series of articles — about English writers, but they tended to look back rather than forward. Shelley, Keats, Tennyson and Swinburne, for instance, were familiar names. When Yeats eventually became known, it was within the context of the Celtic Revival. This turned out to be both an advantage and a disadvantage for the dissemination of his work in the Netherlands. Yeats was first spotted, and warmly received, by Dutch supporters of Irish Home Rule, and this Irish context continued to dominate his image for decades. Long after Yeats had embraced modernism, Dutch critics were still discussing *The Countess Kathleen* and *The Wanderings of Oisin*, disregarding *The Wild Swans at Coole* or *The Tower*.

Dutch articles and books about Ireland and the Irish question began to appear in the first decade of the twentieth century. Their number reached a climax in the late 1910s and early 1920s, when the Irish Free State came into being. Around the time of the formation of Sinn Féin in 1907-1908, the Dutch began to take a lively interest in matters Irish. The growing Gaelic League, founded in 1893, and Sinn Féin drew Dutch attention and sympathy. Several journalists and writers returned from Ireland with idealistic reports of a beautiful green country, with a dreamy and friendly population, desperately fighting for its identity against a much stronger foreign oppressor. According to Dutch commentators the Irish were spiritual or pious, friendly, honest, childlike, gregarious, people in touch with a long tradition and legendary past, dreamers and born poets, steeped in the supernatural. But they were also lazy, unorganized, hot-headed, dirty and neglectful of material progress. They preferred a friendly chat to disciplined work. The Irish were contrasted with the British, who were thought to be serious and hard-working, but over materialistic and possessive. In the eyes of Dutch commentators the virtues of the Irish easily compensated for their vices, which was more than could be said of the British. Living in an island of great natural beauty, with a legendary past, the Irish had kept modern times at bay and retained a purity that had been lost to an industrialized Europe. English repression had damaged the once high and widespread Irish culture, but not irreparably so.

More than once Dutch writers pointed to parallels between the British oppression of the Irish and that of the originally Dutch Boers in South Africa. The Flemish movement was also a frequent point of reference. In the early twentieth century it vehemently defended the identity of Flanders against Walloon or French dominance. It is not surprising, then, that the Dutch found it easy to sympathize with the long-suffering, Irish people. For Catholics and socialists the Irish movement had an additional appeal: for the former Ireland was the centre and last bastion of pristine Catholicism, for the latter it encapsulated the unstoppable rise of poor Irish farmers against their English capitalist exploiters. Most tended to bypass the fact that many of the initiators of the Irish movement belonged to the Anglo-Irish, Protestant, Ascendancy. And Catholics in particular underplayed the heathen aspects of Celtic myths. The Dutch were not blind to the deplorable state of the Irish economy, but they held the view that it went hand in hand with Ireland's cultural dissolution caused by British rule. Culture and economy could be restored if the British oppression was removed. Only then would the former Celtic glory return. Opinions differed as to the measure of independence that was required to achieve this aim.

Single articles appeared in newspapers and magazines, but there were also series of articles and complete books. They covered a wide range of topics: Irish history from Celtic times onwards, old myths and modern Irish culture, the Irish language, politics, everyday life, the scenery and even the weather. The level of seriousness varied: from the comic stories by Cuey-na-Gael about the Irish national character (which were so popular that their author was invited to give readings), through socialist and Catholic propaganda to well thought-out literary essays. In 1911 a Ph.D.-dissertation was published about chronicles of Celtic and Anglo-Saxon history (*De Oudste Keltische en Angelsaksische Geschiedbronnen*; "The Oldest Celtic and Anglo-Saxon Sources of History") by the first

Dutch Celticist, A.G. van Hamel. Following the Gaelic League, Irish language and culture were diligently studied. Van Hamel published several articles about contemporary Ireland and the revival of Gaelic. T.W. Rolleston's *Myths and Legends of the Celtic Race* (1911) was translated into Dutch by B.C. Goudsmit and an anonymous collaborator and published in 1916 as *Keltische Mythen en Legenden.* Work by Douglas Hyde was mentioned and discussed in journals and magazines.

Often Dutch articles or books about Irish politics or culture contained a brief reference to the Celtic Revival and Yeats. They are the earliest Dutch references to Yeats and his work and constitute his introduction to a Dutch audience. Naturally the romantic, biassed conception of Ireland coloured the perception of its literature. Yeats is almost invariably seen as a true scion of the Celtic race and as an ardent patriot. He is dreamy, poetic, conscious of Irish traditions and close to the supernatural. Occasionally the most passionate supporters of the Irish cause blame him for his "Englishness": for writing too much for a cultural élite and not using the language of the people, figuratively but also literally by not writing in Gaelic. A few staunch Catholics reproach him for a lack of piety. Strange though this may seem, Yeats's political views or the poems dealing directly with political issues are hardly ever mentioned. Most writers were satisfied to view him as a Celtic Revivalist and did not look much further.

One of the earliest extensive discussions of Ireland to include Yeats is a series of articles, headed "Ierland's Renaissance" in the much-read column "Van Dag tot Dag" ("From Day to Day") in the daily newspaper *Algemeen Handelsblad.* The unsigned articles were published every day or every other day between 18 September and 26 October 1907. Altogether there were 21 of them, averaging 1500 words. They are a travelogue of the newspaper's editor, Charles de Boissevain, who was then on holiday in Ireland and described his impressions in letters to the paper. His letters are representative of a good number of other Dutch publications.

The first two letters offer a survey of the Irish question in which the author clearly sympathizes with the Irish. He hails the new nationalist élan. On 18 September he writes:

> In Ireland, in the country I love, surrounded by the people I think I understand and among whom I feel so much at home, it strikes me as very unexpected that a new hope, that a new life has arisen, so that one gets the prospect of a better future .... There, west of Wales lies an island which is far less familiar to most English than are France and Germany. If only the British got to know the

people who inhabit this fair island, then the Irish question would soon be solved. For those who find themselves among the Irish people, and thus do not exclusively obtain their information from the Anglo-Irish, soon feel sympathy for the national ideal.[1]

That initially De Boissevain does not think much of the Anglo-Irish or their culture becomes even clearer when he discusses the Gaelic League. De Boissevain began his holiday in Dublin, and in the third letter, published 21 September, he visits the office of the Gaelic League in 24 O'Connell Street, where he is charmed by two young supporters of the Irish cause:

> Oh, how full of soul were the beautiful grey eyes, darkly framed, of the couple of Irish girls who told me what the Gaelic League meant to them, how the League gave a purpose to their lives, how propaganda for the Irish ideal filled all their days with joy.
> This League strengthens characters and encourages altruism. It gives the Irish the true national atmosphere, in which heart and mind develop best and most beautifully, and it reconnects them with their poetic past.[2]

The well-connected journalist also interviews Douglas Hyde (4th letter, 24 September), whose disdain for the anglicization of Ireland he repeats with approval:

---

1. The original Dutch reads: "In Ierland, in het land dat ik lief heb, te midden van het volk dat ik meen te begrijpen en in welks midden ik mij zoo thuis voel, treft mij als iets zeer onverwachts, dat er een nieuwe hoop, dat er jong leven verrezen is, zoodat van een betere toekomst men het voorgevoel krijgt .... Daar ten westen van Wales ligt een eiland, dat den meesten Engelschen veel meer onbekend is dan Frankrijk en Duitschland dit zijn. Leerden de Britten het volk, dat dit schoone eiland bewoont kennen, dan zou de Iersche quaestie dra opgelost zijn. Want wie met het Iersche volk verkeert, en dus niet uitsluitend zijn kennis opdoet bij de Engelsche Ieren, gevoelt dra sympathie voor het nationale ideaal" (all translations from the Dutch are my own).

2. "O, hoe vol ziel waren de mooie grijze oogen, donker omlijst, van het tweetal Iersche meisjes, dat mij vertelde wat *the Gaelic League* voor haar was, hoe de Bond een doel aan haar leven gaf, hoe propaganda voor het Iersche ideaal met vreugde al haar dagen vulde.

Deze Bond sterkt karakters en maakt onzelfzuchtig. Hij geeft den Ieren de ware nationale atmosfeer, waarin gemoed en verstand zich het best en mooist ontwikkelen, en hij brengt hen weder in verband met hun dichterlijk verleden."

Mr. Douglas Hyde, the head of the Gaelic League, shrugs but smiles when he speaks of English writers who learned some of the language, copied a few things, and are now praised ... because they captured the Irish style, because they composed songs and ballads in the Irish style .... But time and again all attempts to render this poetry into English turn out to be wholly in vain ....[3]

De Boissevain then cites and makes disparaging remarks about English translations of old Gaelic poetry and concludes that only when Gaelic will have resumed its position as the national Irish tongue (and he does not doubt this is bound to happen), will great Irish poetry be written again. However, his subsequent stay on Ireland's west coast makes him change his mind. In his 10th and 11th letters (8 and 10 October respectively) De Boissevain has arrived in what is now the Yeats Country. He visits the town of Sligo, sees Knocknarae and Benbulben, Hazelwood and Loch Gill, reads Yeats and meets the local population (including Yeats's father). And he is impressed by the countryside, the people, and the poetry. He feels that he has now reached the heart of the country and punctuates his account with exclamations of "Dit is Ierland!" ("This is Ireland!"). The opening of the 10th letter resolutely sets the tone:

Oh, blessed by wind and rain and silver light is this west of Ireland, against the cliffs of which waves that are miles long come rushing from the Atlantic Ocean with the rolling sound of thunder to glide on here and there into calmer fjords, into long water lanes, deep into the country between glowing hills and the green of ferns and furze, gliding with water that is alive, of such a pure green colour.
   Soft, balmy is the air. The wind, the wondrous sea wind from the great ocean makes itself heard and felt day and night. It envelops us, it sings and sings, now jubilant, now howling.[4]

---

3. "De heer Douglas Hyde, het hoofd van *the Gaelic League*, spreekt schouderophalend, maar met een glimlach van Engelsche schrijvers, die iets van de taal leerden, iets van haar afkeken, en nu geprezen worden ... omdat ze den Ierschen stijl beet kregen, omdat ze liederen en balladen dichtten in den Ierschen stijl .... Maar elke poging om deze poezie in het Engelsch weer te geven blijkt telkens geheel te vergeefs ...."

4. "O, gezegend door wind en regen en zilverlicht is dit westen van Ierland, tegen welks rotskust de mijlenlange golven van den Atlantischen Oceaan met rollenden donderklank aanstromen, om hier en daar in gladder fjords, in lange waterlanen, diep het land in tusschen gloeiende heuvels en groen van farens en *furze*, voort te glijden, te glijden, met levend water zoo rein-groen van kleur.

This is a mysterious country, shrouded in mists or bathed in moonlight, where the present merges with the past, the Sidhe go riding at night, and where women's voices recite ancient poetry. De Boissevain hears and reports the stories of Deirdre and Oisin and reads *The Wind Among the Reeds* (first published in 1899). The way in which he introduces Yeats suggests that this is meant to be, and might well be, a first acquaintance of most of the Dutch reading public with a new Irish poet:

> *The Wind Among the Reeds* is the title of the volume by one of the young poets, by William Yeats, whose verses I heard recited here in Sligo by [a woman] who sees the ideal of a Reborn Ireland rise out of Ireland's past and tradition. His father, artist, painter, poet, simple like a child, naive like an artist, recounted and explained the verses of his son. And the lovely woman said them singing softly.
>
> I heard the wind, the wind from sea in the verses, which got us in an antique mood ....[5]

De Boissevain then goes on to quote in translation Yeats's explanatory notes, included at the end of the first edition of *The Wind Among the Reeds*, about the name and nature of the Sidhe and repeats some of the myths he heard in Sligo. Then, at dusk, so he tells us, with the ever-present wind in the background, he hears a woman's voice, pure and in strange rhythm, recite one of Yeats's songs, which he renders in full in the original. It is "The Hosting of the Sidhe", the poem with which *The Wind Among the Reeds* opens. (De Boissevain does identify Yeats as its author, but does not give the title of the poem in his letter.) He is overcome by the atmosphere the poem has evoked for him and feels enveloped by "flying darkness" ("vliegende duisternis"), "jubilant" ("jubelende") wind, "a pale moonrise above silent waters" ("bleeke maansopgang boven stille wateren") and "invisible powers of the Celtic

---

Zacht, roomzacht is de lucht. De wind, de wondere zeewind van den grooten oceaan, doet nacht en dag zich hooren en gevoelen. Hij omdringt ons, hij zingt en zingt, nu jubelend, dan klagend."

5. "'De wind tusschen de biezen' (*The Wind Among the Reeds*) heet de bundel van een der jonge dichters, van William Yeats, wiens verzen ik hier in Sligo hoorde zeggen door [een vrouw] die uit Ierland's verleden en traditie het ideaal van een Herboren Ierland rijzen ziet. Zijn vader, kunstenaar, schilder, dichter, eenvoudig als een kind, naief als een kunstenaar, vertelde en verklaarde de verzen van zijn zoon. En de liefelijke vrouw zegde ze zacht zingend.

Ik hoorde den wind, den wind van zee in de verzen, die ons in een antieke stemming brachten ...."

west" ("onzichtbare machten van het Keltische westen"). The lighting of a lamp ends his vision and the 10th letter.

In the 13th letter (12 October), while still on the west coast, De Boissevain returns to Yeats. What appeals to De Boissevain in this poet of the Celtic revival, as he calls him, is his love of nature and of the supernatural, of old folklore and Gaelic poetry. He uses the term "Celtic twilight" ("Keltische schemering"), the title of Yeats's 1893 collection of folk-tales, to designate this. There is high praise for Yeats's poetry and folk-tales:

> Without arguing he tells simply and sincerely, and sings of what he saw and heard among the people of the west coast, identifying with their way of thinking and seeing, and without clearly dissociating his beliefs from those of the population.[6]

De Boissevain is apparently unaware of the fact that Yeats could only understand the stories if they were in English, as Yeats himself had not mastered Gaelic. He quotes Yeats, saying that the supernatural can be a source of inspiration with a truth of its own, a swarm of wild bees, ready to produce their sweet honey. And he gives a prose translation of two more poems from *The Wind Among the Reeds*: "Hanrahan Reproves the Curlew" and "To my Heart, bidding it have no Fear". De Boissevain is not shy to change a few words or insert some lines of his own. He quotes these separate poems because for him they express a typically Celtic state of mind: deep despair at a lost past that is reinforced by desolate natural surroundings, while at the same time the past offers consolation and compels one to a kind of nobility. De Boissevain's insertions accentuate this interpretation: he adds lines such as "Oh, I remember the days gone by" ("O, ik herinner mij de dagen van voorheen") and "Not fear but hope!" ("Geen vrees maar hoop!").

In letter 16 (18 October), which signals his leaving the west coast, De Boissevain once more dwells on Yeats and the Celtic Revival. He again stresses the importance of the movement, and of its use of old legends. He warns against losing oneself in fantasies, longing for the unreachable and forgetting the present, but on the other hand he comments that the number of visionary dreamers is only small, so small there is no real danger. Rather than reprove, we ought to protect and honour them, for they are an imaginative elite, "benefactors without whom we would be

---

6. "Zonder te argumenteren vertelt hij eenvoudig en oprecht, en bezong hij wat hij zag en hoorde onder het volk van de westkust, zich vereenzelvigend met hun denken en zien en zijn geloof niet scherp afscheidende van dat der bevolking."

savages on a level with cattle, going about with the eyes turned to the ground" ("weldoeners zonder wie wij barbaren zouden zijn en het vee gelijk dat, met de oogen naar den grond gericht, omgaat").

De Boissevain's Yeats is the Celtic poet and story-teller. He is not the man of the theatre: the letters contain no references to any of Yeats's plays, nor to the Abbey Theatre, which had opened its doors in 1904. He is not the versatile thinker of the essays in *Ideas of Good and Evil* (1903). Nor is he a symbolist and worshipper of the occult: for instance the rose-poems, or stories such as "Rosa Alchemica", "The Tables of the Law", and "The Adoration of the Magi" do not receive any mention. Yeats is a poet in the Shelley sense of the word, a member of an élite of dreamers and visionaries, divorced from everyday Irish reality and living in a higher reality of the Celtic past that is still alive only on the west coast. And even this one side of Yeats is seen in a specific light, given a specific twist: that of the visiting foreigner, impressed with the natural beauty of the Irish scenery. Yeats's scenery in *The Wind Among the Reeds* is not quite the same as that of De Boissevain. It is not only, or even primarily, the pervasive, magnificent presence of nature De Boissevain experiences. In this volume there is surprisingly little pathetic fallacy. Yet de Boissevain quotes the poems that are tainted with it. There are several poems with no nature imagery at all, just as there are poems where the scenery is a series of Irish place names, which may be but are not necessarily inhabited by mythic figures. Yeats's use of specific names gives a grass-roots quality to even the most fantastic poems, which is unlike the abstracted sublimity of De Boissevain's Ireland. Despite his avowed interest in folklore and his praise of Yeats as the passer-on of simple folklore, it is not the simple, folkloristic Yeats he cites. The grand, the melancholy, the heart-sore and other-worldliness are highlighted; the ordinary and the happy are tuned down. De Boissevain's rendering is typical of Dutch taste at this time.

Another early discussion of Yeats can be found in an article by M.P. Rooseboom entitled "The Irish Movement" ("De Iersche Beweging") which was published in 1910 in *Onze Eeuw*, a monthly journal for literature and the arts, science and politics.[7] Rooseboom applauds the Celtic Revival, which he contrasts with the stale state of the arts in England, and places Yeats at the centre of the movement. Rooseboom had apparently met Yeats in person and his description of Yeats's appearance speaks volumes:

---

7. M.P. Rooseboom, "De Iersche Beweging", *Onze Eeuw*, X/1 (1910), 121-42.

Slender and delicate of frame, with a long oval typically Irish face, hollow-cheeked, with a pointed chin, and a shock of hair that shades his pale but still youthful features he is standing there in front of you. But what strikes one most are his eyes, two dark, deep-set eyes of curious shape, staring far away, sombre and dreamy, as if they were seeing the invisible things. It is as if his whole being is made up of those eyes; all other things disappear. It seemed to me that I could hardly look away from those wondrous eyes, that they magnetized me; compared to them all other things seemed so banal in that big crowded drawing room where I met him.[8]

Rooseboom most admirers Yeats's lyric poetry and he quotes some passages from the volume *The Countess Kathleen*. (This volume was published in 1892 and thus predated Rooseboom's article by 18 years.) Rooseboom is wary of Yeats's symbolism and fears Yeats might isolate himself from the Irish cause by writing overly obscure verse or drama. A similar note of warning is sounded by a semi-anonymous critic, "A.B.-d.V.". This critic wrote in the popular literary monthly *Den Gulden Winckel* of 12 December 1912,[9] that Yeats was so wrapped up in Celtic myth he had become blind to political reality:

Yeats distinguishes himself from these last-mentioned, his contemporaries [Lady Gregory and others], by his having no feeling at all for the political side of the Irish question. His mind is wholly taken up with Ireland's past and Ireland's future. The misery of present-day Ireland — more than 40,000 people every year leave the island as emigrants — the dominating influence of the clergy, the destruction of the soil and many other abuses that

---

8. "Slank en tenger van gestalte, met een lang ovaal typisch Iersch gezicht, ingevallen wangen, spitse kin, en een bos haar, zijne bleeke maar toch nog jeugdige trekken overschaduwend, staat hij daar voor u. Maar wat het meest treft zijn zijne oogen, twee donkere, diepliggende oogen van wonderbaarlijken vorm, somber en droomerig ver voor zich uitstarende als ziende de onzienlijke dingen. Het is alsof zijn geheele wezen uit die oogen bestaat; al het andere valt weg. Mij was het alsof ik maar steeds naar die wondere oogen moest zien, alsof ze mij magnetisch aantrokken; al het andere scheen mij daarmee vergeleken zoo banaal in die groote salon vol menschen waar ik hem leerde kennen."

9. "A.B.-d.V.", "Moderne Engelsche Mystiek. William Butler Yeats", *Den Gulden Winckel*, XI/12 (15 December 1912), 177-80.

weigh down Ireland, all of these are merely inessentials to Yeats: a brief span in the history of Ireland.[10]

One may wonder at this. Of course, some of the immediately political poems of the 1910s were yet to come, but the plays should have warned "A.B.-d.V." Notably *The Countess Kathleen*, dedicated to the ardent revolutionary Maud Gonne, exposes the dire position of poor Irish peasants (the soil being barren), and also the corruption of the clergy. It was considered subversive and provocative by its contemporary Irish audience. "A.B.-d.V." does mention this play, but she considers it as no more than a stage version of one of the fairy tales Yeats edited.

One of the most searching analyses of the Irish question in this period is by Pieter Nicolaas van Eyck, a poet and essayist, and the London correspondent for the *Nieuwe Rotterdamsche Courant*, a quality newspaper, between 1920 and 1935. In *Onze Eeuw* of 1921 he published a series of five articles, running to a total length of 148 pages in which he scrutinized Irish history, politics and economy. They are an exhaustive (and exhausting) series in which he made use of detailed figures and the most recent statistics. The articles were afterwards collected and published in book-form.[11] Van Eyck takes the position of most Dutch commentators. He is violently anti-British and makes a strong plea for the rights of the Irish population. His severest criticism is reserved for the members of the Protestant Ascendancy in the nineteenth century, whom he accuses of slavery:

> The world has never produced landowners who were more inhuman than those who formed the Protestant Ascendancy. The slaves of the Roman and Russian landowners represented a certain value for their lords. In the Catholic farmers, of whom there were always more than they could use, the Irish landlords had serfs over

---

10. "Van deze laatsten, zijn tijdgenooten [Lady Gregory c.s.], onderscheidt Yeats zich daardoor, dat hij volstrekt geen gevoel heeft voor de politieke zijde der Iersche quaestie. Zijn geest is geheel vervuld van Ierlands verleden en Ierlands toekomst. De ellende van het tegenwoordige Ierland — meer dan 40.000 menschen verlaten jaarlijks als emigranten het eiland — de overheerschende invloed van de geestelijkheid, de verwoesting van den bodem en vele andere misstanden, waaronder Ierland gebukt gaat, dat alles is voor Yeats slechts bijzaak: een kort tijdperk in de geschiedenis van Ierland."

11. P.N. van Eyck, "De Iersche Kwestie", *Onze Eeuw*, XXI/1 (1921), 217-240, 257-273; XXI/2 (1921), 28-56, 182-222, 233-369 (reprinted in book-form under the same title at Haarlem, 1921).

whose woe they had free control, without ever risking one single penny.[12]

The solution Van Eyck favours is a Dominion status for Ireland, which, so he says, will give Ireland the right to become totally independent if it so desires. Although the focus in these articles is on politics, Van Eyck does slip in a few words about Irish culture. In line with the prevailing Dutch bias, he endorses the spiritual and cultural refinement of the Irish which he contrasts with the bluntness of the British. He seems ambiguous about Anglo-Irish literature: he recognizes the importance of Yeats, Synge and Russell, but thinks the work of the Gaelic League more essential. Yet the fact that here was a revolution in which poets and literati played a significant role was appealing.

Van Eyck's son, Aldo van Eyck, wrote to me in January 1993 that he remembers his father being deeply interested in the Irish question and in Anglo-Irish literature:

A few things can be said about the connection Ireland — P.N. van Eyck — the Netherlands. In fact a great deal .... You probably do not know that several prominent Irish freedom fighters — later ministers — carried on their campaign from an attic room where they hid out in my parents' London home. I specially remember the name of [Desmond] Fitzgerald .... In Ireland in addition to Yeats my parents met with Lady Gregory; A.E. (George Russell), James Stephens and Oliver St.J. Gogarty. I do not believe my father ever met J.M. Synge, whom he greatly admired (perhaps he was no longer alive). I do remember Kate O'Brien coming by in London — several times. Also the Irish library at home — an enormous bookcase filled from floor to ceiling: history, philology, mythology, literature with first impressions and private press editions of many poets with dedications. We were spoon-fed with it all: that Ireland [had] so often [been] led by poets towards freedom. Endless stories. Bloem, Jany Holst and Nijhoff were also well-informed, so that Ireland was often raised when they called round. The Celtic light burnt remarkably bright at our home, but

---

12. "Onmenschelijker grondbezitters dan die de Protestantse Ascendancy vormden, heeft de wereld nooit voortgebracht. De slaven der Romeinsche en Russische latifundia vertegenwoordigden voor hun heer een zekere waarde. De Iersche landlords hadden in de Katholieke boeren, altijd talrijker dan zij gebruiken konden, lijfeigenen, over wier wee zij vrijelijk beschikken konden, zonder dat voor hen ooit één enkele penning op het spel stond."

without pale mysticism. As a result I am nearly an Irish "patriot-
alien".[13]

Yeats's Anglo-Irishness did not stop Van Eyck from accumulating one
of the largest and finest collections of his work in the Netherlands. He
subscribed to the Cuala Press, sometimes ordering several copies of the
same edition. He corresponded with Lily Yeats, W.B. Yeats and his wife
in the 1920s and 1930s and met them when on holiday in Ireland in
1927.[14] After Van Eyck's death his collection was auctioned in 1972
and the catalogue shows he possessed a nearly complete set of Yeats's
work in first editions, English, Irish or American. The catalogue also
features a very large section of other Anglo-Irish writings and political
literature, including the *Sinn Féin Rebellion Handbook* from 1916 in
original wrappers. Van Eyck's advocacy of Yeats's work took place
mostly behind the scenes. He talked and corresponded about Yeats with
literary friends such as Bloem and Roland Holst, who were also avid
collectors of his work. When *The Winding Stair* was difficult to obtain,
Van Eyck manufactured typescripts from his own copy which were
circulated among his friends. On a number of occasions Van Eyck
published on Yeats, and in the last of five articles on the Irish question
he refers to his work:

---

13. "Over de relatie P.N. van Eyck — Nederland — Ierland is wel wat te
vertellen. Veel zelfs .... U weet waarschijnlijk niet dat enkele vooraanstaande Ierse
vrijheidsstrijders — later ministers — vanuit een kamer op zolder thuis in London
waarin zij schuilden, hun acties voerden. Vooral de naam Fitzgerald is mij
bijgebleven .... In Ierland kwamen mijn ouders behalve met Yeats ook met Lady
Gregory; A.E (George Russell), James Stephens en Oliver St.J. Gogarty samen.
J.M. Synge, voor wie mijn vader grote bewondering koesterde heeft hij, geloof ik
niet ontmoet (misschien was hij niet meer in leven). Kate O'Brien is in London langs
geweest dat weet ik nog — meerdere keren. Verder de Ierse bibliotheek thuis — een
enorme kast van vloer tot plafond vol: geschiedenis, taal, mythologie, literatuur met
eerste drukken en private press edities van veel dichters met opdrachten. Wij kregen
het allemaal met de paplepel mee: dat Ierland zo vaak door dichters bij de hand
genomen de vrijheid tegemoet! Eindeloze verhalen. Bloem, Jany Holst en Nijhoff
waren goed op de hoogte zodat Ierland als zij er weer eens waren vaak aan de orde
kwam. Het Keltische licht brandde thuis opvallend sterk, hoewel zonder bleke
mystiek. Ik ben dan ook haast 'n Iers 'patriot-alien'." J.C. Bloem, Adriaan Roland
Holst and Martinus Nijhoff were prominent Dutch poets and contemporaries of Van
Eyck.

14. This correspondence will be published in my forthcoming Ph.D.-dissertation
about the reception of Yeats's work in the Netherlands.

The young poets of 1890, who looked back to their country's past in a reaction to the spirit of the age, felt the sweet, nostalgic charm of the Eire of their ancestors, whose poets across the misty sees saw the glimmering of an Elysium, their Tir na Nog, which also captured *their* dream in its far-off whisper. Later, on the eve of the battle, which began with the deaths of Pearse, Connolly and their comrades, they remembered Ireland as the Shan Van Vocht, the Poor Old Woman, who lures young men from their firesides to the struggle with the Gaul. To glazing eyes she revealed herself as the visible soul of their immortal country. "A terrible beauty is born" wrote the poet of Oisin and Forgael after the executions of 1916, which also for him transformed his country.[15]

Here, again, Yeats is the romantic, patriotic Irish poet, building a future for his country out of its legendary past. Van Eyck also focuses on Yeats's fascination with a Celtic mythology, the play *Cathleen ni Houlihan* and "Easter 1916", but curiously enough, he does not mention Yeats's name.

Two of Van Eyck's later publications also deal with Yeats's reworking of Celtic myth. On 13 August 1929 and 3 April 1930 he reviewed performances of *Fighting the Waves* for the *Nieuwe Rotterdamsche Courant*.[16] Van Eyck himself had been a vital link in the genesis of this play. He had written to Yeats about the masks that were used in performances of *The Only Jealousy of Emer* in Amsterdam in the 1920s. These masks had been made by the Dutch sculptor Hildo Krop and Yeats was so fascinated by them that he decided to write a new version of *Emer*, which resulted in *Fighting the Waves*. Both of Van Eyck's reviews were published anonymously and are not listed in his

---

15. "De jonge dichters van 1890, die uit reactie tegen de geest van hun tijd naar het verleden van hun land terugblikten, voelden de zoete, nostalgische bekoring van dat Eire hunner voorgeslachten, wier dichters aan de overzijde der mistige zeeën de glinstering zagen van een Elyseum, hun Tir na Nog, dat ook hún droom in zijn verre fluistering gevangen nam. Later, toen de strijd zich voorbereidde, die met de dood van Pearse, Connolly en hun kameraden een aanvang nam, herinnerden zij zich Ierland als de Shan Van Vocht, de Arme Oude Vrouw, die de jonge mannen van hun haardsteden trekt naar de worsteling met den Gall. Aan brekende oogen openbaarde zij zich als de zichtbare ziel van hun onsterfelijk vaderland. 'A terrible beauty is born' schreef de dichter van Oisin en Forgael na de executies van 1916, die ook voor hem zijn land transformeerden."

16. P.N. van Eyck, review of *Fighting the Waves* by W.B. Yeats at the Abbey Theatre, Dublin, *Nieuwe Rotterdamsche Courant*, 13 August 1929; review of *Fighting the Waves* by W.B. Yeats at the Lyric Theatre, Hammersmith, *Nieuwe Rotterdamsche Courant*, 3 April 1930.

collected works. The article of 1929 reviews the opening night of *Fighting the Waves* in Dublin, that of 1930 the first London performance. Van Eyck was critical about the play and its staging, in 1930 more so than in 1929, when his review was based on reports that had appeared in Irish papers. He felt the text was swamped by the masks, music and dance and pleaded for greater simplicity. Both times his reviews were awarded a prominent place on the arts-page of the *Nieuwe Rotterdamsche Courant* and both times photographs of the performance were printed with his review. Few theatre performances were awarded so much space and attention, and certainly not performances a Dutch audience had not seen.

A final significant contribution of Van Eyck with respect to Yeats was a translation of "Sailing to Byzantium" which was published by way of obituary in the literary monthly *Groot Nederland* at Yeats's death in 1939.

Van Eyck's series of articles about the Irish question form a climax in the stream of Dutch publications. In the course of the 1920s and 1930s Ireland still received attention from the Dutch press, but not extensively nor passionately pro-Irish. Many commentators felt that the settlement of 1922 was a good, and final, solution to a complicated problem. Yeats's political career in the Free State was unrecorded in the Dutch media. I have found no contemporary Dutch articles about Irish politics that refer to his political career or quote his senate speeches. Instead, Yeats remained the great man behind the Celtic Revival — to those who knew him at all, that is. The notices that appeared on Yeats receiving the Nobel Prize for literature in 1923 and on his death in 1939 make clear that he was still relatively unknown and that only his earliest work had reached a wider audience. The most widely read Dutch daily, *De Telegraaf*, on 16 November 1923, announced the award of the Nobel Prize thus:

> Word has reached us that the Nobel Prize for literature has been awarded to William Butler Yeats, an Irish lyric poet and dramatist, who has been strongly inspired by romantic folklore and legends of Ireland.[17]

---

17. "Nobelprijs voor Letterkunde", *De Telegraaf*, 16 November 1923: "Naar wij vernemen is de Nobelprijs voor letterkunde toegekend aan William Butler Yeats, een Iersch lyrisch dichter en tooneelschrijver, die sterk geïnspireerd is door de romantische folklore en legenden van Ierland."

De Telegraaf further invents a new Irish writer when it points out that Yeats has not only edited the works of William Blake, but also of a certain Cathleen ni Houlihan. On 30 January 1939, the obituarist of *De Telegraaf* sounds a similar note:

> He was one of the leaders of the revival of Irish literature, the "Celtic Renaissance": both of lyric poetry and of drama (the Abbey Theatre in Dublin). He later served his country in politics as well: from 1922 to 1928 he was a senator of the Irish Free State.[18]

In the same obituary "The Lake Isle of Innisfree" is quoted in full in the original.

In the 1920s and 1930s the bulk of the Dutch translations of Yeats's poetry and drama was published. Most popular with translators was material from *The Wind Among the Reeds*, *In the Seven Woods* and *The Countess Kathleen*. The play *The Countess Kathleen* was translated three times, as was "When you are Old and Grey" from the same volume. "The Old Age of Queen Maeve", "The Fiddler of Dooney", "He Wishes for the Cloths of Heaven" and "The Ballad of Father Gilligan" were popular as well. The most productive and successful translator of Yeats's work was Adriaan Roland Holst. Roland Holst began translating Yeats's work in the 1920s and published his last translations in the 1950s. In 1944 he also published a Dutch English-language edition of Yeats's selected poetry.[19] Roland Holst shared Van Eyck's interest in Ireland. His book collection is now kept by the Museum of Dutch Literature and by the Royal Library, both in The Hague. Next to first editions of Yeats, there are works by Synge, Lady Gregory, Padraic Colum, James Stephens and Oliver St. John Gogarty. There are Kuno Meyer's translation of *The Voyage of Bran*, as well as more general books about the history and culture of Ireland. Roland Holst became interested in Ireland at the time the Irish question gained prominence. As a young man he studied at Oxford for a few terms, between 1908 and 1910. His letters

---

18. "William Butler Yeats Overleden", *De Telegraaf*, 30 January 1939: "Hij is een der voorgangers van de herleving der Iersche literatuur, de 'Celtic Renaissance', geweest: zoowel wat de lyrische poëzie als de tooneel literatuur (het Abbey Theatre te Dublin) betreft. Later heeft hij zijn land ook in de staatkunde ten dienste gestaan: van 1922 tot 1928 was hij senator van de Irish Free Sate."

19. The title page of Roland Holst's edition of Yeats's *Selected Poems* gives 1939 as date of publication. The book was in fact published illegally in 1944, during the German occupation.

to friends and family from that period leave no doubt about his fascination with Irish literature. Instead of the political economy he had set out to study, he read Douglas Hyde, Irish myths and modern Irish literature, including Yeats.

As one might expect, both in his translations of Yeats's work and in the *Selected Poems* which Roland Holst compiled, the early Yeats is over-represented. For instance, of the 46 poems in the *Selected Poems*, 20 predate *The Green Helmet and Other Poems* of 1910. The single volume from which most poems have been selected is *The Wind Among the Reeds*.

The influence of the Irish Revival on the early reception of Yeats's work in the Netherlands is all the more striking because of the paucity of other voices. Certainly, people like Van Eyck and Roland Holst collected later work as well, but little was published about this side of Yeats. And although Roland Holst did translate some later poetry, including "A Prayer for my Daughter" and "The Second Coming", these did not evoke any commentary. Only one or two literary critics in the 1920s and 1930s noticed Yeats's development of a new, terse style. A notable exception was Willem van Doorn, who wrote the entries for Yeats and for Irish Literature in the fifth edition of the *Winkler Prins* enyclopaedia, which was published in the 1930s. Van Doorn is also the one noteworthy critic from the professional ranks: he taught English at secondary school.

Before the Second World War contemporary English literature was not a regular part of the academic English curriculum. There was a strong emphasis on philology and if taught at all, literature tended to halt at the end of the nineteenth century. Thus there were no incentives from this side to engage in Yeats criticism. There was one contemporary Ph.D.-dissertation about Yeats, entitled *The Beginnings of the Irish Revival*, by Rebecca Brugsma and published in 1933.[20] She, too, sees Yeats as the central figure of the Revival and concentrates on his early plays. Nothing is said about Yeats's later or non-Celtic work.

From Dutch Celticists equally little was to be expected. The above-mentioned A.G. van Hamel was one of the most prominent Celticists of the period; he was appointed Professor of Celtic studies at the University of Utrecht in 1923, yet he mainly taught Celtic philology. In his publications about contemporary Ireland he proves to be a loyal supporter of the Gaelic League. He considers Yeats and other Anglo-Irish

---

20. Rebecca P.C. Brugsma, *The Beginnings of the Irish Revival*, diss. University of Amsterdam, publ. Groningen, Batavia, 1933.

nationalists as transitional figures. They are only a step on the road towards the final goal, which is a literature in Gaelic. The language of Yeats, Synge and others, though colourful, remains English; Irish culture, however, can only be built on Gaelic. Thus in "The Soul of Ireland's Struggle" ("De Ziel van Ierland's Strijd"), published in *Onze Eeuw* of 1924 he writes:

> Gaelic still lives on among the people in the north and west. There one still hears it with those who in appearance are impoverished and exhausted, but who are descendants of kings and heads of clans. In their conversation the soul of the old Ireland still lives. If the language they speak was lost, the real Ireland would be finished.[21]

In the *Haagsch Maandblad* of 1927 Van Hamel repeats his preference for Gaelic.[22] "Ierland en het Gaelisch" includes a description of an amateur performance of Gaelic plays by Irish teachers, which he saw during one of his visits to Ireland. Van Hamel observes: "I watched them present short plays with a depth of feeling and strength of intensity that left the art of the Abbey Theatre behind."[23] Yeats, in other words, is merely an exponent of a first, Anglo-Irish, phase of Irish nationalism. His work is to be superseded by the real thing, a literature in Gaelic.

Needless to say, Yeats is being sold short by these Irish "patriot-aliens". Not only do they tend to ignore truly political poems such as "Easter 1916" and "Sixteen Dead Men", they also gloss over the irony Yeats displayed with respect to his own Celtic material. No one mentions "The Men Who Dreamed of Faeryland", or the programmatic statement of "A Coat". And of course by the 1920s and 1930s Yeats had already written poems of a totally different stature. But none of these generated much contemporary reaction in the Netherlands. Only such later Yeatsian works as *Wheels and Butterflies* and *Dramatis Personae* were noticed very briefly by Frederick T. Wood based in Sheffield in his "Current

---

21. "Onder het volk in het noorden en westen leeft het Gaelic nog altijd. Daar hoort men het nog bij menschen, uiterlijk verarmd en uitgeput, maar afstammelingen van koningen en clanhoofden. In hun gesprek leeft de ziel van het oude Ireland nog. Ging de taal die zij spreken verloren, het zou met het echte Ierland gedaan zijn." (A.G. van Hamel, "De Ziel van Ierland's Strijd", *Onze Eeuw*, XXIV/3 (1924), 5).

22. A.G. van Hamel, "Ierland en het Gaelisch", *Haagsch Maandblad*, July-December 1927, 593-602.

23. "Ik zag hen Iersche tooneelstukjes vertoonen met een diepte van stemming en een kracht van spanning, die de kunst van het Abbey Theatre voorbij streefden."

Literature" review section in *English Studies*, the international journal founded and edited in the Netherlands.

Only after the Second World War, when the study of English literature began to develop rapidly in the Netherlands and opened up to international influences did the situation change. The brief stay of A. Norman Jeffares as a lecturer at the University of Groningen between 1946 and 1948 was one step in a new direction. His use of detailed biographical data together with his close-reading of Yeats's work, both early and late, formed a clear break with the Dutch tradition up to that time. New Criticism drifted over from England and America, and the second Ph.D.-dissertation to be published on Yeats in the Netherlands shows its influence: it is a close-reading study of "Among School Children" by Abraham Verhoeff, published in 1966.[24]

The Netherlands was slow to discover that Yeats is more than a Celtic Revivalist. The Irish question first brought him to the attention of Dutch critics and for decades the early work determined his image. If one compares the Dutch reception with that in England or America it emerges that English and American critics were more susceptible to new developments in Yeats's work. Jochum in his bibliography of Yeats criticism, for instance, lists a review of *Responsibilities*, written by Ford Madox Ford in 1914, the year in which the volume was published.[25] According to Jochum's short summary of the review Ford finds Yeats in this volume "no longer grotesque and irritating" and suggests an improved version of one of the earlier poems he considers particularly bad, "The Lake Isle of Innisfree". Ford's amended version opens thus: "At Innesfree [*sic*] there is a public-house;/They board you well for ten and six a week." J.W. Cunliffe in *English Literature During the Last Half Century*, published in New York by Macmillan in 1919, also comments on the new direction Yeats seems to be taking in *Responsibilities*.[26] He quotes "A Coat", pointing out that Yeats "seems to take leave of Celtic mythology". And he even refers to "In Memory of Major Robert Gregory", which had only appeared in *The New Review*

---

24. Abraham Verhoeff, *The Practice of Criticism: A Comparative Analysis of W.B. Yeats's "Among School Children"*, diss. University of Utrecht, publ. Utrecht, 1966.

25. K.P.S. Jochum, *W.B. Yeats: A Classified Bibliography of Criticism*, 2nd edn, Urbana and Chicago, 1990.

26. J.W. Cunliffe, *English Literature During the Last Half Century*, New York, 1919.

in 1918 and cites T. Sturge Moore's remarks in the same issue about Yeats's new, sober style.

If one considers translations or foreign editions of Yeats's work the Netherlands lags behind Germany or France. The first Dutch translations *per se*, that is other than in articles about Ireland or in critical analyses, were printed in the 1920s and 1930s in literary journals. The first English language edition to be printed in the Netherlands was Roland Holst's selected poems of 1944. In contrast, there were French translations from 1892 onwards. In 1912 a volume of Yeats's poems in French translation was published, which included "The Man Who Dreamed of Faeryland". German translations began in 1894. In 1916 a German translation was published of stories such as "The Tables of the Law" and "The Adoration of the Magi", which included Yeats's literary criticism as well. As early as 1913 Tauchnitz published an English language edition of Yeats's poetry and drama. The works that were selected run up to 1912.[27]

For a considerable time, even while Yeats published volumes that showed a development beyond the early Celtic material, for Dutch critics he remained coupled with the Celtic Revival. Fairy-tales, poems from *The Wind Among the Reeds* and early plays determined the Yeats corpus. Beginning with De Boissevain's Irish travelogue, discussions of his work almost invariably included reviews of Irish history and culture and contemporary politics. Given the pro-Irish feelings and the call for political awareness, as expressed by Rooseboom and "A.B.-d.V.", one might have expected poems such as "Easter 1916" and "Sixteen Dead Men" to have been hailed by Dutch critics. But they were not. There were no published comment on these poems, nor were they translated or included in Roland Holst's English language edition of Yeats's poetry. Perhaps it was the romance of the Celtic Revival that was most attractive after all. This seems to be confirmed by the Dutch neglect of other work, early and late, that did not have the lustre of twilight.

---

27. See Allan Wade, *A Bibliography of the Writings of W.B. Yeats*, 3rd edn, London, 1968.

A SEARCH FOR A NATIONAL IDENTITY: THREE PHASES OF YEATS STUDIES IN JAPAN

TOSHI FUROMOTO

A scholarly critic in Japan once wrote an essay on the development of our critical faculties entitled "Appreciation, Criticism, and History". As you may guess from the title, the essay described how we mature mentally. At first, the essay maintains, a man's response to a work is just an emotional one without analytical reasoning. But before long he grows dissatisfied with this naiveté. He comes to ask himself what causes his appreciation, and why. The development is inevitable, human beings being doomed to self-awareness. Then the process turns toward criticism, where he seeks a reasonable basis for his appreciation. He tries to show and persuade others about the connection between his primary response and the ensuing judgement. The judgement becomes more or less an objectified activity of criticism. To objectify what has not yet been externalized is a sort of social activity. He comes to share one and the same experience with others by verbalizing it. This critical activity necessarily proceeds to a wider perspective both chronologically and spatially. This is the third phase of critical maturity.

In the case of a critical history of a writer's reception in a certain society, we can see these phases at work. The present article endeavours to show how Yeats's reception in Japan is in accord with this hypothesis. Part of this reception history was described by Oshima's *Yeats and Japan* (1965).[1] I would like to divide the history of Yeats reception in Japan into three phases. The first is the period when readers and scholars were eager to read only the Yeats that suited their tastes. In the second period, eclectic readings are complemented with a critical faculty which focuses on the Yeats that is germane to Japanese culture. In the third period, the Japanese reception rid itself of native slants and biases, instead embracing universal presuppositions and a common inheritance.

---

1. Shotaro Oshima, *W.B. Yeats and Japan*, Tokyo, 1965.

The bibliographies of the earlier Japanese Yeats studies bear out a predilection for certain works and for certain types of approaches to Yeats. We have been left records of a number of interviews with Yeats by Yone Noguchi, Hojin Yano, Makoto Sangu and Shotaro Oshima.[2] These records are now very precious, and provide first-hand information on the poet. The second popular theme for discussion of the period was symbolism. As many of the studies of this period consisted of biographical introductions and summaries of the poet's work, the discussion centred upon Yeats's essays "Symbolism in Painting" and "The Symbolism of Poetry" in *Ideas of Good and Evil*. In discussions of the symbolic tendencies of the Celtic race, these scholars mostly depended on the works by Matthew Arnold, Ernest Renan (*Poetry of the Celtic Races and Other Essays*) and Francis Grierson (*The Celtic Temperament*). A bias towards Yeats's symbolical work is also manifest in the translations made in this period. Apart from the shorter poems, two translations and a production of *The Shadowy Waters* appeared between 1911 and 1915.

Some have accounted for the strong appeal of symbolism to the Japanese by claiming that it was innate in our own culture. We should, however, note that this period was only one generation or so after the Meiji Restoration — the beginning of modernization. The social atmosphere in general welcomed the "profitable and useful" studies, such as law, economics and medicine. In this climate it was no wonder that literature tended to favour a trend away from "mundane cupidity". Scholars of Yeats and symbolism include Koju Kurihara (an 1908 essay, later enlarged and added to his translation of *The Shadowy Waters* in 1914) and Makoto Sangu (1914).

The period around 1910-1920 was a turning point in the Japanese literary tradition. This era briefly enjoyed the liberalism of the "Taisho democracy", and with a sense of freedom spreading among people there appeared two translations of Whitman's *Leaves of Grass*. The translators were poets, rather than scholars, and their works met with severe criticism by Hojin Yano (1920). Apart from being a respected scholar, Yano was also a poet of *tanka* verse (a short poem of 31 syllables), and his public dismissal of Whitman is indicative of the dominance of

---

2. Yone Noguchi interviewed Yeats during his American tour from August 1903 to March 1904; Hojin Yano was in London on 12 November 1926, at Thoor Ballylee on 30-31 July 1926, and in Dublin, from the end of September to 1 October 1927; Makoto Sangu was in Dublin, 3 August 1926; and Shotaro Oshima interviewed Yeats on 5 July 1938.

traditional lyricism at the time, and an unwillingness to acknowledge realistic epic trends.

In all, the reception of Yeats in this first phase favoured expressions of admiration for his works rather than critical rigour. Japanese critics were less analytical than imaginative, and eager to find an affinity of temperament in Yeats. This is exemplified by a poem added to the first serious book-length study on Yeats, by Oshima:

IN TIME OF ROSES TO COME OUT
For Yeats

Traveller pale with passion,
Bury the urn of clear memory
In the timeless pond
Among the unknown forest of the moon.
Thus
When you call up the days past
You'll hear the roses come out beyond the day and night.

Oshima began to write almost at the end of the first phase of Yeats reception, and he remained, in his lifetime, the foremost authority on the poet. It was not until Manji Kobayashi's close reading of Yeats's poems in 1958 provided a frame of reference against which Oshima's literary style could be seen as tending to slide into obscurantism. The subjectivity manifest in Oshima's translations is also prominent in the selection of Yeats's poetry, with detailed notes, made by Yano.[3] Published in 1928, it disregards *The Tower* and presents Yeats as the poet of *The Wind Among the Reeds*, *Oisin* and *The Shadowy Waters*, neglecting the poetry after *The Green Helmet and Other Poems* (1910).[4]

In the second phase, critics and scholars became aware of the advantage of approaching Yeats from the Japanese point of view, focusing on such topics as Noh, Zen and Buddhism. Already in the discussion of symbolism, some had noticed some affinity between the Japanese mind and the Celtic, but the appearance of *Four Plays for Dancers* (1921) and the preface to Fenollosa's translation of *Noh, Certain Noble Plays from Japan* (1916) gave impetus to this kind of approach.

---

3. Kazumi (Hojin) Yano, *Selected Poems of Yeats*, Kenkyusha, 1928 (with a 46 page introduction and 100 pages of notes).

4. For a more recent translation of Yeats see Tetsuro Sano, *W.B. Yeats*, Kyoto, 1981 (an edition containing two plays, and a selection of poetry and prose, together with a Preface and notes).

As early as 1922 Yone Noguchi wrote an essay entitled "Yeats and the Noh"; and in 1928 Jiro Nan'e wrote of Yeats's interest in Noh, "it will be a quite superficial view if any, looking at the similarities in appearance, may think that fanciful Yeats tried to imitate a Noh out of mere curiosity aroused by exotic interest". Nan'e emphasized that "what Yeats learned from Noh were not only the stylistic and formal devices but also the noble essence of this suggestive art which is simple, mysterious and beyond artistic restrictions; a sort of apocalyptic message shaken out of heightened beauty and life". A little later, in 1932, Tadaichi Hidaka wrote "Yeats and Japanese Noh Plays" for a booklet of *Nihon no Noh-gaku* (Noh Plays), and Hojin Yano in 1948 and Makoto Sangu in 1949 wrote about the relationship between Yeats and Japan.

Among these pioneering works, one cannot ignore Kan Kikuchi's works. He is almost the only contemporary Japanese man of letters mentioned in Hojin Yano's interview with Yeats, and again in Oshima's. Yeats seemed to have read one or two works of his. In 1917 Kikuchi wrote "A Note on Synge's Plays", contrasting Synge's characters in the real world with those of Yeats and A.E. in the land of fairies". The latter he called "intangible like smoke". Kikuchi maintains that Deirdre's decision in Synge's play to seek intensity of life in the world of conflicts rather than just wait for the age and ugliness is a tragic element unknown to the Japanese. Kikuchi says that Japanese writers too often write about elopement and double suicide without exploiting the irony which is hidden in the successful union of the lovers. Instead, they seem to think that one success is enough to last trance-like to the end.

With a younger scholar, Kikuchi wrote in 1925 a book on modern English and Irish plays, which is not listed in Oshima's bibliography. Several chapters are devoted to Irish plays and Irish temperament. Yeats is discussed up to *The Land of Heart's Desire* and *Where There Is Nothing*. The latter, he says, is full of Eastern thoughts and reads like the salvationist message of Nirvana. But nowhere are there references to Noh plays. The relation between Noh and these two Yeats plays struck the Japanese only after *Four Plays for Dancers* and Yeats's own admission of the influence of Noh on his drama.

The resemblance between Yeats's plays and Noh was subsequently acknowledged by most critics and scholars. But the first in-depth study of the subject was not produced until 1966, with Hiro Ishibashi's booklet *Yeats and Noh*.[5] Isibashi had read a paper of that title in 1963 at the Yeats Summer School in Sligo, but she published it after Oshima's book,

---

5. Hiro Ishibashi, *Yeats and the Noh: Types of Japanese Beauty and Their Reflection in Yeats's Plays*, Dublin, 1965.

Yeats and Japan (1965). Oshima's book has chapters on Noh, Zen and Eastern thought. There were no exchanges of insights on the subject between the two scholars and no recognition was made on either side. In their discussion of the characteristics of Noh, both essays are not dissimilar; the former concentrates more on the structure of Noh while the latter focuses on the background to Yeats's interests such as Fenollosa, Michio Ito, Yone Noguchi and Kaoru Osanai on his notes to producing *The Hour-Glass* in Noh style.

These two works proceeded the comprehensive studies by Masaru Sekine.[6] Sekine collaborated with Christopher Murray on *Yeats and Noh* (1990).[7] This book is, in a sense, a completion of Sekine's own works and exhaustive on those topics launched but left suspended by previous scholars. Sekine has staged both Yeats and Noh, and combines a scholarly knowledge of the subject with the experience of a director. The similarity in the texts of *The Dreaming of the Bones* and *Nishikigi* had been explained in Oshima's *Yeats and Japan*, but Sekine analyses them in action. Sekine calls Noh a "dance theatre".[8] He considers action — in the form of dance — to be the essence of Noh. Sekine also stresses the importance of the Shinto tradition for Noh. This may not strike the student of Noh and its origins as anything new — the ideas of cleansing life's dirt, the renewal of life is one of the principal concepts in Shinto — but in the essays by Oshima and Ishibashi, Shinto was not discussed at all, while both Zen and Buddhism were. On one thing most of these studies agree, namely that Yeats did not learn directly from Noh, but that he came to confirm what he was looking for. This is an important point, and we shall return to it later.

Another characteristically Japanese approach is to view Zen elements in Yeats. Oshima explicated Zen ideas such as "Satori", "Non-Committal" and "Emptiness". The first was defined by Oshima as follows: "When a man in a state of super-unconsciousness is confronted with reality, all things cease to trouble him".[9] He goes on to say:

---

6. *Ze-Ami and His Theories of Noh Drama*, Gerrards Cross, 1985; and "Four Plays for Dancers: Japanese Aesthetics and a European Mind", in *Yeats the European*, ed. A.N. Jeffares, Gerrards Cross, 1989, 232-37.

7. Masaru Sekine and Christopher Murray, *Yeats and the Noh*, Gerrards Cross, 1990.

8. Sekine and Murray, 29.

9. Oshima, 64.

Only after having experienced all sorts of human sufferings can a man enter upon Satori, the state of pure experience and enlightenment. And to reach Satori means to reach gaiety which is the absolute freedom of mind and soul.

As for the notion of Non-Committal, Oshima observes:

Wu wei does not mean to sit idle and to do nothing. It means not to interfere with others' affairs, or even with one's own as long as they flow of themselves from the inner fountain of the Tao.

Oshima contrasts emptiness with intellectual preoccupation:

Hamlet [represents] European intellectual yearning after knowledge ... tormented by his analytical intelligence .... In Mahayana Buddhism ... the supreme wisdom can be attained only by the cognition of non-duality, or the negation of the knower and the knowable.[10]

Satori, Non-committal and Emptiness are experiential phenomena which, by their nature, defy rational analysis. Oshima, or for that matter anyone who tries to give a rational account of these essences of Zen, is therefore in a difficult predicament. An example of this difficult can be seen in the two books by Shiro Naito.[11] Naito takes up important ideas in Zen such as "Becoming and Being", "Emptiness", "Silence", "Ignorance", and "No-mind-ness". Quoting amply from Daisetsu Suzuki, the most distinguished Zen scholar, he tries to show that the later Yeats found the ideas of tragic gaiety and Unity of Being in the East. Suzuki's explanations are revealing, but they do not necessarily lend themselves to verification or to scrutiny. Naito suggests we should "see the similarity or common characteristics between Zen Buddhism and Yeats's proper thought as formed before he was acquainted with Zen". He maintains that "it is impossible that, without such sympathetic premises, Eastern thought would have influenced the Western poet".[12] Here we find the same pattern of thought as we found in the examination of Yeats's interest in Noh plays. This pattern may be universal, for,

---

10. *Ibid*., 66, 73 and 91.

11. Shiro Naito, *Yeats and Zen*, Kyoto, 1984; and *Yeats's Epiphany*, Kyoto, 1990.

12. *Yeats and Zen*, 85 and 87.

generally speaking, only what we really and urgently need comes in sight; in other words, by finding it we come to realize what we need.

After Oshima's books, two impressive books were written in Japanese, which together with Oshima's can be said to represent the orthodox tradition of Yeats studies in Japan, by Yukio Oura, and Hisayoshi Watanabe. Oura focuses more on the later Yeats than Oshima had done, although the latter does admit the greatness of the later Yeats. Oshima's key-word in speaking of the later Yeats is "reality". He found Yeats settled in a certain harmony or balance. Oura, on the other hand, is more specific about the nature of Yeats's "reality". Oura thinks that reality is a space where diverse forces are in conflict. The "contradictory elements", mixing and merging in Yeats to the end, contributed to the production of "a unique character carrying a chaos within, reflecting reality itself". He continues: "The interest in reality and the romantic yearning for dreams and visions, interfering with each other, developed an interesting dualism in Yeats".[13]

Rather than analysing the notion of "reality", Watanabe focuses on Yeats's religious sense, claiming that

> to understand [the gyres] and "The Second Coming" is not to make them consistent with the pattern of the combination of the cones, but to identify or try to identify oneself with the poet's will or energy to challenge and conquer that huge violent force of "history". It is to think over what that intensity of the passion means — as if fear and joy have been put into one inseparable entity — and to realize that this passion is trying to transform that inevitability of the huge force of history into the creation of one's will. This is what we cannot name but "a sort of religious passion".[14]

The development of these critical studies corresponds to Yeats's transformation from a poet immersed in the Celtic Twilight to one "walking naked" in harsh reality. The romantic and subjective reading has been replaced by a tighter and starker one. The completion of this third phase comes somewhat later with works in English.

When Earl Miner published *The Japanese Tradition in British and American Literature* (1958), my first reaction was both of admiration and of an inexpressible sense of defeat. It was a kind of study which might

---

13. Yukio Oura, *W.B. Yeats, Poet of the Lonely Tower*, Kyoto, 1961, 47 and 78.

14. Hisayoshi Watanabe, *W.B. Yeats*, Kyoto, 1982, 48.

have been written but could not by a Japanese. Other non-Japanese critics who have contributed to Yeats scholarship in Japan are G.S. Fraser and Anthony Twaite, who together with the Japanese studies we have been looking at, paved the way for the Japanese Yeatsians to express themselves in English. Along with Sekine and Murray's comparative study of Yeats and Noh, a study of Yeats's aesthetics by Okifumi Komesu is a fine example of the completion of this third phase.[15]

This last phase has also seen the publication of other valuable studies, particularly by Sumiko Sugiyama and Yoko Chiba.[16] The title of the latter's article might suggest that it belongs to the second phase of Japanese Yeatsian studies, but in fact the paper is a product of years of training the critical faculty, diligent reading and familiarity with the texts, which could be gained regardless of nationality. I do not mean to suggest that racial temperament has nothing to contribute to the study of literature, but the question here is one of personal talent rather than racial (national) character. Just as in the case of an individual, the development of a critical climate follows a pattern towards objectivity with regards to the liberation from various limitations and self-restraints. It is time for us to stop thinking in terms of being specifically Japanese; for true nationality must be based upon the individual freed from national idiosyncrasy and upon an ability to look at oneself through an ever-widening perspective of history.

---

15. Okifumi Komesu, *The Double Perspective of Yeats's Aesthetic*, Gerrards Cross, 1984.

16. Sumiko Sugiyama, "What Is *The Player Queen* All About?", in *Irish Writers and the Theatre*, ed. Masaru Sekine, Gerrards Cross, Totowa and New York, 1986, 179-207 (also see her *Yeats: Fatherland and Song*, Kyoto, 1984, and "The Dream of Eros: Yeats's *His Dream*", *Irish University Review*, XIX/2 [Autumn 1989], 227-39). Yoko Chiba, "Ezra Pound's Versions of Fenollosa's Noh Manuscripts and Yeats's Unpublished 'Suggestions and Corrections'", *Yeats Annual No 4*, (1986), 121-44.

"EASTER 1916" IN THE 1990s:
A SOUTH AFRICAN PERSPECTIVE

NICHOLAS MEIHUIZEN

In "Passion and Cunning: An Essay on the Politics of W.B.Yeats", Conor Cruise O'Brien presents, we may recall, an amusing anecdote regarding the poet's nonchalant attitude towards matters political. In an Arts Club speech Yeats referred to Mussolini as Missolonghi, the place in Greece associated with Byron's death. When corrected, the poet responded in measured tones: "Does ... it ... really ... matter?"[1] O'Brien may suggest that the anecdote offers a true reflection of a particular Yeatsian pose; however, relatively recent studies, such as Elizabeth Cullingford's *Yeats, Ireland and Fascism* (London, 1981), and Cairns Craig's *Yeats, Eliot, Pound and the Politics of Poetry* (London, 1982), have shown the poet's highly informed engagement with the political dimension. The value of this engagement is surely apparent in "Easter 1916", a poem even esteemed by Harold Bloom, in his otherwise largely antipathetical book on Yeats.[2] This article, although it will focus specifically on Yeats's poem, will first consider the explicit and implicit responses to "Easter 1916" generated by the highly politicized South African literary scene. The South African perspective underlines, albeit in an oblique manner, the credibility and pertinence of Yeats's political observations.

Sally-Ann Murray's "Easter 1989" is a response to and critique of "Easter 1916".[3] Set in present-day Durban, the poem is worlds apart from Yeats's; at the same time it does evoke moments from Yeats's poem. Thus instead of Dublin streets in the first section of "Easter 1989", we find a Durban lecture room. (Incidentally, the slightly

---

1. *In Excited Reverie: A Centenary Tribute to W.B.Yeats 1865-1939*, eds A. Norman Jeffares and K.G.W. Cross, London, 1965, 246.

2. Harold Bloom, *Yeats*, London, 1970.

3. For the full text of "Easter 1989" see the Addendum to this article. The poem was published in *English Academy Review*, 6 (December 1989), 128-29.

out-of-focus quality of the near-coincidence of the two names, Durban/Dublin, characterizes the glancing disparity achieved by Murray in the remainder of the poem.) The lecture room is filled with barely awake first-year students who seem far less capable than Yeats's revolutionaries of relinquishing the "casual comedy". Apart from the Durban social environment, the hard facts of the political environment intrude on the class-room setting. If Yeats introduces various revolutionaries, Murray introduces one in particular, Sandile Thusi, who is on hunger-strike:

> First class of the day. Heavy-eyed
> with sleep, first years yawn through Yeats
> in unrelenting heat. Outside,
> pale blue and vivid yellow wait.
> A sky that tumbles the sun,
> a sea that plashes the beach:
> minute by minute Durban
> streams into the room as I speak
> of metaphor and history,
> romantic myths and Irish pride.
> Minute by minute while Sandile
> Thusi dies.

But, despite his sacrifice, Thusi is no purveyor of "terrible beauty". The symbols of circumscription in the first section of the poem conspire to ensure this. Police, police vans, the implacable injustice of the state of emergency regulations, and the complacency and helplessness of the populace, epitomized by the "colleague" who merely heads for the beach once he has, apparently, eased his conscience by appealing to the Minister of Law and Order, ensure the fact of Thusi's non-elevation into the transformative heroic realm as imaged in Yeats's poem:

> ... Blue uniforms bide
> their time in yellow vans at
> the campus gate. Class ends. We have tea,
> then send to Minister Vlok a fax
> urgently requesting that he release
> or charge all detainees. After which
> a colleague heads for Durban Surf Life-
> Savers' Club — white males only, such
> is life — to practise in a five
> man rowing team. Pull together.

The remainder of the poem corroborates the initial position set up by Murray. Indeed, the only affirmative statement in the poem is the final line of the third section, and even this line, in its portrayal of the claustrophobic situation, is qualified by heavy irony: "His action is a statement of hope for the future".

In the fourth section of "Easter 1989" Yeats's soothing murmuring of names is transformed into an activity which brings "rash comfort". And Yeats's impersonal "stone", at once a symbol of the foundation of a nationalist spirit and an emblem of feelings numbed by rigid adherence to "one purpose alone", attains a personal specificity. This specificity is limiting in its implications through its relation to Thusi's mother:

> her son's constancy becomes
> at once a shield and an injury,
> the rock foundation and the stone that numbs
> her heart.

She is seen to bear the burden of nationalist sacrifice and experience the chilling numbness, not of hate, but, ironically, of love. Despite her sacrifice, Thusi's fame is not heroic, but "awkward", heralding, it may be, the questionable worth of an isolated "martyred stranger". And if in Yeats's poem "change" results from the Easter uprising, in "Easter 1989" the situation is characterized by stasis. This stasis is not created, as might be expected, by the tension between the charging or releasing of prisoners, but by the tension between imponderable police silence and at least *some* form of legal activity, where to charge or release, paradoxically and stultifyingly, might both take on a positive light:

> Many others wait with her for police
> to charge or release their children.

In the final section of Murray's poem, human rights protesters, drum-majorettes and student charity activities serve as backdrop to Thusi's "communion", underlining a moment of spirituality in the midst of the indefatigable tide of life. That Thusi's only food will be spiritual, double-blessed because of the propitious time of the year, Easter, suggests something of the moral integrity of his position. Contrasted with this image of integrity is the Minister of Law and Order, who gains easy absolution through artifice and deceit. He can, through corrupt temporal power, justify his position by fabricating a charge, or by promising *ad infinitum* to review the case. The final image in the poem is of marching protesters actually receiving some concession from the riot police

214   *Nicholas Meihuizen*

regarding laws of trespass. This small triumph, however, only highlights the general impasse.

The sombre ending of "Easter 1989" displaces the sense of hard-won pride presented in Yeats's poem, by explicitly comparing the situations in the two poems, and pointing to the inexorable differences:

> But what has changed so utterly? the students ask.
> Yeats has no real answers for the class.

The ending clinches Murray's overall strategy: by presenting a series of slightly out-of-focus near-parallels with Yeats's poem, she in fact undermines any sense of solution to be derived from such parallels.

Playing on the remoteness of Yeats's Ireland from present-day South Africa, Murray also seems to question the relevance of poetry itself in a political situation:

> minute by minute Durban
> streams into the room as I speak
> of metaphor and history,
> romantic myths and Irish pride.
> Minute by minute while Sandile
> Thusi dies.

"Easter 1916", first published on a large scale four years after the uprising,[4] might surely be viewed as isolated from the events it commemorates. In that case, Murray's critique exposes more than superficial historical, geographical and social differences, but also points to the old problems underlying the very nature of artistic engagement in political issues.

This observation is most pertinent in South Africa today, and is expressed in one way in James Matthews's poem "They Say".[5] In the poem Matthews presents himself as the beleaguered poet who, because of his political situation, is unable to satisfy his artistic needs. His critics in the poem make a distinction between a prescriptive attitude which furthers political causes, and an attitude apparent in the type of poetry which merely describes political situations without offering any "solutions". Matthews is accused of writing descriptive verse of no pragmatic value to the revolution:

---

4. In *The New Statesman*, 23 October 1920, and *The Dial*, November 1920.

5. For the full text of "They Say" see the Addendum to this article. The poem is taken from James Matthews, *No Time for Dreams*, Athlone, 1981, 43.

> they say
> writing poetry at
> this stage of
> our struggle is
> absurd, and writing
> black protest poetry
> is even worse
> people need direction
> and not words
> relating the situation
> as it is
> things that everyone
> knows all about
> poets, black poets,
> have written themselves
> into a dead end

Matthews, who is in fact committed to political change, feels that such criticism is "acid" eating the "flesh" of his poetry. The nature of his imagery in this instance suggests that at a fundamental subjective level he deeply values artistic autonomy.

The position he portrays has been the subject of much recent discussion in South Africa, prompted by a paper by ANC intellectual Albie Sachs, once a political hard-liner who advocated that culture is an instrument of the struggle, but who now urges freedom of expression in the arts.[6] Sachs suggests that an artistic position which is ideologically free can better argue the complexity of socio-political situations, and thus provide us with a richer appreciation of the socio-political environment. Sachs articulates a position long since held in Marxist circles. One thinks of the young Edmund Wilson's essay "Marxism and Literature", apart from ideas expressed by Lenin, Trotsky, and, indeed, Marx himself.[7]

To reach the perspective of artistic freedom advocated by Sachs, one cannot simply bypass issues and situations that bring a tremendous weight of coercive power to bear on one's life. One has to face these situations — as Matthews does, as Murray does, and, indeed, as Yeats does. Seamus Heaney indicates this aspect of the problem in his essay "Feeling into Words", when he writes of his poetic need "to search for images

---

6. The paper can be found in *Spring is Rebellious*, eds Ingrid de Kok and Karen Press, Cape Town, 1990, 19-29.

7. For this essay, see *Twentieth-Century Literary Criticism: A Reader*, ed. David Lodge, London, 1972, 241-46.

and symbols adequate to [the Irish] predicament".[8] The search would be for a "field of force" in which "it would be possible to encompass the perspectives of a humane reason and at the same time to grant the religious intensity of the violence its deplorable authenticity and complexity". Heaney quotes Shakespeare and Yeats: "The question, as ever, is 'How with this rage shall beauty hold a plea?' And my answer is, by offering 'befitting emblems of adversity'".[9] The ethos of the bog people, at once richly familiar, spiritual and barbaric, provides Heaney with an adequate context with which to face events in Northern Ireland, as the poem "Punishment" attests. (The poem, it will be remembered, links the fate of a bog queen figure with "the exact/and tribal, intimate revenge" carried out on present day-girls who have been fraternizing with English soldiers.[10])

In "Easter 1916" Yeats faces his situation in a more direct way, a way also followed by Sally-Ann Murray, in fact. He does not seek a correlative mythology as Heaney does; he dramatizes his present-day situation, mythologizing it in the process. But despite the heroic nature of aspects of this mythologizing, "adversity" is very much in evidence in the poem. Adversity is detected in the consequences of political violence which Yeats presents. Through his careful examination of these consequences Yeats is able, in Heaney's words, to "encompass the perspectives" of both a "humane reason" and "religiously intense" violence. Neil Corcoran in his study of Heaney emphasizes the "authenticity" of Heaney's vision: the atavistic emotions and responses in his vision of violence "criticize the shallowness and presumption of most rationalist and humanist responses".[11] Yeats, although drawing in an indirect and somewhat backhanded way on atavistic emotions and responses, achieves an inclusiveness of vision similar to that achieved by Heaney. This vision bypasses the merely rationalist and humanist responses of what amount to, in the end, prescriptive notions of literature which seek unambiguous cause and effect, and explicitly presented praise or censure.

Harold Bloom is puzzled by "Easter 1916" because it is, in his view, so uncharacteristic of Yeats. He feels that the poem "excels in a sober coloring of accurate moral description, a quality normally lacking in

---

8. Seamus Heaney, *Preoccupations: Selected Prose 1968-1978*, London, 1984, 56.

9. *Ibid.*, 57.

10. Seamus Heaney, *New Selected Poems 1966-1987*, London, 1990, 72.

11. Neil Corcoran, *Seamus Heaney*, London, 1986, 116.

Yeats", and that it is "a model of sanity and proportion".[12] Perhaps more than anything in Yeats, the poem does mirror the sober responsibility of conventional morality. But here, in the mechanics in which the poem does this, an interesting notion arises. Violence assumes a positive value in the poem, but not through the political ends which it achieves, which are presented in a highly qualified manner by Yeats anyway. It is through accommodating the violence within a responsible social framework that Yeats is able to arrive at the sane proportion of vision so praised by Bloom.

It would seem that Yeats is elaborating on a position which dates back to 1907, when he wrote of the clarifying influence of "memory of danger" (*E&I*:259). A similar notion is expressed in his final years in "Under Ben Bulben", in which a fighting-mad man "completes his partial mind" (*CP*:398; *PNE*:356). Here Yeats underlines his inherent belief that conflict is a necessary aspect of life. He does not have in mind, of course, the blind political conflict that leads to the mother murdered at her door, but existential conflict as propounded in *A Vision*, and, of all Yeats's sources, perhaps best summarized in Blake's "Without Contraries is no progression".[13]

How does "Easter 1916" achieve its noteworthy degree of proportion? It seems to me that Yeats, in the intensity of the moment, attains a conception of the violence not mitigated by the comparatively simplistic and one-sided idealism apparent in, for example, "September 1913". In "September 1913" violence is equated with heroism without any qualifications. We find memory of danger in action, as it were, bitterly taunting the wearers of motley with visions of a romantic past: "But let them be, they're dead and gone,/They're with O'Leary in the grave" (*CP*:121; *PNE*:115). Confronted with actual violence, Yeats is far more cautious in his response to heroism. Thus the qualifications in "Easter 1916" are numerous. Yeats tells of his scepticism in the face of the motley of the casual comedy; he tells of the lost promise of lives cut short by the violence; he tells of the dangers of political idealism; he even questions the value of the sacrifice in the light of England's possible granting of Home Rule after the war. But he nevertheless acknowledges a transformation in Irish spirit: a "terrible beauty" is very actively "born" in the immediacy of the present tense.

It is, finally, the birth of the beauty which interests me. Some form of integration or individuation creative of beauty, of proportion, has

---

12. Bloom, 314.

13. William Blake, *Complete Writings*, ed. G. Keynes, London, 1972, 149.

taken place, an individuation that does not exist independently of the violence, but like Yeats's Vision of Evil, must incorporate the violence, the bad, in order not to compromise human nature by undervaluing the good.[14] In other words, in Jungian terms, the shadow has to be integrated within our natures if we are at all to bring some proportion to the forces which constitute our lives.[15] Yeats's task is not mere description, then, but an active moral engagement, which transforms violence into an important facet of what is to become the existential process of the Vision of Evil. It seems to me that this process, already apparent in *Per Amica Silentia Lunae* of 1917, deeply informs Yeats's approach in the poem; it is fundamental in the meditative weighing of opposite perspectives.

It appears that Murray, despite her skilfully ironic assimilation of Yeatsian elements (which must surely qualify, as the irony acknowledges its source of power, at least the attitude conveyed in the conclusion of her poem — an instance of de Manian "blindness and insight" perhaps), too readily limits Yeats. Yeats's discourse *is* pragmatically effective once the crude prescriptive notions of the "opinionated mind" are set aside. I think not only in terms of a theory of an existential process, which tells of the necessity of opposites, but of a meditative process which is actively able to embrace contraries. It is the resultant comprehensiveness and depth of vision of this process, embodied in "Easter 1916", which is so important, and which is so necessary in any society, but especially in politically tempestuous societies such as present-day South Africa. For in South Africa today poetry and politics are still both undermined by a pervasive dualism, which, incorporating and mirroring the polarizing simplifications of apartheid, has held us so long in its thrall.

---

14. George Bornstein, *Yeats and Shelley*, Chicago, 1970, 201-202.

15. Carl Gustav Jung, *The Archetypes and the Collective Unconscious*, tr. R.F.C.Hull, London, 1959, 20.

Easter 1989

First class of the day. Heavy-eyed
with sleep, first years yawn through Yeats
in unrelenting heat. Outside,
pale blue and vivid yellow wait.
A sky that tumbles the sun,
a sea that plashes the beach:
minute by minute Durban
streams into the room as I speak
of metaphor and history,
romantic myths and Irish pride.
Minute by minute while Sandile
Thusi dies. Blue uniforms bide
their time in yellow vans at
the campus gate. Class ends. We have tea,
then send to Minister Vlok a fax
urgently requesting that he release
or charge all detainees. After which
a colleague heads for Durban Surf Life-
Savers' Club — white males only, such
is life — to practise in a five
man rowing team. Pull together.

Solidarity at a special Forum
in the Students' Union. Placards are raised
for Sandhile, prominent men speak for him
and other hunger strikers. He is praised
in the same breath as Shaka, Bambatha, Biko, Tambo and
Mandela:

Sandile Thusi is a researcher at the University of Natal.
He was involved in church youth groups while still at school.
He was first detained in June 1986.
He was released without charge after 11 months.
He was detained again on June 16 1988.
He has not been charged.
He has been on a hunger strike for 34 days.
His action is a statement of hope for the future.

Head bent, his weeping mother lights
the wire-bound candle. Silence. Prayers.

Flame haloes glow, then wane. Might
faith not waver in the glare
of press and politics? Caught as she is in the camera's eye
her son's constancy becomes
at once a shield and an injury,
the rock foundation and the stone that numbs
her heart. To murmur his name
is rash comfort: all must face the danger
that this awkward fame
may fashion for the cause a martyred stranger.
Elderly, held by another son,
the mother is striking in her ordinariness
when the TV crews have done.
Many others wait with her for police
to charge or release their children.

Yesterday saw a Black Sash protest;
the *Daily News* spread drummies on page one.
Two weeks tomorrow, the *Nucleus* will focus
on rag gags and festive beauties. By then,
Sandile will have eaten a communion
wafer. But in the matter of sustained detention the Minister of
    Law
and Order might absolve himself of sin, and the need for
action,
by drumming up a charge, perhaps, or
promising daily to review the case.
Today, people walk, chant, toyi toyi from the meeting
behind banners. People who place
their collective faith not alone in a fleeting
glimpse of suits and mercedes benz
as campus leaders leave the grounds to wield
their combined power against the state but in the march of
justice. The protest ends
without incident when riot policemen yield
to the delegation, honouring a gentlemen's
agreement with regard to trespass.
But what has changed so utterly? the students ask.
Yeats has no real answers for the class.

                                        Sally-Ann Murray

They Say

they say
writing poetry at
this stage of
our struggle is
absurd, and writing
black protest poetry
is even worse
people need direction
and not words
relating the situation
as it is
things that everyone
knows all about
poets, black poets,
have written themselves
into a dead-end

they say
my neighbours do
not even read
what i've written
and that poetry
will not bring
about any changes
in our situation
a revolution can
do without poets
poets should switch to
things more constructive
furthering a revolution
offer a solution
to the problem
their contempt
is acid eating
the flesh of
my poetical work

James Matthews

POLITICS WROUGHT TO ITS UTTERMOST

ROBERT MOHR

W.B. Yeats felt a life-long ambivalence toward political thinking and action. As a young man he was mostly indifferent. Later, when he came under the influences of William Morris and, more emotionally, Maude Gonne, he was both politically active and actively critical of the way political thought could cause the heart to be "Enchanted to a stone/To trouble the living stream" (*CP*:204;*PNE*:193). In "The Leaders of the Crowd", he set himself diametrically opposed to propagandists and rhetoricians who were intolerant of those who see differently and see more:

> How can they know
> Truth flourishes where the student's lamp has shone,
> And there alone, that have no solitude?
>
> (*CP*:207-08; *PNE*:197)

One cannot but agree with John Harrison that it "was not politics or current affairs that constituted reality for Yeats, but the life of the imagination in artistic creation".[1]

Yet, in spite of his critical stance, Yeats was actively engaged with political concerns in art and government. The question arises how he managed this tension between a life of the imagination and a life of political activity. The answer lies in his transforming political action into an enactment of imaginative processes. Literal events were brought to the imagination, which then transformed those events into variations, which in turn showed the complex reality which underlay literal action. Without denying the concrete event, but by using it, the imagination could free concrete reality from literal seizure in any single form. This ethos is well demonstrated in the two overture poems at the beginning of Yeats's *Collected Poems*: "The Song of the Happy Shepherd" and "The Sad

---

1. John Harrison, *The Reactionaries*, London 1966, 43.

Shepherd". The two present a kind of morality tale about the right and wrong regard for one's life story, for one's history of sorrow.

The "happy shepherd" allows his personal, "fretful words" to be reworked and reworded into a variant story by the whorls of a sea shell:

> And they thy comforters will be,
> Rewarding in melodious guile
> Thy fretful words a little while
> Till they shall singing fade in ruth
> And die a pearly brotherhood;

(CP:8;PNE:1)

The "sad shepherd", however, insists that his personal tale shall be exactly re-echoed in the same language he utters it:

> *I will my heavy story tell*
> *Till my own words, re-echoing, shall send*
> *Their sadness through a hollow, pearly heart;*
> *And my own tale again for me shall sing,*
> *And my own whispering words be comforting,*
> *And lo! my ancient burden may depart.*

(CP:9;PNE:2)

His insistence wins him the shell's amnesia and a profoundly bitter isolation.

The happy shepherd is happy precisely because he allows the shell to rework the facts imaginatively. His happiness derives from the courage to let his will slip away, to let himself be re-imagined — "in melodious guile" — and then to assume a different perspective toward his "own" story. Then, though he dies, he goes seeking the company of the "hapless faun" of Arcady, Pan, without being paralyzed by panic, a desperate state to which the sad shepherd is increasingly subjected as his poem progresses. This moral pastoral of the two companion poems sets the political tone and provides guidance through the *Collected Poems*. Their first and primary direction focuses one's attention on the transfiguring power of the imagination, which breaks down the confines of individual history. Imaginative vision recognizes the inevitability of death, perceives the chthonic realm upon which life rests and toward which the happy shepherd departs: "I must be gone: there is a grave ...."
He accommodates what the insistently literal-minded sad shepherd utterly misses: the melodious guile, the mirthful spirit which stirs life's sorrow into song. Imaginative song has power to discover potentiality in actual events, to mine the variants in what has happened. Variants show the

pattern beneath the literal events and bear out meaning. Yeats understood that the poet is not a political historian nor a journalist. If he is to be as his happy shepherd, pleasing even to Pan, he must enter the imaginative heart where his "sorrow" is re-worded by "Some echo-harbouring shell".[2]

The other direction toward which the first poem points is downward into a grave, among poppies, dream, reverie. This movement of the poetic imagination toward death is an essential insight to Yeats. In a now famous letter to Olivia Shakespear in 1927, he concludes that "only two topics can be of the least interest to a serious and studious mind — sex and the dead" (*L*:730). The humour of the remark to Mrs Shakespear belongs to those "mirthful songs" and the "melodious guile" in "The Song of the Happy Shepherd". The seriousness of the statement, especially the point about the dead, however, belongs to the grave ethos at the core of the two poems. The poet knows that, while concrete reality provides building material, no concrete thing or event is to be taken literally as the only form of that particular reality. Representations of reality keep changing into variant forms. The imagination twists images, turns things inside out, upside down; it breaks images down in a kind of alchemical scourging before it rebuilds them. The clearest metaphor for this imaginative process is death. Death unbinds the frozen image and frees it into its variations. Variations show the complexity of ideal reality, while any one variant presents only a politically limited view. Thus the imagination "pathologizes" its images in order to make a clearing for fresh images. Yeats wrote precisely to this point in his *Journal:* "all progress is at the outset 'pathological'" (*Mem*:190).

Perhaps the leap from these two early poems to the main focus of this essay, the four poems which open *The Tower*, can best be made by looking at a passage Yeats wrote in his *Autobiography*. Here he touches upon the dissolution of character and of the active will. He foresees the ecstasy toward which tragedy moves the soul, the ecstasy which comes from contemplating vast things that appear horrific to mortal eyes and which the living see only imperfectly. Here, as in "The Tower", Yeats declares that the soul imagines human reality, and that reality can be seen by the mind only after its will "perishes":

A poet creates tragedy from his own soul, that soul which is alike in all men. It has not joy, as we understand that word, but ecstasy,

---

2. *W.B. Yeats: The Poems*, ed. Daniel Albright, London 1990, 415, notes that "this shell acts as a sounding-box or resonator, transforming words into melody, private emotion into beauty. It is therefore a symbol of the poetic imagination."

which is from the contemplation of things vaster than the individual and imperfectly seen, perhaps, by all those that still live. The masks of tragedy contain neither character nor personal energy. They are allied to decoration and to the abstract figures of Egyptian temples. Before the mind can look out of their eyes the active will perishes, hence their sorrowful calm. Joy is of the will which labours, which overcomes obstacles, which knows triumph. The soul knows its changes of state alone, and I think the motives of tragedy are not related to action but to changes of state. I feel this but do not see clearly, for I am hunting truth into its thicket and it is my business to keep close to the impressions of sense, to common daily life. Yet is not ecstasy some fulfillment of the soul in itself, some slow or sudden expansion of it like an overflowing well? Is not this what is meant by beauty?

(*Au*:471;*Mem*:152-53)

This passage develops a sense for the "feel' of tragedy, which the poet creates "out of his bitter soul", even while he keeps close to common daily life. In the first four poems of *The Tower*, the imagination "pathologizes" the images that pass before it, whether they have happened in fact, were created solely by itself, or belong to legend. All are translated into imaginative material and then scourged in order to liberate the imagination from paralysis stemming from a literal identification with those images and events. Through the imagination's alchemy, Yeats is able directly to confront the most horrific events, which, he feels, a less flexible political sensibility might not be able to approach, so savage would be the indignation.

Yeats orders these four poems in reverse sequence of their composition: "Sailing to Byzantium" (Autumn 1926), "The Tower" (finished on 7 October, 1925), "Meditations in Time of Civil War" (1922), "Nineteen Hundred and Nineteen" (1919). When one reads the four poems in the order Yeats placed them, they carry one into a descent from the most refined to the most debased, from the "golden bough" where the Emperor's golden nightingale is set, to "that insolent fiend Robert Artisson" and all the insane cruelties which surround his lurching image.

Although "Sailing to Byzantium" (*CP*:217-18;*PNE*:204) gathers poet and reader into a shining image of "the artifice of eternity", the first two stanzas present the human condition from which the poem rises. The first word, "that", encompasses everything that "is begotten, born, and dies". "The young/In one another's arms, birds in the trees" and "The salmon-falls, the mackerel-crowded seas" are all set in apposition to "that". And what do these dying generations do? They "neglect" what lasts in spite of the wear of time and the weight of death upon them. Stupidly — and I use the word thinking of the characterization of Robert Artisson at the end of "Nineteen Hundred and Nineteen", "his great eyes without thought/Under the shadow of stupid straw-pale locks" — stupidly, they neglect what most interests the ageing poet. Theirs "is no country for old men" such as his imagined self. He must create a lasting image, a "monument of unageing intellect", if he is to avoid the horrible prospect of dying or of becoming what he imagines an aged man to be:

> An aged man is but a paltry thing,
> A tattered coat upon a stick, unless
> Soul clap its hands and sing, and louder sing
> For every tatter in its mortal dress,

Yeats writes "soul" without the article, because it is a being *per se* rather than a part like the head or the heart. Soul is independent and acts autonomously. And the aged man, who gives experience and image to soul, can either dwindle into tattered refuse or be gathered into an eternal image, depending upon what the soul does. The outcome hinges upon the word "unless". An argument between realities wages in these two stanzas. Does one remain "caught in that sensual music" as do the neglectful dying generations, or does one turn to "there", to "the holy city of Byzantium". "There" the poet hopes to find not the "singing school" of the young and the birds "at their song" of passionate decline, but the soul's song "of its own magnificence", which he may study in contemplation in "the holy city of Byzantium".

Even though he has escaped the pall of death, the agony abides, and the poet asks the sages to come out of the mosaic, artificial, unburning, agonizing fire, to "be the singing-masters of my soul". The barrier to this instruction lies in the distance between his mortal self and the immortal sages pictured in the mosaic. Therefore he asks them to make the journey, "perne in a gyre", from their eternal artifice into his mortal reality. Once in the mortal state, the sages and their fire can consume what they burn:

> Consume my heart away; sick with desire
> And fastened to a dying animal
> It knows not what it is; and gather me
> Into the artifice of eternity.

At this point his heart is the *massa* which requires the transforming alchemical fire. It is sick, dying and ignorant of itself, and the sickness which is killing it and keeping it ignorant is the very "desire" that animates "the dying generations". Mortal desire coagulates the heart, so the heart must be burned away. "Once out of nature", the alchemical poet "shall never take [his] bodily form from any natural thing". Incarnation is finished in this vision, and the unimaginable state beyond mortality is imagined, though not without a touch of humour, a wink at the reader and a nod toward the nodding Emperor. The agony has led to the blessed state although its image may disappoint. Thus the poet keeps all eyes upon mortal limits.

The eyes are kept focused upon mortal limits at the opening of "The Tower" (*CP*:218-25;*PNE*:205):

> What shall I do with this absurdity —
> O heart, O troubled heart — this caricature,
> Decrepit age that has been tied to me
> As to a dog's tail?

Yeats has returned to the image of the "tattered coat upon a stick". The sick and dying heart is troubled by "decrepit age" even while the imagination has grown more vital than ever:

> Never had I more
> Excited, passionate, fantastical
> Imagination, nor an ear and eye
> That more expected the impossible —

The link between the heart and the imagination, which emerged in "The Song of the Happy Shepherd" — the shell of the imagination and the truth in the heart — is troubled by the body's dying. The poet fears that he "must bid the Muse go pack", the muse who inspired "once the growing boy", who is linked to "the ageing man" at the end of "Meditations in Time of Civil War". He fears he must "be content with argument and deal/In abstract things", those "monuments of unaging intellect", in a kind of defeat, or else "be derided by/A sort of battered kettle at the heel", another sound of decrepitude. The first stanza sets up the same problem which troubles the old man in the first stanza of "Sailing to Byzantium".

Against mortal decay, he sets his "excited, passionate, fantastical/Imagination". But out of what does the imagination begin? Part two, the longest section of "The Tower", takes place upon the battlements of the tower, where the surrounding landscape reflects some decline. Entering a reverie, he stares upon two ruins, "the foundations of a house, or where/Tree, like a sooty finger, starts from the earth". These emblems of history, human and natural, arouse his imagination "under the day's declining beam", to call "Images and memories/From ruin or from ancient trees". The imagination is stimulated to somehow transform the images of ruin into a new excitement.

Yet all the images which the imagination calls forth have some cruelty or suffering in them which must be accommodated. The serving man to Mrs. French cruelly "Clipped an insolent farmer's ears/And brought them in a little covered dish". And the sickness of desire for "a peasant girl commended by a song" (Anthony Raftery's song about Mary Hynes) drives men mad and leads them to ruin, and one to death:

> But they mistook the brightness of the moon
> For the prosaic light of day —
> Music had driven their wits astray —
> And one was drowned in the great bog of Cloone.

Yet the men's madness and the blindness of the poet who made the song do not seem strange. The vision of beauty belongs paradoxically to the unseeing poets, like Homer and Raftery, and the maddening tragedy is perennial: "the tragedy began/With Homer that was a blind man/And Helen has all living hearts betrayed." Yeats's ambition too comes out: "O may the moon and sunlight seem/One inextricable beam,/For if I triumph I must make men mad." To make men mad is part of the imagination's pathological work, required by soul. "Madness" makes facing life's extremity possible.

The imagination conflates stories which the poet has heard with ones he has created. He recalls his own story "Red Hanrahan" in a stanza that captures all the errancy, madness, decrepitude, horror, and sick desire suffered by its protagonist:

> And I myself created Hanrahan
> And drove him drunk or sober through the dawn
> From somewhere in the neighbouring cottages.
> Caught by an old man's juggleries
> He stumbled, tumbled, fumbled to and fro
> And had but broken knees for hire
> And horrible splendour of desire;
> I thought it all out twenty years ago:

At the end of the account he portrays Hanrahan rising in a frenzy and following "those baying creatures towards —/O towards I have forgotten what — enough!" Hanrahan had followed the baying hounds to Slieve

Echtge where he met the beautiful Echtge in the other world and failed to speak. Ironically, the painful memory is forgotten one and a half stanzas before Yeats evokes "the Great Memory". The poem comes to a crescendo at the first "towards", which points to the feminine soul-figure, and then recoils from that painful memory of failure. The poem is working through the imaginative difficulty of facing painful events and memories.

Yeats retreats toward safer ground but stays with sorrowful and troubling images: "I must recall a man that neither love/Nor music nor an enemy's clipped ear/Could, he was so harried, cheer." Although, according to Yeats's own note, this tower ghost "lived about a hundred years ago" (*PNE*:595), "there's not a neighbour left to say/When he finished his dog's day: /An ancient bankrupt master of this house". Then the poet lengthens his reach to draw images explicitly from the Great Memory, images which break upon his sleep.

> Before that ruin came, for centuries,
> Rough men-at-arms, cross-gartered to the knees
> Or shod in iron, climbed the narrow stairs,
> And certain men-at arms there were
> Whose images, in the Great Memory stored,
> Come with loud cry and panting breast
> To break upon a sleeper's rest
> While their great wooden dice beat on the board.

At this point he has joined fact and the imagination with the Great Memory. The images lead into one another, call each other up from the memory, and cluster around the protruding tower. And the pathological images evoked by the imagination in the poem move the poet to his question: "Did all old men and women ... rage/As I do now against old age?" He himself states that he has "found an answer in those eyes/That are impatient to be gone". But he does not tell the answer although his isolation, highlighted by the impatient eyes that abandon him to death, suggests the leaning toward rage and an affirmation. Left with the one image of Hanrahan, whose imagined lecheries have greater force than the poet's literal experience, Yeats asks another question even closer to his heart: "Does the imagination dwell the most/Upon a woman won or woman lost?" It could be an evening's game question at the Court of Urbino, only the answer is sought not from the high thought of Urbino but from the depth of Hanrahan's amorous plunges:

> Bring up out of that deep considering mind
> All that you have discovered in the grave,

For it is certain that you have
Reckoned up every unforeknown, unseeing
Plunge, lured by a softening eye,
Or by a touch or a sigh,
Into the labyrinth of another's being;

The wisdom he seeks is a secret of death, discovered by the deep considering mind when it probes the grave. And Yeats associates the grave with "the labyrinth of another's being" into which Hanrahan has plunged and been lured many times.

"Labyrinth" recalls the "twisted, echo-harbouring shell" of the imagination in "The Song of the Happy Shepherd" and the narcissistic "trumpet-twisted shell" in Book I of *The Wanderings of Oisin*. It calls up the lines for the unfolding of the cloth at the beginning of *The Only Jealousy of Emer*:

A strange, unserviceable thing,
A fragile, exquisite, pale shell,
That the vast troubled waters bring
To the loud sands before day has broken.

(*CPl*:282)

All these labyrinthine shell images link the self-gazing soul, the imagination, a white bird, and a woman's beauty. Since Hanrahan is reputed, within Yeats's imagination, to have plunged into this labyrinth, he should be best suited to answer the question whether the imagination dwells most upon the woman won or the woman lost. Yet Yeats and his readers know that Hanrahan turned from Echtge in weak speechlessness. The imagined opportunity for union with soul was lost, and since that moment the imagination has dwelled upon the loss. Just as the images are stored in the Great Memory and are imagined forth from there, so are they lost when the memory of failure recurs. Standing upon the battlements of his tower and sending "imagination forth/Under the day's declining beam", Yeats realizes that the imagination embodies everything and that, by mere changes of state within the soul, the images can be called up in their clusters or lost in anxiety. What is an aged man before the power of the imagining soul? What is the lover who becomes paralyzed in the soul's presence?

Death fills the memory in Part Three of "The Tower". It begins with the poet writing his will. Recoiling from Hanrahan's failure, he begins by favouring "upstanding men that climb". They will inherit his pride of freedom, his pride reflected in the dawn's energy, nature's bounty, the swan's courage to sing into its death.

Encouraged by his assertion of pride, he declares at the climax of the poem his faith in the soul's created images as opposed to Platonic abstraction:

> And I declare my faith;
> I mock Plotinus' thought
> And cry in Plato's teeth,
> Death and life were not
> Till man made up the whole,
> Made lock, stock and barrel
> Out of his bitter soul,
> Aye, sun and moon and star, all,
> And further add to that
> That, being dead, we rise,
> Dream and so create
> Translunar Paradise.

Man makes everything out of his bitter soul. It is an understatement to say that the "man" Yeats imagines is not Paudeen or Biddy, who do create a withered sort of world but do not create death and life nor the cosmos. The man he imagines transcends time and mortality. He is closer to Yeats's idea of Shelley as described in "The Philosophy of Shelley's Poetry": "he could hardly have helped perceiving that an image that has transcended particular time and place becomes a symbol, passes beyond death, as it were, and becomes a living soul" (*E&I*:80). The image becomes a transpersonal, living soul, something the poet imagines and that exists beyond his control. As Yeats wrote in his *Journal*, "is not one's art made out of the struggle in one's soul?" (*Mem*:157) And in an unfinished dialogue of 1915, *The Poet and the Actress*, Yeats writes:

> Now the art I long for is also a battle, but it takes place in the depths of the soul and one of the antagonists does not wear a shape known to the world or speak a mortal tongue. It is the struggle of the dream with the world — it is only possible when we transcend circumstances and our selves, and the greater the contest, the greater the art ....[3]

These passages bring out the soul's transpersonal dimension. One of its antagonists "does not wear a shape known to the world or speak a mortal tongue". Dream happens in a psychic space and is the human activity that best reflects the soul's imagining. About the word "dream" in the

---

3. Quoted in Richard Ellmann, *The Identity of Yeats*, New York 1964, 105.

dialogue just quoted, Ellmann says, "Yeats employs the word 'dream' now to mean the highest, most vigorous imaginative exercise".[4] The same can be said about Yeats's use of dream ten years after in "The Tower". "Being dead" we dream and create a paradise beyond creation. Death, dream, the imagination, the soul, the poet are all woven together so that "Man makes a superhuman/Mirror-resembling dream". This is the human phenomenon wrought to its uttermost.

All the bitter images called out of the soul have led to this insight to the soul's creative imagination, its translunar, superhuman dimension, and the option which Soul offers to the ageing poet's soul

> to study
> In a learned school
> Till the wreck of body,
> Slow decay of blood,
> Testy delirium
> Or dull decrepitude,
> Or what worse evil come —
> The death of friends, or death
> Of every brilliant eye
> That made a catch in the breath —
> Seem but the clouds of the sky
> When the horizon fades;
> Or a bird's sleepy cry
> Among the deepening shades.

The poet's hope "to study in a learned school", to sail to Byzantium, culminates in a deepening and a slowing. In his essay on John Synge's plays, Yeats made the general observation that "in all drama which would give direct expression to reverie, to the speech of the soul with itself, there is some device that checks the rapidity of dialogue" (*E&I*:333). This may be applied to "The Tower" which ends with a "slow decay of blood" in a watery atmosphere of decline. "A bird's sleepy cry/Among the deepening shades" recalls the earlier image of the swan who

> must fix his eye
> Upon a fading gleam,
> Float out upon a long
> Last reach of glittering stream
> And there sing his last song.

---

4. *Ibid.*, 106.

The poet's soul is moved by its images toward death and that learned school outside of nature where it joins the other "deepening shades". At the same time the man and all his companionable images fade into darkness and death. As the poem began in a state of anxiety concerning ageing and death, it ends in a condition of mortal decline, the soul looking toward the eternity which "Sailing to Byzantium" imagines.

The imagination's transformative methods, demonstrated in "The Tower" and "Sailing to Byzantium", are applied to a more overtly political content in the seven lyrical parts of "Meditations in Time of Civil War" (*CP*:225-32;*PNE*:206-12) and the six sections of "Nineteen Hundred and Nineteen". In the first poem, the Big House, the inherited glory of the rich, has fallen into decline and is reflected economically by an image of an empty shell:

> now it seems
> As if some marvellous empty sea-shell flung
> Out of the obscure dark of the rich streams,
> And not a fountain, were the symbol which
> Shadows the inherited glory of the rich.

That sea-shell has become a familiar image for the imagination which rewords one's story. As a symbol shadowing the ancestral houses, the shell has emerged ingloriously from the "obscure dark" and appears empty. The present glory of the rich has not sprung "out of life's own self-delight", but has come inherited and empty. The first image in the poem marks a decline in social and political status.

But out of what began the glory of the rich? And what has brought about its decline? The third stanza answers the first question and suggests the answer to the second, an answer which is elaborated later in the fourth lyric, *My Descendants*:

> Some violent bitter man, some powerful man
> Called architect and artist in, that they,
> Bitter and violent men, might rear in stone
> The sweetness that all longed for night and day,
> The gentleness none there had ever known;
> But when the master's buried mice can play,
> And maybe the great-grandson of that house,
> For all its bronze and marble, 's but a mouse.

By some violent, bitter impulse, the soul is moved to create temporal images which reflect its own magnificence. So those who imagine and those who construct the imagined house are violent and bitter. Soul and man's violent compression of creative energy, a "bloody press", the alchemical fire, can rear a great edifice out of inert stone. Other phrases in the poem capture this sense of violent creative struggle: "An acre of stony ground,/Where the symbolic rose can break in flower" in *My House*, and "a changeless sword,/By pen and paper lies,/That it may moralise/My days out of their aimlessness" in *My Table*. Yeats's moralizing upon the sword leads him to conclude that "only an aching heart/Conceives a changeless work or art". And the "most rich inheritor" of the sword knows "that none could pass Heaven's door/That loved inferior art". Therefore he sustains the greatness of the sword's symbolic adversity by sustaining "such an aching heart" within himself. That is the secret to keeping the sword "changeless", keeping it from becoming empty of force as the inherited houses have become empty shells. Harnessed violence and bitterness supply the drive to rear a great house, to forge a changeless sword, to write a poem. And a heart which aches from the pressure of sustaining such force within itself can enjoy the sustained "sweetness that all longed for night and day". The beauty, the sweetness, the gentleness, "slippered Contemplation", and Childhood's delight are all imagined within a space cleared by a violent and bitter impulse. Those delights are sustained only by an impulse opposed to ease. Decline is held off by an oppositional tension.

When Yeats attributes to the imagining soul the violence and bitterness underpinning the glory of the rich and his own anxieties about social and aesthetic decline, he seizes upon a vessel strong enough to contain both desperate and explosive contents. Within this psychic enclosure he can ask, "And what if my descendants lose the flower/Through natural declension of the soul"? And he can utter the unspeakable curse against his own progeny. "Declension of the soul" in man seems inevitable. The poet knows that things and people "flourish and decline". This political insight forms the wedge which begins to crack the poem, the tower, sanity, even the world. The language of failure and ensuing desolation wells up and nearly overwhelms the balance between delight and violence: torn petals, declension of the soul, roofless ruin, cracked masonry, crying desolation and desolate sky. The poet tries to re-establish equilibrium by evoking Primum Mobile, yet this made "the very owls" which "may build in the cracked masonry" of his tower and cry desolation. These owls foreshadow the bees whom he invites to come build in the starling's empty nest. They build upon human decline. While the poet counts himself "most prosperous" among his wife and friends at the moment, he foresees imminent decline and imagines his tower as "these stones", a monument of what has passed. The unacceptable has been imagined.

Everything gets caught up in the sweep of destruction. First the
masonry of his tower begins to loosen and he makes his invitation to the
bees to "come build in the empty house of the stare", a refrain following
upon each image of instability and senseless violence. For the violence
that is unleashed is not creative but destructive, and he admits his
powerlessness in its general wake. The pronoun reference widens beyond
"I" to include "we", which refers directly to his wife and himself, but
also draws in his reader, his friends, his countrymen, and mankind itself,
as the immediate expands into universal metaphor:

> We are closed in, and the key is turned
> On our uncertainty; somewhere
> A man is killed, or a house burned,
> Yet no clear fact to be discerned:
> Come build in the empty house of the stare.

Acts of violence become abstract as the mood of destruction sweeps away
individual responsibility. An unidentified man is killed in an unspecific
place, and no attributable facts can be applied to the act. Discernment has
vanished and man is reduced to carnage: "that dead young soldier in his
blood". Enmity has overtaken love and thrown off the balance between
violence and the "sweetness that all longed for night and day", "those
things the greatest of mankind/Consider most to magnify, or to bless".

At this point Yeats has confronted a possible source for the senseless
brutality, fantasy. But he leaves the word vaguely defined:

> We had fed the heart on fantasies,
> The heart's grown brutal from the fare;
> More substance in our enmities
> Than in our love;

Is he saying that fantasies have nourished enmity? Are fantasies dreams
of freedom from political oppression that have spawned hatred? And is
this enmity akin to or different from the bitterness that goes with
greatness? Or are fantasies insubstantial dreams stemming from a
glorious inheritance that yet fail to maintain the creatively controlled
violence which built the inheritance initially? Are fantasies isolated
dreams of comfortable indulgences that neglect social responsibility, like
the musing ladies in Part VII whose "minds are but a pool/Where even
longing drowns under its own excess"? More questions have been
prompted than can be answered within the poem's maelstrom.

Once unleashed, the heart's brutality sweeps everything into madness and death in the last section of "Meditations", *I see Phantoms of Hatred and of the Heart's Fullness and of the Coming Emptiness*. The heart's fullness resembles the "aching heart" which "conceives a changeless work of art" and the "soul's beauty". Resembles; however, the balance has fallen off and the "ache" declines into "brutality". In his reverie, Yeats leans "upon broken stone" of the battlements and gazes at the moon which is transformed by his mood (state of soul) to look "unchangeable", frozen in the image of "a glittering sword out of the east", poised for apocalyptic reaping. In this mood, "Frenzies bewilder, reveries perturb the mind;/Monstrous familiar images swim to the mind's eye". The mind's eye opens to images "in the Great Memory stored", as he says in Part II of "The Tower".

And what swims in the mind's eye is a "rage-driven, rage-tormented, and rage-hungry troop" that cries, as time collapses, for vengeance for the murder of a fourteenth century heretic, Jacques Molay. But this troop is driven toward more than just vengeance. It turns upon itself in suicidal fury and, consequently, toward a kind of black out: "Trooper belabouring trooper, biting at arm or at face,/Plunges towards nothing, arms and fingers spreading wide/For the embrace of nothing." The poet nearly falls in with the frenzied troop:

> and I, my wits astray
> Because of all that senseless tumult, all but cried
> For vengeance on the murderers of Jacques Molay.

The poem hovers for a moment over images of gentle "sweetness", which finally

> Give place to an indifferent multitude, give place
> To brazen hawks. Nor self-delighting reverie,
> Nor hate of what's to come, nor pity for what's gone,
>
> Nothing but grip of claw, and the eye's complacency,
> The innumerable clanging wings that have put out the moon.

These hawks of nature, like the indifferent multitude, claw at delicate images of beauty, regardless of culture's "self-delighting reverie" ("what is passing"), or the cultured poet's "hate of what's to come" or his "pity for what's gone". Even his poetical image of the moon poised impressively as "a glittering sword out of the east" is merely "put out" by grip of claw, eye's complacency, clanging wings, all images of the "filthy modern tide" which is anathema to the poet. He prompts into memory those lines in "Ego Dominus Tuus" that ask, "What portion in the world can the artist have/Who has awakened from the common dream/But dissipation and despair?" (*CP*:182;*PNE*:181). Unlike Lionel Johnson and Ernest Dowson, Yeats does not dissipate, but he nearly despairs. As he turns away from the horrible fantasy and shuts the door, he wonders "how many times I could have proved my worth/In something that all others understand or share". He might have made an effective contribution to society that would have reversed the insane tide, or joined a revolutionary army:

> But O! ambitious heart, had such a proof drawn forth
> A company of friends, a conscience set at ease,
> It had but made us pine the more.

Perhaps that is what fantasy does. It makes "us pine the more", because its hunger is increased by feeding or because it grows frustrated at the impossibility of realizing the imagined political utopia. The poet despairs of the world's improvement and turns his back. Yet he does not despair of the lonely, abstract joys that have sustained him since boyhood, and it is to those he turns in bemused resignation:

> The abstract joy,
> The half-read wisdom of daemonic images,
> Suffice the ageing man as once the growing boy.

The despair is not complete because he has the sufficient consolation of philosophy, an umbrella that protects him from the collapsing heavens. He turns from the soul's seeming perverse delight in destruction, which leaves the man in the cold dark, and returns to the enclosure of his tower, evoking at the last moment the innocence of childhood. There is, however, one last poem in this quartet in which the soul makes its raid upon life's cherished images, and there the cock's comb is scalped.

"Nineteen Hundred and Nineteen" (*CP*:232-37;*PNE*:213) opens on a note of loss and picks up the division between the multitude and genius: "Many ingenious lovely things are gone/That seemed sheer miracle to the multitude". It then indulges in a nostalgic look at those ingenious things, couching everything in the past tense. "There stood ... an ancient image ... and gone are Phidias' famous ivories":

> We too had many pretty toys when young:
> ....

> O what fine thought we had because we thought
> That the worst rogues and rascals had died out.

The phrase, "pretty toys", is not intended to overtly trivialize and undermine the political accomplishments cited, but it does initiate a potentially explosive irony which builds until the end of the third stanza. The sarcastic observation, "what matter that no cannon had been turned/Into a ploughshare" draws back the hammer, and the mere mention of "Parliament and king" nearly springs the trigger.

When the trigger does spring, the tense shifts to the present and the psyche's most horrific images pour into view, perhaps the most terrible images in Yeats's poetry:

> Now days are dragon-ridden, the nightmare
> Rides upon sleep: a drunken soldiery
> Can leave the mother, murdered at her door,
> To crawl in her own blood, and go scot-free;
> The night can sweat with terror as before
> We pieced our thoughts into philosophy,
> And planned to bring the world under a rule,
> Who are but weasels fighting in a hole.

While the actual murder of Mrs Ellen Quinn at Gort by the Black and Tans feeds the horror of this passage, that blame insulates neither Yeats nor the reader from implication. The imagination implicates everyone in the event. The literal acting out of such horrors signifies more the ignorance of pathological psychic fantasy than an awareness of its necessity. The denial of the soul's pathologizing puts it under pressure and causes these horrific irruptions, a fact confirmed in war-time behaviour, as Yeats is well aware. War is the literalization of the soul's pathological fantasy, a kind of breakdown in psychic reality. Yeats quickly moves the focus from a literal event to metaphoric imagining — "the night can sweat with terror" — and recalls a time before philosophy brought the consolation and illusion of "rule". But he recognizes with horrible insight that those who brought the world under rule "are but weasels fighting in a hole". And "we" who are weasels reflect "the rage-driven, rage-tormented, and rage-hungry troop" in "Meditations in Time of Civil War". No one escapes involvement in the horror.

Yeats asks, "who can read the signs nor sink unmanned/Into the half-deceit of some intoxicant/From shallow wits"? What comfort is there left to one "who knows no work can stand .... No honour leave its mighty monument"? The only comfort left to one who sees through all

triumph is to turn to psychic reality, to the soul's enduring, to the non-
human reality beneath worldly forms.

> He who can read the signs ...
> ... who knows no work can stand,
> ....
> No honour leave its mighty monument,
> Has but one comfort left: all triumph would
> But break upon his ghostly solitude.

The last line needs some amplification. It refers to the idea that in the
afterlife, the soul refines itself by purging the memory of all worldly
accomplishments and blunders which would hold it back from
reincarnation and impede its progress toward the original Unity. In these
lines the needs of soul to shed the vestiges of mortal care come forth,
and psychic comfort derives from the soul's immortality, whereas "man
is in love and loves what vanishes". There is nothing more to say. The
assertion of psychic over material reality is final, though "none dared
admit, if such a thought were his", because he and his cherished works
of beauty would fall under brutal hands and be burned or crushed, as
demonstrated at the end of the story "Rosa Alchemica".

What more is there to say? The soul pathologizes all that man loves
until all burns away and the soul is free from mortal, material fetters to
return to .... To what? Is there a goal, a Unity toward which the soul
yearns? Is that goal clearly defined? Is the material mechanism of the
universe a barrier to be surpassed as soon as possible in order that the
soul be teleologically correct? Does the soul simply hate what man loves
and want to shed it, and, if so, are political man and transcendent soul
primarily at odds? Or are man's images food for the soul's
self-knowledge, and pathologizing a kind of eating? The poem does not
answer all these questions; the human comedy cannot be simply resolved.
The poem proceeds to set up a tension between man's works and soul's
impulse to fly from all worldly forms right until its last, horrible,
world-attached image, Robert Artisson, "lurches past". The poem ends
in disgust but also on a note of regret for the loss of what the poet's
"laborious life imagined". Irony and ambivalence attend the soul's leap
"into the desolate heaven".

The second part of "Nineteen Hundred And Nineteen" savours a
shining image of the human dance and then watches that image whirled
off:

> When Loie Fuller's Chinese dancers enwound
> A shining web, a floating ribbon of cloth,
> It seemed that a dragon of air
> Had fallen among dancers, had whirled them round
> Or hurried them off on its own furious path ....

The human dance evokes the dragon who hurries both dancers and dance upon its "own furious path". It becomes a part of the dance's momentum out of itself. This is not the Western dragon of evil, the dragon that rides upon our days like nightmare, but the Eastern dragon of fortune whose prosperous blessing a shopkeeper would seek. Yet the dragon is an ambiguous image, more akin to the Western Wheel of Fortune that both elevates and crushes men's estates than to the Medieval Wyrm who brings only evil. This dragon has both beneficent and terrible sides and carries both into life in a circular dance:

> So the Platonic Year
> Whirls out new right and wrong,
> Whirls in the old instead;
> All men are dancers and their tread
> Goes to the barbarous clangour of a gong.

The terrible aspect of the dragon and the dance comes to the fore in "Nineteen Hundred and Nineteen" because the poem meditates upon a terrible moment in history when "many ingenious lovely things" are being hurried into destruction by "the barbarous clangour of a gong". The music has grown barbarous, the dance has become an unwinding, and all that the soul imagines through human work — "master-work of intellect or hand" — is dissolved in the scorching wind of the soul's alchemical fire.

Man clings to his own works and becomes caught within their labyrinthine whorls:

> A man in his own secret meditation
> Is lost amid the labyrinth that he has made
> In art or politics;
> Some Platonist affirms that in the station
> Where we should cast off body and trade
> The ancient habit sticks,
> And that if our words could
> But vanish with our breath
> That were a lucky death,
> For triumph can but mar our solitude.

Death is implicit in all of the soul's images, and a clean letting go signifies the whirling dragon's luck bestowed upon man's work, which is letting the soul make its images through him. The soul is the active imagination while man is but an image. The phrase "own secret meditation" recalls to mind "The Sad Shepherd", who insisted that his *"own words"* and his *"own tale"* remain unchanged. He ends lost and forgotten by the shell of the imagination which "changed all he sang to inarticulate moan" in his own ears. The happy shepherd, having accepted the "rewording" of his own "fretful words", ends by gladly going into the grave where he "would please the hapless faun ... with mirthful songs before the dawn". His is a lucky death. His demise frees the soul into a solitude unmarred by mortality's clinging vestiges.

For human attempts "to mend/Whatever mischief seemed/To afflict mankind" are "crack-pated" dreams that mankind should not be afflicted, that mankind should be spared the destruction of all cherished images. "We were crack-pated when we dreamed" that a political vision of goodness could keep the whirl of barbarous destruction from breaking out of the very images which embodied the good. And Primum Mobile, the gyre, the winding stair, and bird flight all intensify the case.

> We, who seven years ago
> Talked of honour and of truth,
> Shriek with pleasure if we show
> The weasel's twist, the weasel's tooth.

The night can and does "sweat with terror as before/We pieced our thoughts into philosophy", a terror reducing us to "weasels fighting in a hole". It sweats from the great transforming heat that "can bring wildness, bring a rage/To end all things", a heat which leaves man, if he clings to things, "caught/In the cold snows of a dream", as Yeats is caught at the end of *The Road at My Door* and at the end of Part III, when the "winds of winter blow".

Corrosive mockery then is applied to all proud "triumph", to all dreams of the great, the wise, the good. "Wind shrieked — and where are they?" The leveling wind is not romantically embraced nor identified as collaborator in some apocalyptic agenda the poet imagines. In human eyes it appears as "that foul storm", and his honour obliges him "to help good, wise or great" or else be accused of trafficking in mockery:

> Mock mockers after that
> That would not lift a hand maybe
> To help good, wise or great

> To bar that foul storm out, for we
> Traffic in mockery.

Sinking into mockery would be to "sink unmanned/Into the half-deceit of some intoxicant/From shallow wits". If one must face the scourge, then one must do so with full sense of the terrible loss of the goodness, greatness, and wisdom of man's "monuments". Therefore, the dross of mockery too must be scourged. This leads to the final maelstrom from which the ultimate epiphanic image emerges, much as it emerges at the conclusion of "The Second Coming".

Part VI of "Nineteen Hundred and Nineteen" opens on a note of violence like a great *forte* chord: "Violence upon the roads: violence of horses". And the outcry of violence is followed by a brief interlude of delicacy:

> Some few have handsome riders, are garlanded
> On delicate sensitive ear or tossing mane,
> But wearied running round and round in their courses ....

Delicate handiwork decorates the images of violent power only momentarily to remind us what "ingenious lovely things" are being whirled away. And the horses' weariness signals the cue for their collapse. No punctuation gives pause after the interlude before the poem suddenly breaks into violence:

> All break and vanish, and evil gathers head:
> Herodias' daughters have returned again,
> A sudden blast of dusty wind and after
> Thunder of feet, tumult of images,
> Their purpose in the labyrinth of the wind;
> And should some crazy hand dare touch a daughter
> All turn with amorous cries, or angry cries,
> According to the wind, for all are blind.

The secret purpose of Herodias' daughters courses in "the labyrinth of the wind", and that labyrinth may be an exactly opposed reflection of man's labyrinth, which appeared in the second stanza of Part III: "A man in his own secret meditation/Is lost amid the labyrinth that he has made/In art or politics". That labyrinth is man made whereas the windy labyrinth is antithetical to all man's images. The perverse, corrosive effect of these daughters is to cast life "into the frog-spawn of a blind man's ditch" ("Dialogue of Self and Soul", II), so that fresh images may be spawned out of a bestial fecundity. The image of the divine "rough beast" or Leda's swan or the "insolent fiend", Artisson, terrifies to the pitch of insanity, as the "flaming breath,/Comes to destroy/All those antinomies/Of day and night" ("Vacillation", I). The antinomies keep a balance. Once the balance is destroyed, life breaks open to the influx of a terrible divine fertilization. Depending upon how they are blown by the secret purposes of the labyrinthine wind, all men are struck morally blind and succumb to every amorous or angry impulse.

The dance of the daughters of Herodias is crystallized in the consortium of Robert Artisson and "the love-lorn Lady Kyteler". Robert Artisson is not a man but a "fiend", a demonic incubus, a *daimon*, who enters human reality through the "love-lorn" incantations of the Dame. This inhuman soul-image fertilizes the imagination from the dark underworld, a reverse of the golden shower which fell upon Danae in her tower, just as the "white rush" fell on Leda, or as the Dove visited the Virgin. This is an image of the soul's mysterious pathological fertility.

Robert Artisson is the dark, stupid, evil offspring of Art, an apotheosis of the artist, perhaps, who copulates with the anima, here embodied in Lady Kyteler. Or perhaps he is the anti-Muse who, rather than inspires, merely "lurches past, his great eyes without thought". Does Yeats mean that the imagination in the new age is guided by this blind impulse? Does the muse or the Son of Art now delight only in dismembered animals, only the feathers without the bird, just the cock's scalped comb? Yeats has imagined a lurching fiend who is just as relentlessly horrible as the rough slouching beast in "The Second Coming". There can be no turning away from the pathological image. The poet has seen and expressed his own transpersonal artistic anti-self, and that image pathologizes a culture or portends a cultural change characterized by moral inversion. Where from this darkness, this stupidity, can the imagination go, once all its cherished images have been broken? It cannot ignore its pathological insight. It needs somehow deliberately to incorporate pathologizing in further imagining, and it does so in the voice of madness or partial madness. "For wisdom is the property of the dead,/A something incompatible with life" ("Blood and the Moon", IV).

The imaginative transformation of painful, terrifying political events makes facing those events possible for Yeats. A brutal act remains meaninglessly brutal unless it can be placed into a larger psychic frame wherein time and humanity move, or dance. This is the purpose behind Yeats's transformation of painful fact into imaginative recitation, just as it has been the purpose of this essay to draw the point out. If the imagination can recast events into variants and thereby gain meaningful perspective upon even the most horrible events, then Yeats may have been correct in refusing to write overtly political poetry but instead a poetry that can contain more powerful content than political writing ever could imagine handling. In imaginative work, politics can be wrought to its uttermost and yet hold its form.

NOTES ON CONTRIBUTORS

C.C. Barfoot, English Department, Leiden University, published *The Thread of Connection: Aspects of Fate in the Novels of Jane Austen and Others* (1982); has most recently edited or co-edited *The Great Emporium: The Low Countries as a Cultural Crossroads in the Renaissance and the Eighteenth Century* (1992), *Theatre Intercontinental: Forms, Functions, Correspondences* and *Shades of Empire In Colonial and Post-Colonial Literatures* (1993); and *In Black and Gold: Contiguous Traditions in British and Irish Poetry* and *"Een Beytie Hollansche": James Boswell's Dutch Compositions* (1994).

Elizabeth Butler Cullingford, Department of English at the University of Texas at Austin, is the author of *Yeats, Ireland and Fascism* (1981) and *Gender and History in Yeats's Love Poetry* (1993). She also edited *Yeats: The Middle Poems* (1984) in the Macmillan Casebook series. She is currently working on a study of the myth of Carthage in Irish culture, from the seventeenth century to the present day.

Toshi Furomoto, Department of American Studies and Celtic Studies, Kobe University Japan, is the author of *Literature of the Anglo-Irish: The Descendant of Celt* (in Japanese, 1993). He has also translated W.H. Auden and co-translated Yeats's *Collected Plays* into Japanese; and edited an anthology of poems on Yeats, *The Widening Gyre* (private edition).

Peter van de Kamp, Regional College in Tralee, founder and director of the Kerry International Summer School of Living Irish Authors, co-authored (with Peter Costello) *Flann O'Brien: An Illustrated Biography* (1987), and edited *Katharine Tynan: Irish Stories: 1893-1899* (1993), and *Turning Tides: Dutch and Flemish Verse in English Versions by Irish Poets: 1880-1994* (1995). He is currently writing the biography of Katharine Tynan; and with others is editing the *Collected Works* of James Clarence Mangan.

Peter Liebregts, English Department, Leiden University, has published, besides articles on Paul Scott, Alexander Pope, W.B. Yeats, Padraic

Fallon, Ezra Pound and Donna Tartt, *Centaurs in the Twilight: W.B. Yeats's Use of the Classical Tradition* (1993). He is currently working on a study on Ezra Pound and the Greek tradition, and on a translation of Philostratus' *Life of Apollonius of Tyana*.

Augustine Martin, Professor of Anglo-Irish Literature and Drama at University College Dublin, founder/director of the James Joyce Annual Summer School (UCD), has written widely on various aspects of Anglo-Irish literature. His publications include *Anglo-Irish Literature: A History* and *W.B. Yeats*, while he has edited *The Collected Poems of W.B. Yeats*, *James Joyce: The Artist and the Labyrinth*, and the section on Prose of the Literary Renaissance in the *Field Day Anthology of Irish Literature*. He is currently working on the official biography of Patrick Kavanagh, and, as general editor, on the *Collected Works* of James Clarence Mangan.

Nicholas Meihuizen, Department of English at the University of Zululand, has published numerous articles on Yeats, including "Mr Yeats Meets the Queen of the Faeries: Yeats and the Anima"; "Birds and Birdsong in Wordsworth, Shelley and Yeats"; and "Yeats, Jung and the Integration of Archetypes". His essay "Landscapes of the Soul: Neoplatonic Environments in Blake and Yeats" appeared in Nigel Bell's *Literature, Nature and the Land: Ethics and Aesthetics of the Environment* (1993).

Robert A. Mohr has recently finished his doctoral dissertation on W.B. Yeats and the psychoanalytic writer James Hillman at University College Dublin. He published "W.B. Yeats and James Hillman, a Study in Soul-making" in *PaGes: Proceedings of the Postgraduate Colloquium* (1993), and has prepared several articles for publication which shall be forthcoming.

Maureen Murphy, Professor of Curriculum and Teaching/English at Hofstra University, is Past President of the American Conference for Irish Studies, and the Chairperson of IASAIL, and is on many other boards and councils. She has written on Irish history, literature, folklore and the Irish language. She is the editor of *A Guide to Irish Studies in the United States* (1979, 1982, 1987) and Máire MacNeill's *Máire Rua: Lady of Leamaneh* as well as co-editor of *Irish Literature: A Reader* (1987) and *James Joyce: A Centenary Tribute* (1988). Her current project is a book on the Irish Servant Girl in America.

Andrew Parkin, Professor of the Department of English and Fellow and Trustee of Shaw College at the Chinese University of Hong Kong, taught at the University of British Columbia in Vancouver for twenty years. Besides many articles and reviews on drama and poetry, he has published *The Dramatic Imagination of W.B. Yeats* and *Dion Boucicault: Selected Plays*. He edited *The Canadian Journal of Irish Studies* for fourteen years, and also edited a scholarly edition of Yeats's *The Herne's Egg*. He has published poetry in several journals, and two volumes of poetry, *Dancers in a Web* and *Yokohama Days, Kyoto Nights*. His anthology of Hong Kong poetry in translation is forthcoming from O.U.P.

Hedwig Schwall teaches Anglo-Irish literature at the Katholieke Universiteit Leuven and German at EHSAL Brussels. Her principal research interests are psycho-analytical methods of reading literature. She has published on early Irish literature, German expressionist poetry and painting, Yeats, Rilke and Cézanne. She is currently finishing a study on theatricality in Yeats, based on her doctoral dissertation.

Roselinde Supheert studied English and Musicology at the University of Utrecht, Linguistics at Clare College, Cambridge, and English and American Literature at Vanderbilt University, Nashville, Tennessee. She has taught English and American literature and translation at the Universities of Utrecht and Groningen. Her Ph.D.-dissertation on the reception of Yeats's work in the Netherlands is in preparation.

www.ingramcontent.com/pod-product-compliance
Lightning Source LLC
Chambersburg PA
CBHW020345270326
41926CB00007B/315